Not in the Heavens

Not in the Heavens

The Tradition of Jewish Secular Thought

David Biale

PRINCETON UNIVERSITY PRESS

PRINCETON AND OXFORD

Published by Princeton University Press, 41 William Street, Princeton, New Jersey 08540
In the United Kingdom: Princeton University Press, 6 Oxford Street,
Woodstock, Oxfordshire OX20 1TW
press.princeton.edu

Library of Congress Cataloging-in-Publication Data

Biale, David, 1949–
Not in the heavens : the tradition of Jewish secular thought / David Biale.
p.   cm.
Includes bibliographical references and index.
ISBN 978-0-691-14723-9 (hardcover : alk. paper)
1. Judaism—History—Modern period, 1750- 2. Secularization (Theology)—
History of doctrines. 3. Judaism and secularism. 4. Secularism. 5. Jews—Cultural
assimilation. 6. Jews—Identity. I. Title.
BM195.B53 2011
296.3′7—dc22   2010006054

British Library Cataloging-in-Publication Data is available
This book has been composed in Janson Text
Printed on acid-free paper. ∞
Printed in the United States of America

1   3   5   7   9   10   8   6   4   2

To the memory of my sister, Leah Korer, who chose a different path,

And for my children, Noam and Tali, who have inherited the legacy

Contents

Preface   ix

Introduction: Origins   1

Chapter 1
God: Pantheists, Kabbalists, and Pagans   15

Chapter 2
Torah: The Secular Jewish Bible   59

Chapter 3
Israel: Race, Nation, or State   92

Chapter 4
Israel: History, Language, and Culture   135

Conclusion: God, Torah, and Israel   176

Epilogue: Legacy   181

Notes   195

Index   221

Preface

One of my father's favorite memories of his mother—my grandmother—was that she was the first Jewish woman in the Polish town of Włocławek to grow her own hair. It was a small but significant rebellion. Since ancient times, the Jewish code of female modesty required married women to cover their hair, either with a scarf or, for Eastern European Jews of means, by a headdress encrusted with jewels, called in Yiddish a *shterntikhl*. In the nineteenth century, a new fashion of wigs swept the Jewish world, splitting the ultra-Orthodox, who denounced the new head coverings as "Gentile wigs," from the merely Orthodox, who believed that Jewish women were still within the bounds of tradition with their heads covered by someone else's hair. By taking off this *sheitel*, my grandmother declared her independence from a long-standing custom and thus, by a female gesture, heralded the beginnings of secularism.

Her declaration was hardly born of a well-conceived ideology or of conscious intent to overthrow the religion of her ancestors. She, like my grandfather, was in most respects a thoroughly Orthodox Jew, nominal followers of a pietistic Hasidic sect. Yet, in the first decades of the twentieth century, the winds of radical change began to blow through the ten-thousand-strong Jewish community of Włocławek, some two hundred kilometers northwest of Warsaw. Despite his Hasidic leanings, my grandfather joined the Mizrahi, the party of religious Jews who supported the Zionist movement. He was also instrumental in creating a Hebrew gymnasium in the town. The renaissance of the Hebrew language, so often associated with secular Zionism, did not seem to him to contradict the dictates of the Jewish religion.

These halting gestures toward modernity left a deep impression on my father. In the interwar period, when Polish Jews embraced a host of conflicting ideologies he, with his sister, joined Hashomer Hatzair, the Zionist youth movement that espoused socialism and a romantic return to nature. His younger brother gravitated in the opposite direction, also to Zionism but instead to the Revisionist Betar, the hard-line nationalists who wore military uniforms and rejected social revolution. Both movements, despite their differences, were staunchly secular, viewing the Jewish religion as complicitous in the sufferings of the Jews. The arguments around the Shabbat table of the Bialoglowsky household in the 1920s were consequently fierce. But since the parents themselves had already taken the first steps toward the modernity that their children now completed, a total rupture never took place. On the contrary, a spirit of tolerance prevailed that partially eased the path, often so rocky for others, between religion and secularism.

The early twentieth century was a time, like our own, of great quests for identity. For my grandparents, and even more for my father and his siblings, the old ways of being Jewish were no longer relevant in a modern world. Many, of course, continued to adhere to them, but growing numbers did not. The attractions of a greater world beyond the shtetl and the disabilities of being Jewish called out for new solutions. Many abandoned not only the Judaism of their parents but Jewish identity altogether. For others, universalism and assimilation were inadequate. In 1913, a young, assimilated German Jew named Franz Rosenzweig, on the verge of converting to Christianity, attended Yom Kippur services and, having experienced a kind of epiphany, concluded: "so I remain a Jew." For my father and his comrades, the *violation* of Yom Kippur became the way to proclaim a new identity. The young members of Hashomer Hatzair famously demonstrated their antinomian contempt for their elders by celebrating Yom Kippur with a ball provisioned with nonkosher food.[1] But in all these cases—secularization or the return to religion—identity had become fluid, up for grabs.

This admittedly anecdotal and personal account of one family's journey provides the backdrop for the theme of this book. For many, rejection of religion in favor of a secular life was not the result of ideology but instead a response to the dislocations of modernity: secular education, urbanization, migration, and the breakup of traditional society. Thus, my maternal grandparents abandoned traditional Judaism almost without reflection when they immigrated to America in 1912. It was not so much a revolution of ideas as it was the flight from traditional communities, rabbinic authority, and the daily routine prescribed by Jewish law.

For others, such as my father and his siblings, however, the secular revolt was deeply ideological, driven by new cultural ideals and political programs. They wanted to escape from what they considered the oppression of an obscurantist, medieval religion and to create a new Jew and a new society. A world without religion promised them liberation from their disabilities as Jews. Secularism became a way of resisting their minority status, something that they shared with other minorities in multiethnic states and empires. Their ideologies ranged from Communist to Zionist, from Yiddishism to assimilation. But one thing characterized all of them: a generational revolt against a world in which the Jewish religion, economic plight, political impotence, and cultural backwardness seemed wrapped up together in one unsavory package.

The Yiddish memoirist and Zionist Puah Rakovsky (1865–1955) described the contradictory ideological trajectories of late-nineteenth- and early-twentieth-century eastern European Jews, much like the different courses taken by Tevye's daughters in Sholem Aleichem's famous story.[2] While she herself was a socialist Zionist, her son became a Communist revolutionary and ended up in Soviet Russia. Her youngest daughter (by a third marriage) ended up in Palestine, but her younger sister joined the Bund (the Jewish Workers Movement in Poland). It is clear in Rakovsky's account that all these choices within the family, despite their ideological differences, were common responses to the religious, economic, and political crisis of this transitional period of Jewish history.

In this book, I aim to investigate the ideas of those who chose an ideological path to the secular. To be sure, as the story of my Polish Jewish grandparents shows, and as Shmuel Feiner has recently demonstrated for the eighteenth century, the secularization of Jewish society often *preceded*, rather than followed, the intellectual expression of secularism.[3] But a full account of this social transformation, which is really the story of modern Jewish history writ large, is a story too big to be told here. Similarly, this is not a book about the many varieties of secular Jewish culture, which range from fiction and poetry to art, theater, film, and museums and include everyday practices and material culture. That, too, would be a work too sweeping for my admittedly limited ambitions. Instead, I set my sights more narrowly on ideas expressed primarily in essays and other programmatic and philosophical works, albeit with occasional reference to other literary creations. And finally—and regrettably, since it was largely men who shaped the intellectual tradition of Jewish secularism (with several important exceptions to be discussed below)—this story, begun with my grandmother's act of rebellion, cannot fully embrace the female experience, just as it must eschew that of unlearned men.

Nor is this a work about secular thinkers who happened to be Jewish or came from Jewish origins—those whom Isaac Deutscher famously labeled "non-Jewish Jews"—unless their work dealt substantively with questions of the Jewish past or present. Karl Marx is a useful limit case. Marx was baptized as a child and was not above using crude anti-Semitic invective against his Jewish enemies. But he also associated with Jews and even frequented Jewish spas where, at one, he struck up a friendship with the Jewish historian Heinrich Graetz.[4] Nevertheless, Marx's only sustained engagement with the Jewish question was in his notorious essay of that name.[5] "On the Jewish Question" is a complex work that can be read equally as defending Jewish emancipation and as trafficking in anti-Semitic stereotypes of Jews as "the principle of money."[6]

For the purposes of this book, Marx's signal contribution was the distinction he drew between the "Sabbath Jew" and the "everyday Jew." He wished to shift the debate from the Jewish religion to the secular life of the Jews, and it is in this sense that he plays a role in the history of Jewish secularism. But in the final analysis, Marx was not really interested in the Jews as real people; they were a placeholder in his argument. It is true that generations of secular Jews, including Deutscher, would include Marx in their pantheon. In fact, a systematic study of the reception of Marx as a Jew still awaits its author. Unlike Baruch Spinoza, who, while he apparently also disavowed his Jewish affiliation, did so by writing a whole treatise attacking the Bible, Marx as a thinker—as opposed to the later image of Marx—remains peripheral to the intellectual tradition I wish to reconstruct in this book.

A plausible argument might be made that secular Jews, like Marx, Sigmund Freud, and the French sociologist of religion Émile Durkheim, were able to create their original theories because they stood at a conscious distance from the conventions of society.[7] If a certain alienation is necessary for creativity, then the condition of modern Jews both as part of and apart from European culture must have played a role in the spectacular contribution of Jewish thinkers to modernity. But it is not my intention to search out the hidden Jewish cast of thought in those who otherwise had little systematic or explicit to say about their Jewish identity or Jewish culture. Neither am I interested in speculating about how a "talmudic mentality" might have unconsciously shaped thinkers who never opened a tractate of the Talmud, or how some abstract "Jewish essence" informed a writer who did not acknowledge such sources. Unhistorical theories of this sort often veer off into a kind of racial determinism.

The tradition of Jewish secular thought that will preoccupy us in these pages is therefore distinctively different from Deutscher's "Non-Jewish Jews" since it rests on those whose writings engaged explicitly with the metaphysical, textual, political, and cultural dimensions of the Jewish experience, if for no other reason than to refute them. Many of these authors may not have consciously regarded themselves as contributing to such a body of literature, although some surely did, but taken collectively, they make up a modern tradition that challenged and even sought to replace the religious tradition called "Judaism."

• • •

This book owes its origins to the work of Felix Posen, that rarest of philanthropists who takes deep intellectual interest in the causes he supports. His quest to make better known the secular turn in modern Jewish culture and to uncover the social, political, and intellectual sources of Jewish secularization have had an enormously stimulating effect on a generation of Jewish Studies scholars. This book was undertaken initially with a grant from the Posen Foundation that allowed a year of uninterrupted research and writing away from my usual academic duties. The foundation was highly generous in its support without ever constraining or directing me in developing my ideas where the spirit took me.

I also owe a great debt to the participants in the yearly Posen Foundation conferences and even more to those who took part in the 2009 Posen Summer Seminar in Berkeley. I especially want to thank my co-facilitators of this seminar, Naomi Seidman and Susan Shapiro. Naomi, in particular, has been a faithful and unfailingly honest interlocutor. I was also fortunate to convene two ad hoc seminars of former students and colleagues to criticize early drafts of the book. For their participation, I thank Steven Aschheim, Amos Bitzan, Menahem Brinker, Benjamin Lazier, Arthur Samuelson, Naomi Seidman, Abe Socher, and Azzan Yadin. Jerome Copulsky and Yuval Joboni offered some trenchant comments of their own. And Peter Gordon shared the manuscript with his seminar on secularization at Harvard University, which resulted in some very useful feedback from both Peter and his students. Finally, two able graduate students, Shaun Halper and Elena Aaronson, helped me with the research.

Not in the Heavens

Introduction: Origins

In "The Non-Jewish Jew," the Polish social revolutionary Isaac Deutscher, who began his education as a yeshiva student, argued that those who rejected their ancestral religion and their people in favor of secular universalism had historical precursors. In a paradoxical formulation that captured something of his own identity, Deutscher wrote: "The Jewish heretic who transcends Jewry belongs to a Jewish tradition."[1] This "Jewry" is Judaism—not only the religion but all of the traditions built up over nearly three millennia. Yet, in transcending Judaism, the heretic finds himself or herself in a different Jewish tradition, a tradition no less Jewish for being antitraditional. Secular universalism for these heretics paradoxically became a kind of Jewish identity.

Many of these ideas originated in the European Enlightenment, but they also often had a Jewish provenance or at least were believed by secular Jews to have such a provenance. Deutscher, for example, started his famous essay on an autobiographical note, remembering how, as a child in the yeshiva, he had read the story of the heretic Elisha ben Abuya (or Aher—the Other—as he is known). Elisha's favorite student, Rabbi Meir, became one of the towering legal authorities of his generation, yet he never renounced his wayward teacher. By raising the question of the relationship of the Orthodox Rabbi Meir and the heretic Elisha, Deutscher implied that even the heretic remains somehow connected to that which he rejects, for the source of his heresy may lie within that tradition. For Deutscher, Elisha was the prototype of his modern heroes: Spinoza, Heine, Marx, Rosa Luxemburg, Trotsky, and Freud. They were all heretics, yet their heresy might be understood as a rejection that grew out of the Jewish tradition itself.

Like Deutscher, I want to argue that Jewish secularism was a revolt grounded in the tradition it rejected. The relationship between the premodern and the modern, in which the first is associated with religion and the second with the secular, remains one of the most fraught for students of religion. According to a common master narrative of the Enlightenment, also sometimes called "the secularization theory," modernity represented a total rupture with the past as innovation was privileged over tradition, science over superstition, rationalism over faith. In what Mark Lilla has called "the Great Separation," religion was divorced from the state, with the secular sovereign taking the role of God.[2] Religion may continue to exist in modernity, but it has become one choice among many and is no longer hegemonic.[3] All of us are free to choose and if such choice is an inherent meaning of secularism, then even those choosing to be religious are, in a sense, secular.[4]

In recent years, this dichotomous break has come under new scrutiny, especially given the persistence of religion in the modern world.[5] The contemporary resurgence of religion is clearly a complex response to secularism, just as secularism was—and still is—a response to religion. These two mortal enemies are very much defined by and through the other. And not only does it appear that religion and secularism in modernity are deeply implicated in each other, but it may well be that their contemporary entanglement owes something to the way the secular emerged out of the religious, not so much its polar negation as its dialectical product.

One example of this process can be found in the history of the very word "secular."[6] The term comes from the Latin *saeculum*, meaning "century" or "age." Christian theology held that between the First and Second Comings, the world was in a "middle age." Following Augustine's *City of God*, the church saw itself existing apart from this age, wandering on the earth but not a part of it. That which belonged to this age belonged to the earth. Thus, to be a part of the *saeculum* meant to belong to the unredeemed world. The term conflated time and space: a "temporal" power was a power pertaining to this world (the Hebrew word *olam* carries a similar double meaning: "world" and "eternity"). But "secular" also distinguished those clergy who were "of this world," as opposed to those who took "religious" (i.e., monastic) vows. *Seculatio* referred to the process of leaving the monastery. In this sense, "secular" in the medieval vocabulary could not be divorced from the context of religion.

By the seventeenth century, the word began to lose its linkage with a religious context and came to stand in sharp opposition to it. As the seventeenth-century Cambridge Neoplatonist Henry More wrote: "The Sun and the Moon have either a Spiritual signification or a Secular."[7] As a product of modern scientific thinking, this world became detached from the divine, the natural from the supernatural. Seventeenth and eighteenth-century political theorists also began to use the word "secular" to imagine a state free of religion (however, the word "secularism" was a nineteenth-century invention). And, finally, with the Reformation, the Wars of Religion and the French Revolution, "secularization" took on the meaning of church property appropriated by the temporal power. Thus, the word "secular," originating in a medieval religious milieu, came to signify a world opposed both metaphysically and politically to religion.

A number of scholars have accordingly argued for a dialectical path that secularism followed out of religion. Amos Funkenstein used the term "secular theology" to describe this relationship.[8] According to his argument, the seventeenth-century proponents of rationalism and the scientific revolution adopted the medieval scholastic divine attributes—God's omniscience, omnipotence, and providence—and invested them with earthly meaning. The desacralization of the world was thus accomplished with the tools of theology. Similarly, Karl Löwith proposed that the secular idea of progress owes much to the secularization of Christian apocalypticism.[9] And Carl Schmitt argued that modern "political theology" secularized the power of a transcendent God in the power of the state.[10] If these scholars found the origins of modernity primarily in medieval Catholicism, Peter L. Berger, building on Max Weber, suggested that the roots of the secular lay rather in Protestantism, which had shrunk the medieval realm of the sacred and created a heaven empty of angels.[11] Berger also observed that this Protestant move, in turn, had its roots in Old Testament monotheism, since the ancient Israelites had already banned the gods from the world: monotheism thus became the first step toward secularization.

This last argument—albeit without specific reference to Berger—found a thoroughgoing exponent in Marcel Gauchet in his challenging book, *The Disenchantment of the World*.[12] In a magisterial account of human history, Gauchet argued that the secular began with what Karl Jaspers called the "axial age," when Judaism, Zoroastrianism, and Buddhism banished the idols. Thus, the emergence of the "major" or "universal" religions was the first stage in the eventual disintegration of religion: the greater and more transcendent the god, the freer are humans. Monotheism dissolves the unity of the world into oppositions: God versus the world, the one versus the many, the sensible versus the intelligible. In this way, the modern dichotomy of "secular" versus "religion" is itself a product of religion. For Gauchet, monotheism by itself did not destabilize religion since Judaism and Islam assumed God's continued presence in the world. Only Christianity, in its doctrine of incarnation, postulated God's radical otherness, which required the mediation of God's son. Only Christianity created a religion of interiority and abdicated the world to its secular rulers. The monotheistic religions—and Christianity in particular—thus produced their own secular subversions.

All of these sweeping arguments suffer from a notable defect: they assume that secularization was a homogeneous process rooted in Christianity. But even within Europe itself, different local conditions created different types of secularization. Puritan England gave rise to a different form of the secular than did Lutheran Germany. Catholic Poland scarcely secularized at all until a late date, while Catholic France cut off the heads of its clergy when it underwent its revolution. Moreover, this focus on Christianity— and particularly on its western European expressions—fails to acknowledge that secularism has many and varied manifestations outside of Europe. In far-flung places like China, India, and Turkey, modern secular movements reflect, in one form or another, the religious contexts—Confucianism, Hinduism, and Islam—out of which they sprang. To attend to secularisms in the plural is to pay attention to the specific traditions that they reject but that inevitably shape their character.[13]

In this book, I will argue that Jewish secularism is a tradition that has its own unique characteristics grounded in part in its premodern sources. While the Christian origins of the word "secular" are connected to the dichotomous way Christian theologians saw the "City of God" and the "City of Man," Judaism never made such a sharp distinction: the profane world is not irredeemably polluted. While traditional Jewish sources repeatedly hold that this world is not the same as the next (or the one above), nevertheless, a strong *worldliness* informs much of the biblical, rabbinic, and medieval philosophical traditions. Even the Kabbalah, the most theosophical genre of Jewish literature, held that forces within this world mirror those above and vice versa; the two worlds can never be separated.

The origins of the Hebrew word for "secular" suggest this cultural specificity. One of the biblical roots for "polluted" or "defiled" is *hol*, which came to mean "secular" in modern Hebrew.[14] But *hol* in the Bible can also mean something intermediary between the sacred and the polluted, namely, the profane. So, for example, when David demands bread from the priest Ahimelech, he is told: "I have no profane bread (*lehem hol*), only consecrated bread

4

(*lehem kodesh*)."[15] In the later rabbinic division of the week, the days other than the Sabbath or festival days are referred to as *hol*. The profane is merely that which is everyday, neither holy nor defiled.

The Bible also makes a strict distinction between priests and nonpriests. It refers to the latter as a *zar*, or stranger (i.e., one who is a stranger in the domain of a temple). Onkelos, who translated the Bible into Aramaic, rendered this term as *hiloni*, the word that Joseph Klausner, the twentieth-century historian of Hebrew literature, adopted to refer to secular Jews, a usage that soon entered the vernacular of modern Hebrew.[16] In the midrash on Leviticus, a high priest tells a *hiloni* that he can only walk with the priest if he consents not to enter graveyards, which are forbidden to priests.[17] This "secular" Jew thus occupies an intermediary status between the priest and someone who is ritually defiled. The secular here is part of a continuum that presupposes the holy, not its negation.

Another word that demonstrates the continuum between past and present is *apikoros*, one of the key rabbinic terms for a heretic. The word *apikoros* is evidently derived from "Epicurean," but it probably did not carry the later meaning of "hedonist." Instead, the philosophical followers of Epicurus believed in the existence of the gods but denied that they interfered in or interacted at all with our world. The world was made up of atoms, which collided with each other in random fashion. If the rabbinic *apikoros* had such a philosophical outlook, he not only would have denied revelation but would have professed something like an ancient version of materialism. Since an early rabbinical text says that one should study in order to "know what to answer the *apikoros*," we can assume that the rabbis of late antiquity faced a real challenge from such heretics.[18] In the talmudic discussion of the Mishnah, the rabbis generally understand the *apikoros* as one who insults the rabbis: "what use are the rabbis to us, they study for their own benefit" and "what use are the rabbis since they never permitted us the raven nor forbade us the dove" (the point here is that the Torah already contains all the knowledge necessary for its interpretation).[19] The *apikoros* is therefore the one who rejects the rabbis as superfluous authorities, foreshadowing the attack by modern secularists on latter-day rabbis.

While we should not automatically equate the *apikoros* as defined here with modern secularists, the similarities are nevertheless striking and have to do in part with the similarities between some forms of Greek philosophy and modern sensibilities. As Berger has suggested, the heretic of premodern times becomes the secularist of the modern era: insofar as we autonomously "choose" (one of the original meanings of the Greek *haireisis*) our orientation to religion, we are all heretics."[20]

As Berger and Gauchet both insist, the Hebrew Bible represented a decisive moment in the prehistory of secularism. But is the appeal to the Hebrew Bible a sufficient explanation for the particular character of Jewish secularism? After all, the strict monotheism that Judaism shares with Islam did not predispose the latter to a secular revolution. It was specifically where the Jews had contact with European modernization—either in Europe itself or in areas under the influence of European colonialism—that Jewish secularism developed. The historical tradition may have provided the kindling, but the European Enlightenment lit the match. The argument that I will make does not preclude these external influences but is aimed at revealing how secular Jewish thinkers built their philosophies on the religious tradition they sought to replace.

That the earlier tradition fueled and shaped the particular form of Jewish secularism does not, however, mean that the two are identical. To say that they are, as Gauchet seems to at times, effaces what is new and revolutionary about modernity. But I want to argue that aspects of premodern thought not only anticipated their modern successors but at times even furnished arguments that might be appropriated, adapted, and transformed to fit a secular agenda. Even if these ideas in their original contexts were not intended for such a purpose, the social context of modernity cast them in a new light, making it possible to view them as genuine precursors. To use a different metaphor, these premodern ideas were like genes that required the social and political environment of modernity before they could be expressed. They were less the proximate causes of Jewish secularism than they were providers of the dominant *mentalité*—the language and particular flavor—of that secularism when modern forces caused it to emerge.

While the processes of modernization and secularization were typically experienced as ruptures, rather than as continuities with the past, no revolution takes place in a vacuum. The new is always incubated in the old. It is also in the nature of rebels to search for precursors, to legitimize their innovations in traditions of their own. Whether identified by actors themselves or by later observers, the nexus between religion and secularism forms a crucial element in any story of modernization.

Let us consider one of the most famous stories in the Talmud, in which the second-century sage Rabbi Eliezer finds himself in a minority of one in opposition to the other rabbis.[21] He invokes various miracles on his side, but the majority is unimpressed. Finally, he insists that if the law is according to his opinion: "let the heavens prove it." Immediately, a *bat kol*, a heavenly voice, affirms that his reading of the law is the right one. Against this seemingly iron-clad defense, Rabbi Joshua, the leader of the majority, stands on his feet and declares, quoting Deuteronomy 30:12: "It [the Torah] is not in the heavens." The Talmud asks: "what does 'it is not in the heavens' mean?" A later authority, Rabbi Yermiya explains: "Since the Torah was given at Sinai, we no longer listen to a heavenly voice." The Torah is now on earth and, so, it is the majority—a majority of rabbis, that is—who will decide its meaning. The text finds the principle of majority rule in another biblical quotation: "according to the majority you shall incline" (Exodus 23:2). It is thus the Torah itself, the divine revelation, that both affirms a secular principle ("it is not in the heavens") and teaches majority rule.

This story is sometimes cited as evidence of a rabbinic declaration of independence from God. And it is indeed that, but it is also more complicated. The rabbis enact their independence not only in the story itself but also in the quotations they bring from the Torah to support their case. The verse in Exodus utterly contradicts the rabbis' use of it. In its original context it says: "You shall not side with the many to do wrong, nor shall you pervert your testimony by following after the many." The verse clearly means that a witness should adhere to what he believes right rather than following after the majority opinion. But the rabbis turn this negative statement into a positive one: one *should* incline after the majority. It is almost as if to declare their independence from heaven, they needed to radically subvert heaven's own revelation.

Through the lens of this pregnant story, we can witness the tensions in rabbinic thought between divine revelation and human autonomy. But this is hardly secularism *avant la lettre*. Subvert the Torah the rabbis do, but they are far from discarding it altogether. They clearly believed that some communication from heaven is possible: hence, the *bat kol*.[22] In addition, they argued that their own law—the oral law—was revealed at Sinai together with the written law. Their legislative innovations were not mere human inventions but were grounded in revelation. It was probably this last idea that undergirds the Rabbi Eliezer story, since if rabbinic interpretation—majority rule—had its origins in Sinai, then a belated heavenly voice must surely count for less. Moreover, no one in this story—or in others—doubts either the existence or the authority of God. Immediately after Rabbi Joshua's statement, God is said to laugh: "My sons have defeated me, my sons have defeated me." God acquiesces in his own defeat. So, the majority, too, invokes a divine voice, but this time on its own side.

In addition, as Jeffrey Rubenstein has rightly pointed out, the larger story in which this passage is embedded belies the seeming secularism of the text.[23] Following their victory, the rabbis ban Rabbi Eliezer and burn everything that he declared pure. Yet the Talmud clearly takes the side of Rabbi Eliezer since various miraculous catastrophes occur after he is banned. The point seems to be that the victorious majority must not shame the minority. Otherwise, divine punishment will be visited on those who do so. If the rabbis claim sovereign authority for themselves, their own text undermines that claim.

However, we should not be too hasty in minimizing the radical import of our text. The story reveals a sense that the destruction of the Temple created a new world in which human autonomy loomed large, an idea that we might usually associate with modernity. The rabbis asserted that, without the Temple, prophecy had ceased, left only to children and fools.[24] The end of prophecy guaranteed their interpretive monopoly, at least if they could suppress other voices. And then there is the very legal dialectic itself: the law was not given definitively but is instead open to contradictory interpretations, each of which, to quote another famous story, is "the words of the living God."[25] In all of these expressions, the Torah has now become the property of its human interpreters.

The relationship between this text and modern Jewish secularism is therefore not direct, in the sense that it neither leads to nor causes the revolt by later secularists against the tradition. One might argue that it is a symptom of a certain mentality, a willingness to stake out an independence from scripture, even in the thick of a traditional culture. It is this mentality that may have predisposed certain Jews, once they became infected with modernity, to break from the religion. And the text is also available to those moderns who would use it to give their philosophies a historical pedigree, much as Isaac Deutscher's invocation of Elisha ben Abuya is an example of such a search for a secular forebear among religious heretics.

The religious tradition may have prepared the ground for modern secularism in other ways. For example, Gershom Scholem famously argued that the antinomian seventeenth-century messianic movement led by Shabbtai Zvi sowed the seeds of the Jewish Enlightenment by shattering rabbinic authority. Here, the relationship between the premodern and the modern might be called dialectical since one of the most mystical movements in Jewish history becomes the ground for its opposite, modern rationalism. Another example of this type, to be examined later, is Moses Maimonides' "negative theology," in which God becomes so transcendent that a later thinker—Spinoza—could turn him into his opposite, the equivalent of the world.

Since the creators of Jewish secularism were intellectuals, some of them products of yeshiva education, it was only natural that they would find their inspiration in books, starting with books from within the religious tradition. Later, the books of earlier secularists, notably Baruch Spinoza, fulfilled a similar role. Jewish secularism as an intellectual tradition is therefore the product of the writers of books basing themselves on other books even as they rejected the books on which they were raised. Intertextuality is the key to this literature.

What we find here is the Jewish analogue to another of Funkenstein's definitions of secular theology: nontheologians practicing theology. In the Jewish case, these literati, starting with Spinoza, were often not rabbis; indeed, they were self-conscious rebels against the rabbis. This literary chain reaction had a peculiar character. The creators of Jewish secularism were primarily Ashkenazi (i.e., northern and eastern European Jews). Theirs was a revolt of sons against traditionalist fathers. But the tradition in which they found inspiration was often that of the Sephardic (Spanish) Jews, especially the philosophical tradition mediated through Islam.[26] One might argue that in revolting against their fathers, they turned instead to their "uncles."[27] The most prominent of these uncles was Moses Maimonides, the towering figure whose thought will figure prominently in the chapters to follow.

This uncle-nephew relationship continued with the adoption of Spinoza, the Sephardic son of Marranos, as their radical progenitor. Isaac Deutscher related that one reason he came to question religion was that his father gave him Spinoza to read. Deutscher's father had himself earlier written a book on Spinoza and had thus already embarked on the road away from religion before his son.[28] The younger Deutscher's path to secularism through Spinoza was not unique, and the enigmatic Dutch philosopher will, not surprisingly, be a central figure for much of this book. Spinoza stood on the cusp of modernity, indeed, arguably as the first secular philosopher. While he would no doubt have resisted the title "secular Jew," since he evidently relinquished all ties to the Jewish people, he was embraced by generations of Jewish secularists as their model and precursor.

Because Spinoza was not only the first modern philosopher but equally the last medieval one, he points back to the premodern Jewish tradition before he points forward to his modern inheritors. It was often by adopting Spinoza as one's spiritual father that later Jewish secular thinkers indirectly came into dialogue with the medieval tradition, even if they never explicitly mentioned it. Spinoza will therefore serve as a fulcrum for the first three chapters of this book, providing the bridge between the religious tradition and its secular progeny.

I have used the term "secularism" repeatedly without having defined it, and a preliminary definition would seem to be in order. Since, as I have already suggested, there are many varieties of secularism depending on their cultural context, we may be justifiably hesitant before giving a global or essential definition of Jewish secularism. Such a definition will instead have to emerge phenomenologically from the sources. But, following Talal Asad, we can distinguish two separate, if related, meanings of the word.[29] In his vocabulary, "secular" refers to a metaphysical position: the rejection of the supernatural in favor of a materialist view of the world. The word "secularism," on the other hand, refers to the political doctrine of separation of church and state.[30] For the secularist, following Immanuel Kant, law should derive not from an external divine source but from autonomous human decisions. To remove religion from the state means to leave humans in full command of their political fate. While materialism thus defines the metaphysical philosophy of the secular, humanism defines the political theory of secularism.

These categories are not entirely adequate by themselves, and adoption of one does not necessarily entail adoption of the other. Consider, for example, the eighteenth-century Enlightenment philosopher Moses Mendelssohn, who certainly believed in the existence of the deity and in its role in the world but who nevertheless outlined a secularist theory of the separation of religion from the state. Moreover, there are many Jews today—as well as in the past—who claim to believe in the existence of God but also define themselves as secular, by which they mean that they do not

identify with any of the religious movements of Judaism and do not follow
the revealed law. To translate a modern Christian term, they are the "unsynagogued." These Jews are religious in terms of abstract belief but secular
in terms of practice. On the other hand, there are those who *do* belong to
synagogues and practice Jewish law but are secular in their beliefs. One can
reject God's existence but still live according to his law. ⌉

For many of the thinkers we will consider, the metaphysical and the political went hand in hand. Zionist thinkers will necessarily play a major role
in this book since the movement originated as a profoundly secular revolution against the perceived religion of exile. But Zionism as both a political
and cultural movement was itself the product of a moment in history—before and after the turning of the twentieth century—that produced many
ideological challenges to traditional life.⌈Fed by mass emigration, urbanization, and economic upheaval, social revolution and nationalism in both
their Jewish and non-Jewish forms captured the Jewish street. Bundism, territorialism, communism, and liberalism joined Zionism as political answers
to the crisis of late-nineteenth- and early-twentieth-century Jewish life. All
sought salvation in some form of politics, and all did so in conscious opposition to traditional religion.[31] The power of such politics was such that even
the Orthodox felt compelled to form their own political movements, if only
to defend themselves against the antireligious alternatives.⌉

In addition to the metaphysical and political "formations of the secular," two others seem critical: history and culture. Secular Jews often describe their relationship to their identities in terms of history. They may
identify with the Hebrew Bible not as a work of religion but, instead, as a
prescription for social justice or as a document of culture. They may find in
the narrative of Jewish history a collective past that informs who they are
today, even if their beliefs and practices have no connection with Judaism
as a religion. This attention to history is not, however, merely academic or
antiquarian. Rather, it is a form of what Maurice Halbwachs called "collective memory."[32]⌈Although Jews have always defined themselves according
to mythic memories—the Exodus from Egypt, the destruction of the Temples—modern Jews have created their own secular versions of collective
Jewish memory, often grounded in nontheological readings of the Bible as
well as in later history.[33]⌉

Moreover, for many modern Jewish intellectuals, this past was prologue
to a secular Jewish culture in the present. The fin de siècle was as much a

moment of cultural revolution as it was political. Secular writers sometimes claimed that the historical culture of the folk, as opposed to that of the rabbis, could inspire a nonreligious renaissance of Jewish culture in the modern period. Others translated the non-Jewish cultures of their surroundings into a Jewish idiom. To do so, some argued for a secularization of Hebrew, the ancient language of the Jews that had long been associated with the religion of Judaism. Others found salvation in the Jewish dialects of Yiddish and Ladino. And, finally, there were those who created a new Jewish culture in European languages, whether Russian, German, English, or French. Divorced from religion, language became the handmaid of history for constructing a secular culture.

Judaism as a religion is a modern invention no less than Jewish secularism. In an effort to define this religious formation, many modern Jewish thinkers have searched for an "essence" or "essences" of Judaism, a reduction of its many beliefs and practices to an eternal core. Already in the Middle Ages, philosophers tried to articulate "principles of belief," ranging from thirteen to one. The Zohar, the chief work of the medieval Jewish mysticism, proposed a tripartite definition, proclaiming that "Israel and the Torah are one," that God and Israel are identical, and that the Torah is nothing but God's name.[34] In this fashion, a kind of Jewish version of the trinity emerged. The trope took on new life in the modern period. Updating the Zohar's argument, a range of thinkers suggested that Judaism rests on three concepts: God, Torah, and Israel. Thus, for example, the American Jewish theologian Mordecai Kaplan, in his *Judaism as a Civilization*, refers to the "well-known trilogy, God, Israel and Torah."[35] Or more recently, the Reform rabbi Leo Trepp writes: "The Covenant unfolds through the interaction of God, Israel and Torah. They are one and inseparable: God has an ongoing direct relationship with Israel, structured by Torah."[36]

Jewish secularists typically reject the idea that Judaism has an essence. The past is no more harmonious or homogeneous than the present, and indeed, the secularist insistence on the pluralism of the past can serve as an argument for pluralism in the present. Nevertheless, I will argue that these three originally medieval categories provided the questions to which secular thinkers responded with new answers. To quote Hans Blumenberg, "the [modern] philosophy of history is an attempt to answer a medieval question with the means available to a post-medieval age."[37] In this way, even if a modern thinker did not explicitly invoke the past, it was often that historical tradition that provided the very structure for the Jewish "post-medieval age."

The chapters that follow are therefore organized around the categories of God, Torah, and Israel. Each chapter starts by examining how the traditional categories might have contained in a nutshell the source of their later secularizations. In chapter 1, we will see how the God of the Bible lost his personality in the philosophy of Moses Maimonides and then became nature in the renderings of Spinoza and his disciples. The medieval Kabbalah provided the source for another modern vision of God, as "nothingness" or "void." And, finally, paganism suggested another alternative to the God of tradition. In chapter 2, we turn to secular readings of the Bible, but first pausing to observe how the Bible itself and some of its medieval interpreters already prepared the ground for such readings. Stripped of its status as revelation, the Bible now emerged as a historical, cultural, or nationalist text. Chapters 3 and 4 treat the final category, Israel. Chapter 3 concerns itself with the new definitions of Israel as a nation, a definition that has its roots in earlier Jewish history. But the way secular thinkers shaped this definition was equally grounded in modern ideas: race, nationality, and the state. Chapter 4 turns to another way of defining the traditional category of Israel: history, language, and culture. Culture in particular is a modern concept that, in the hands of Jewish secularists, comes to take the place of religion. In the modern transformations of each of these traditional categories, we will find the Jewish analogues of Funkenstein's secular theology, the construction of secular ideas with the tools of theology.

Although the argument of this book is that secularism has its dialectical ground in the tradition it overturns, not every thinker I discuss necessarily spelled out his or her debt to the tradition. But by offering secular answers to the questions raised by the categories of God, Torah, and Israel, I want to claim that all these thinkers are in dialogue, however implicitly, with premodern Judaism. Moreover, not all these thinkers necessarily addressed all three categories. Some struggled profoundly with the question of God, while others were indifferent to it. The tradition of secular Jewish thought might perhaps better be called *traditions*, in the plural.

Jewish secularism may be seen as the attempt to fashion a countertradition,[38] an alternative to Judaism as a religion that has its own intellectual lineage. While it may sometimes seem as if the story of secularization is a narrative of the world we have lost, secularism is not only a negative; it is also an effort to fashion a new identity out of the shards of the past. This lineage consists of a chain of ideas that arose in rejection of the religious tradition yet were still tied to that which they overturned. It is my aim in this study to make explicit the warp and woof of this countertradition and, in so doing, illuminate the identity that Jewish secular thinkers have sought to create.

Chapter 1

God: Pantheists, Kabbalists, and Pagans

It is often said that Judaism has no orthodoxy (correct belief), only ortho-praxis (correct practice). The commandments, as spelled out in the Bible, elaborated by the rabbis, and codified by medieval sages, were the foundation for the Jewish religion to a far greater extent than theology. Belief in God as the source of these laws was, of course, a given, but without the elaborate dogma and its attendant heresies that one finds in Christianity. One might argue that this theological reticence provided part of the mentality in the modern period for those secular Jews who denied God's existence altogether. If one's culture was little preoccupied with the divine being's biography, personality, and attributes, how much easier then to imagine a world without him. Yet it would be a mistake to equate secularism with atheism. Many secular Jewish thinkers did not abandon the idea of God, even as they stripped him of his biblical personality and rabbinic authority.

In this chapter, we will follow three trends of secular thought, each grounded dialectically in premodern texts. The first is the transformation of the biblical God into nature, a trail first blazed by Baruch Spinoza in the seventeenth century and then followed by a series of thinkers whom I will call generically "Spinoza's children," from Salomon Maimon and Heinrich Heine to Sigmund Freud and Albert Einstein. We shall see how Spinoza and his children stood on the shoulders of the premodern Jewish tradition, especially the philosophy of Moses Maimonides. The second group of thinkers—Hayim Nahman Bialik, Gershom Scholem, and Franz Kafka—whom I term "secular Kabbalists," built upon the medieval mystical doctrine of God as "nothingness" to describe a world either devoid of the divine or at most haunted by his shadow. If Spinoza's children might be loosely called pantheists, since they hold that God is equivalent to nature, the secular Kabbalists have affinities with the ancient Gnostics, who believed that the true God is hidden and inaccessible. Finally, we will conclude briefly with a third trend, the secular revival of pagan gods as a weapon for dethroning the God of Judaism.

Precursors

Who was the Jewish God against whom Spinoza and his acolytes revolted? In his *Theological-Political Treatise*, Spinoza showed little doubt that the Bible's idea of God was the opposite of a philosophical one, an anthropomorphic deity exhibiting human emotions (jealousy, anger, and occasionally even love). But it is worth noting that the Bible is not theologically monolithic and that the biblical God at times anticipates the God of the philosophers. While the Torah, the historical books, and the prophets demonstrate God's hand in history, God is often present only as a "cloud of glory" (the Priestly formulation) or in the form of his name (the book of Deuteronomy).[1] According to the Priestly school, no one—even Moses—can look at God and live (Exodus 33:20). Some biblical texts speak of God's anatomy, but others make it clear that he cannot be compared in any way to human beings. The purely transcendent God of the philosophers has its roots, if not its fully realized form, in the Bible.

It is in the post-exilic Writings (that is, after the return from the Babylonian exile in the sixth and fifth centuries BCE) that one finds a thoroughgoing skepticism about the God of history. In many of the works that can be dated to the Persian or Hellenistic periods, such as Esther, Job, and Ecclesiastes, God is transcendent or even completely absent.[2] He no longer walks among humans, as he did in the literature of the First Temple period, and his communication with them has become indirect, if not mute. The verities of the formative period of the nation no longer seemed to hold. Perhaps under the influence of Greek philosophy, but perhaps also as a result of their own internal history, the Jews no longer produced books like Deuteronomy or Isaiah. To be sure, God's perceived silence gave rise not only to works of religious skepticism but also to new genres of literature, like apocalypticism; yet here, too, God's will could only be divined from reinterpreting old prophecies or inventing pseudepigraphic new ones.

For the Second Temple period, God's perceived absence from the world thus prompted a literature far removed from the classical books of the Bible. The book of Esther, for example, famously does not mention God at all. Even though one could theoretically interpret the victory of the Jews over their Persian persecutors as evidence of divine intervention, the text itself attributes it to the machinations of the seductive Esther and her canny uncle, Mordecai. Esther is first and foremost a tale of politics in the Diaspora, and its lessons are thoroughly secular.

Other works similarly do not contest the existence of God but do question his role in the world. For the author of Ecclesiastes, everything is determined by God, but "man knows none of these in advance" (9:1). The writer finds no meaning in the world, starting and concluding that "all is futile." Although the coda to the book recommends revering God and obeying his commandments, one has the sense that this pious ending was tacked on to make the less-than-Orthodox text more palatable. Exactly what the philosophical position of the author actually was remains hotly contested, and he may or may not have been the follower of a Greek school of philosophy like that of Lucretius or Epicurus. But the book was certainly ripe for the picking by a modern secularist. For example, the nineteenth-century Jewish historian Heinrich Graetz, in a remarkable letter to Karl Marx, recommended his commentary on Ecclesiastes to his antireligious interlocutor on the following grounds:

> [I]ts author [i.e., the author of Ecclesiastes] is a rude realist in a world of fantasies turned towards the heavens, who had the courage to say outright that in a certain sense *this world* should to be more important than that doubtful *other world* (*Jenseits*), and who, nineteen hundred years ago[,] already preached the rehabilitation of the flesh [Graetz writes the last phrase in French].[3]

Graetz was certainly no secularist, but he knew enough of Marx's philosophy to understand that such a secular interpretation of Ecclesiastes would appeal to the founder of scientific socialism, who had written his doctoral dissertation on Democritus, Epicurus's predecessor.

A book with similar doubts about the divine is Job, which radically challenges prophetic theology.[4] The prophets had taught that punishment is the direct consequence of sin. Job's friends articulate the same argument in an attempt to understand his suffering, but he rejects their explanations. He has committed no sin to justify his downfall. The theology that might be called the hallmark of biblical Judaism now turns out to be a conventional cliché, irrelevant to man's true predicament. It is Job's questioning of God that is authentic, not the pious and self-satisfied pontificating of his friends. In the end, of course, God does reveal himself to Job, but his answer is anything but theologically satisfying: "Where were you when I created the world?" Indeed, God's answer, although delivered in words, is more a demonstration of power than it is an argument.

For the rabbis of late antiquity, God was also largely an absent character. To be sure, they spoke of God's presence (*shekhina*) going into exile with the Jewish people. But the Almighty himself remained sequestered in his heavens. As the story of Rabbi Eliezer, discussed in the introduction, conveys, God did on occasion speak through a *bat kol* (heavenly voice), but in general the rabbis believed that prophecy had ended. It was this agnostic view of God that may have prompted in reaction a nonrabbinic literature of heavenly palaces in which a mystic journeyed to the heavens to behold the divine throne.

It was no doubt the reticence of the rabbis that gave rise to the view that Judaism has no prescribed theology. But the confrontation with Islamic philosophy and the challenge of the Karaites (those Jews in the eastern Mediterranean starting in the eighth or ninth centuries who rejected the authority of the rabbis) caused medieval Jewish thinkers to define core Jewish beliefs in theological terms. Saadiah Gaon's tenth-century *Book of Beliefs and Opinions*, the first work of medieval Jewish philosophy, was also the first to articulate such beliefs. Moses Maimonides (1138–1204) took this effort further by distilling Judaism's "beliefs and opinions" into thirteen principles. Perhaps his motivation was to match Islam's simple profession of faith with a Jewish parallel. Several of Maimonides' successors tried to outdo him by reducing the principles of faith to three—and then finally to one.[5] These philosophical exercises to define a Jewish "dogma" were just that—exercises—and Maimonides' *Guide of the Perplexed* was widely regarded as dangerous to Jewish practice. If anyone was liable to excommunication because of belief, it was more likely Maimonides and his followers than simple believers.[6] But medieval Judaism never developed an Inquisition. In general, the question of God and correct belief about him remained the province of a tiny coterie of philosophers. Yet when modern thinkers encountered this philosophical tradition, it could become the catalyst for a radical trajectory never envisioned by its progenitors.

Medieval Jewish philosophy thus prepared the ground for the radical subversion of the biblical God, which explains why later generations of secular rebels would embrace not only Spinoza but also Maimonides, read as if through the eyes of Spinoza. Indeed, in the eighteenth and nineteenth centuries, the great Andalusian rationalist became *the* medieval model for modern secularists.[7] Those rebelling against rabbinic authority often surreptitiously read his *Guide of the Perplexed* as a subversive work. On the face of it, though, Maimonides was an improbable candidate for this role. One of the harshest Jewish critics of astrology, Maimonides had no use for the science that seemingly did away with divine providence. And his *Guide* is perhaps the most thoroughgoing attempt to reconcile faith with reason. As the greatest codifier of Jewish law in the Middle Ages, Maimonides was anything but a rebel against tradition. On a number of different levels, though, Maimonides' philosophy contains radical ideas that excited violent opposition in his lifetime and were available for even more radical reinterpretation in the modern age.

To give a full account of Maimonides' thought would lie far outside the scope of this book,[8] but in this chapter and the two following, we will encounter five aspects that seem particularly relevant to secular appropriation: negative theology, nature, biblical exegesis, the historical interpretation of the commandments and political theory.

If the God of the Hebrew Bible was both transcendent and immanent— that is, present in the world—Maimonides' God was utterly transcendent, so removed from the world as to have nothing in common with it. Maimonides arrived at this position by a radically allegorical reading of the Bible. Not only did he reject biblical anthropomorphisms (attributing to God a hand or a mouth), he rejected the attribution of *any* human or earthly characteristics to God: "[A]nything that entails corporeality ought of necessity to be negated in reference to Him and . . . all affections likewise should be negated in reference to Him."[9] God lacks a body as well as all emotions and other human qualities. This leads Maimonides to negate all positive statements about God. One cannot, for example, say of God that he is good. To do so would arouse comparisons with goodness in our world: is God better or worse than person X? In addition, to posit of God that he is good raises the possibility that he might, at some particular time, lose that quality, just as any human being who is good might, at some point, become evil. No matter how superlative God is in goodness, the very nature of goodness is that one can be deprived of it. And that is inadmissible for God, who doesn't change and lacks nothing.

The only way that Maimonides can find to insulate God from the relative nature of our world is to describe him by negations: he has no body and has no emotions. But what about qualities like goodness? The correct way to state it is by a "negation of a privation": God does not lack goodness. This statement is not the same as saying that God is good. Instead, it says that whatever God has with respect to goodness, it is not something that would cause a lack.

The argument through which Maimonides arrives at this negative theology is complicated and need not detain us here.[10] What is important for our purposes are its consequences. Maimonides' God, who can only be described by negatives, is as far from the God of the Bible as one might imagine. This is a thoroughly transcendent God, one that would appear to be utterly remote from our world, since he cannot share anything with our world and remain God. This is a God who can only be worshipped by philosophers, insofar as such worship consists of meditation on negations.

Although Maimonides holds that a chain of negations leads ultimately to the affirmation of God's unity (albeit in the form of a negative proposition), it could just as well—against Maimonides' intention—lead to the final, big negation of atheism: a God so transcendent that "he" cannot be described is virtually a God that doesn't exist. It was perhaps in reaction to the heretical potential in Maimonides' theology that led the thirteenth-century Kabbalists to run to the other extreme and describe God in the most frankly human terms imaginable, including the erotic. The Kabbalists' anthropomorphic myth of the divine confirms in a negative way the atheistic threat of Maimonides' God.

By abstracting God from the world, Maimonides cleared the way for an autonomous realm of nature. Not that nature operates outside of divine providence, but it does so under what medieval scholastics called "general providence," or the laws of nature. The world, says Maimonides, represents God's "attributes of action," which means that all we can know of God are the effects of his creation. But the mechanism by which he accomplished this creation is unknown to us. We can infer nothing about the Creator from these laws except that they are self-evidently the product of a rational Creator. Maimonides thus articulated a medieval version of the modern religious argument from design: since the universe appears to be rationally ordered, it must have been ordered by an intelligent designer.

As a follower of Aristotle, Maimonides believed that the world is governed by necessity: everything that happens in it is a necessary product of the laws of nature, an anticipation, as well, of Spinoza's universe. This determinism was a reaction against one school of Muslim philosophy that held that everything in the world requires a unique intervention by God: a stone cannot fall unless God wills it to do so. The medieval Aristotelian position, which anticipated eighteenth-century deism, removed God from nature and left only his laws. The system works on its own, while God himself remains utterly transcendent. Insofar as God is said to "cause" actions within nature, it is really just a figure of speech or a formal statement. Physics stands separate from metaphysics.

This argument from necessity produced a head-on clash with the biblical doctrine of miracles. How could God suspend the laws that he himself had created if these laws were necessary and sufficient? Many medieval thinkers gave scientific or naturalistic explanations for these miracles and thus brought them under general providence. So, too, did Maimonides, but his answer to this conundrum was more subtle.[11] There is no such thing as a thoroughly deterministic system, he argued. In giving the laws, God had to make certain choices. Should a particular sacrifice involve six lambs or seven? Should one slaughter an animal from the neck or from the throat? These choices no longer fall under the necessity dictated by reason. They are arbitrary. Thus, within any system of rational necessity, there is a small residue of contingency, of arbitrary choice: "Know that wisdom rendered it necessary—or, if you will, say that necessity occasioned—that there should be particulars for which no cause can be found."[12] It is from this realm of contingency that God performed—or, "if you will, that necessity occasioned"—most of the miracles in the Bible.[13] In this way, Maimonides was able to preserve traditional miracles and not reduce them to merely naturalistic explanations, but nevertheless incorporate them into a naturalistic philosophy. And it is striking that he equates God with necessity, a position that would be adopted by Spinoza.

Given this naturalistic approach to the Bible, it is not surprising that Maimonides and his followers would interpret events in the Bible along purely natural lines. For instance, the tablets of stone given at Mount Sinai were only "written" by God in the same sense that he planted the cedars of Lebanon, that is, by a purely natural process.[14] According to Moses Narboni, one of the commentators on the *Guide*, the stones themselves from Sinai had images of a bush, presumably like that of the burning bush.[15] If the stones had such an image, it would not be surprising to discover that they also had the forms of letters. From this position to Spinoza's later argument that the Bible is not a supernatural document seems a small step indeed.

His confrontation with Aristotle had caused Maimonides to depart radically from conventional Jewish beliefs about God and nature. To be sure, Maimonides was very far in his own mind from disavowing the existence of God. On the contrary: his doctrine of the negative attributes was designed to exalt God's unity and uniqueness. Atheism was not a medieval sin. But this was the house that Spinoza built on Maimonides' foundation. It is true, as Catherine Chalier has pointed out,[16] that Maimonides stood for everything that Spinoza rejected, especially his allegorical method of reading the Bible and his belief that Moses possessed a philosophical understanding of God. Yet, as we have seen, the twelfth-century philosopher took radical positions that his seventeenth-century successor could adopt and adapt for his own purposes. The two were at once diametric opposites but also dialectical twins, just similar enough to be two sides of the same coin. Spinoza's revolution had its feet firmly planted in the Middle Ages.

Spinoza's Revolution

Baruch/Bento/Benedict Spinoza (1632–1677) was born into the curious Portuguese community of seventeenth-century Amsterdam. The vast majority of these exiles from the Iberian Peninsula descended from converts to Christianity who had returned to Judaism. Following the 1391 pogroms in wide areas of Spain, many Jews had converted to Christianity, either willingly or under coercion. During the fifteenth century, some (the percentage is a matter of dispute among historians) of these *conversos* continued to practice aspects of Judaism in secret. Fear of these "Judaizers" (pejoratively called Marranos) prompted the establishment of the Inquisition, starting in 1478, and ultimately led to the expulsion of the Spanish Jews in 1492. Many of these Jews moved to Portugal, which, in turn, forced them to convert in 1497. Because the Inquisition was not established in Portugal until 1536, it is believed that a significant percentage of those forced to convert in 1497 practiced crypto-Judaism. Their identities, by definition, were hybrid: Christian on the outside and quasi-Jewish in private. But even their

Judaism had its own unique features, since they had to maintain their religion in secret. So, when many escaped to countries where they could practice Judaism openly, they had to deal with the contradictions between their crypto-Judaism and the rabbinical religion of such communities as those of Amsterdam, Hamburg, Italy, and the Ottoman Empire.

Much has been written about the dislocations caused by these contradictions.[17] It is thought, for instance, that the Sabbatian messianic movement of the 1660s attracted many Marranos, partly for its promise of a redemptive solution to all contradictions and partly, once Sabbatai Zvi converted to Islam, because his experience seemed to mirror their own. As one former Marrano put it: "it is fated that the Messiah should become a Marrano, just like me." With their affiliations to both Judaism and Christianity attenuated or fluid, some former *conversos* who returned to Judaism had as much difficulty accepting their new religion as they had their old. This, in turn, led a few to reject both in favor of something new: a religion of reason—or no religion at all. The communal authorities of the Portuguese "nation," as these Jews called themselves, concerned that *conversos* returning to Judaism might still be infected by heterodox ideas, in turn threatened or enacted writs of excommunication against a series of real and imagined renegades.

There were, it must be said, not many such cases; most former Marranos either embraced orthodox rabbinic Judaism or returned to Christianity. But the handful of cases known to us were spectacular in their own time and also echoed profoundly through the centuries. Three of these left special marks: Uriel (originally Gabriel) da Costa, Juan (or Daniel, after he returned to Judaism) de Prado and Baruch or Bento (later Benedict) Spinoza.

Consider Prado (1612–1669), who was born in Spain as a Christian but who undertook active Judaizing, that is, attempting to convert others to crypto-Judaism. Fleeing to Amsterdam in 1655, he was almost immediately excommunicated by the Jewish community for denying fundamental Jewish beliefs, such as resurrection of the dead. It seems that when still in Spain, he became convinced that all religions have equal access to truth; but once in Amsterdam, he expressed the view that only reason might lead to truth and that all religions were equally worthless. How exactly Prado maintained these heretical ideas while agitating in Spain for *conversos* to embrace Judaism remains a mystery, perhaps best explained by a psyche torn by contradictions. But when he was excommunicated in Amsterdam, Prado refused to accept his fate, arguing instead that he should be allowed to remain in the Jewish community despite his heterodox ideas. As Yirmiyahu Yovel has pointed out, this made Prado the first secular Jew, since he wished to be counted as a Jew even as he rejected Judaism.[18] To belong to the "Hebrew nation," Prado seemed to imply, did not require religious faith or practice.

Spinoza seems to have associated with Prado and was excommunicated a year later, in 1656, for unspecified heinous beliefs. He lived out the rest of his life making his living as a lens grinder, composing philosophical works, and corresponding energetically with a number of intellectuals, including a loyal band of followers. He did not seek another communal identity, thus becoming, through his principled individualism, perhaps the first modern man. Yet Spinoza would probably be astonished to find himself described as "the first secular Jew." As a number of recent commentators have noted, he was intent on dissolving all particularistic ties and creating a universal identity for himself as a philosopher. Rebecca Goldstein has argued that Spinoza's *Ethics*, his major philosophical work, which was published after his death, was an attempt to solve the problems of identity faced by the former Portuguese Marranos in Amsterdam.[19] Torn between Christianity and Judaism, Spinoza argued not for either a choice between the two or a synthesis of them, but for something far more radical, which Goldstein, following Thomas Nagel, calls "the view from nowhere."[20] By exposing the falsity of all partial or particular identities, Spinoza believed that only a universal identity based on an infinite God was philosophically tenable.

On the other hand, as Willi Goetschel has argued, it may not be accurate to say that Spinoza opposed in a binary fashion the particular and the universal.[21] Since no limited human mind can fully comprehend the infinite mind of God, and since our minds are always connected to our particular bodies, the "view from nowhere" can only be a theoretical construct. No matter how much we seek to transcend our particularity, we can no more escape it than we can our physicality. We always view the universal through the particular.

Goldstein may well be right that Spinoza's aspiration to discover a universal identity grew out of the struggles for identity in seventeenth-century Amsterdam, even if Spinoza himself might have rejected such a historical explanation as a "betrayal" of his philosophy. If so, then she has correctly identified one of the *particularistic* aspects of Jewish universalism: it is born from the desire to overcome the particularism of Jewish identity, but in doing so, it retains a residue of what it seeks to overcome. Indeed, the vehemence with which some secular Jews reject Judaism and embrace abstract universalism certainly appears to be peculiarly—if not uniquely—Jewish, and Spinoza was its first major exemplar.

In his fixation on the question of God, Spinoza departed from the rabbinic tradition, but he stood firmly within a medieval philosophical framework, even as he pointed forward toward modernity. Spinoza adopted the medieval idea of "substance" and used it to show that God could only be equivalent to the universe. We won't follow his argument in detail, but it runs in brief as follows: there can only be one substance, which is God.[22] That substance is infinite and absolute. All finite modes are derived from it and are contained in it, but they have only transitory or accidental existence. Absolute or infinite substance has two attributes that are known to us (although others must exist): thought and extension (space). Since nothing can exist outside of this infinite substance, all ideas and all physical entities must be part of it. Thus, the universe is equivalent to God, or, in Spinoza's famous Latin phrase: *Deus sive natura* ("God or nature"). The two concepts God and nature are interchangeable.

In the *Ethics*, Spinoza appends a note attacking those who would anthropomorphize God: "Some assert that God, like a man, consists of body and mind, and is susceptible of passions. . . . [T]hey wander far from the true knowledge of God."[23] If God had a body, he would necessarily be limited, no matter how big his limbs, which would contradict his infinitude. God's body—the universe—is of a different nature from the limited bodies we encounter in the world. Somewhat further on, he acerbically refutes those who think that if we attribute intellect and will to God, these qualities must be something like human intellect or will: "there would be about as much correspondence between the two as there is between the Dog, the heavenly constellation, and a dog, an animal that barks."[24] When we use the term "intellect" with respect to God, we are only using a metaphor, just as we call the heavenly constellation that looks to us like a dog by that name.

Although Spinoza's God is quite different from Maimonides', these arguments are squarely in the Maimonidean tradition: it is inadmissible to attribute to God any human qualities, since God and humans are literally incommensurable. It is therefore likely that it was Maimonides, as well as Maimonides' disciples—especially Levi ben Gershon and Moses Narboni—who were Spinoza's main medieval interlocutors.[25] One might say that Spinoza took over the divine attributes of action from Maimonides and argued that they are all that there is to God. There is no essence outside of them, no transcendence beyond their immanence. God *is* the universe—and nothing else. One might also say that once the transcendent God became so abstract that he could not be grasped; he vanished from sight, leaving only the universe. Maimonides' negative theology collapsed on itself with Spinoza, turning into its precise opposite: radical transcendence begat pure immanence.

This radical "dehumanizing" of God leads Spinoza to positions that generations of readers have found uncomfortable. In the last part of the *Ethics*, he writes: "God is without passions, neither is he affected by any emotion of pleasure or pain. . . . Strictly speaking, God does not love anyone."[26] Therefore: "He who loves God cannot endeavor that God should love him in return."[27] The intellectual love of God that Spinoza taught must of necessity remain unrequited, for the beloved in question is not like a human lover. One can and must love nature without expecting anything in return.

Because nothing can exist outside of the one substance, it is impossible to speak of God as acting out of his free will upon the world. Instead, the very laws of the universe are the actions of God, and as laws, these actions are necessary and determined.[28] Since God *is* nature, the only laws that he can give are the laws of nature (of course, since Spinoza denied that God had volition, he could not actually "give" anything). Thus, the revelation at Mount Sinai could not have been divine. The difference between natural and biblical laws lies in the necessity of the former and the contingency of the latter: a biblical law can be transgressed, a law of nature cannot. So, for example, God's commandment to Adam and Eve not to eat of the fruit of the Tree of Knowledge could not have been a true law because had it been, they could not have violated it, any more than that they could have violated the law of gravity.[29]

In light of this view of nature, Spinoza was probably the most deterministic of any philosopher since Aristotle, and even more than Aristotle who allowed for accidents or contingencies. Medieval scholars had debated long and hard about God's powers and whether he could suspend the laws of physics (e.g., cause the sun to stand still), mathematics (make $2 + 2 = 5$), or logic (suspend the law of excluded middle, i.e., that a proposition is either true or false).[30] While the doctrine of biblical miracles required that God be able to do the first, the second two were generally regarded as impossible. But even miracles requiring the suspension of the laws of physics seemed to many to be problematic, and there were those, such as Maimonides, who held that God took miracles out of "the realm of the possible" rather than suspended the laws of nature.

The desire to explain the biblical miracles by resorting to naturalistic explanations was not, then, an entirely modern idea. But Spinoza took it to a new extreme. Not only are the laws of nature immutable, but everything that happens within nature happens necessarily and without an external cause. Calling an event within nature a miracle is nothing but an admission that one doesn't understand its immanent cause. Or, as he puts it:

> If there were to occur in Nature anything that did not follow from her laws, this would necessarily be opposed to the order which God maintains eternally in Nature through her universal laws. So this would be contrary to Nature and Nature's laws, and consequently such a belief would cast doubt on everything and would lead to atheism.[31]

Far from proving the existence of God, miracles undermine it! The real atheists are those who mistake the Bible's stories for truth, not the scientists who give them naturalistic explanations. That the Bible revels in such miracles is but one piece of evidence that it was written not by a philosopher but by a prophet who spoke the uneducated language of his audience.

Spinoza's radical philosophy began to appear in print only toward the end of his relatively short life, with the *Ethics* seeing the light of day posthumously. The *Theological-Political Treatise* came out a full fourteen years after Spinoza was excommunicated by the Portuguese synagogue in 1656, so we cannot know for sure what were the "abominable heresies that he practiced and taught."[32] Did he already hold the same views at age twenty-three that were to scandalize generations of readers, not to speak of those who never opened even one of his books? As Steven Nadler has pointed out, the *herem* (ban) on Spinoza was unprecedented in the violence of its language and its severity: unlike other such bans, it had no time limit. Nadler has made a cogent case that Spinoza, like his predecessor in heresy, Uriel da Costa, questioned the immortality of the soul, thus casting doubt on the possibility for redemption, especially for those Marranos who had abandoned Judaism. Since many of those in the Amsterdam community still had relatives in Spain and Portugal who, unlike them, had not returned to Judaism, they would be understandably hostile to any suggestion that these relatives could not be saved in the next world.

Whether or not this was the cause of the ferocious *herem*, Spinoza's position on the immortality of the soul remained ambiguous. The only explicit statement he made on the afterlife in the *Ethics* is this: "The human mind cannot be absolutely destroyed with the body, but there remains of it something which is eternal."[33] A great deal of debate has arisen over this passage, with some claiming that Spinoza did believe in personal immortality, while others see this statement as evidence that after death the mind becomes one again with the mind of God.[34] In the latter case, the mind separated from the body loses its individuality. But if this was Spinoza's position, it puts him surprisingly in a medieval tradition, especially that associated with Levi ben Gershon, or Gersonides (1288–1344). Gersonides held that the immortality of the soul lies in the congruence between the "acquired intellect" (that is, the knowledge that one's mind has acquired) and the "active intellect" (the eternal truths of God).[35] Insofar as the contents of one's mind unite with the active intellect, one becomes immortal, but this is a form of immortality that would appear to be impersonal and, in this sense, similar to Spinoza's doctrine.

Several things become immediately apparent from this summary of Spinoza's position. First, Spinoza was a radical monotheist—in fact, so radical that the oneness of God is equivalent to the world. Second, he was no atheist, if by atheism we mean the denial of God's existence. Even if we grant, with Yirmiyahu Yovel, that Spinoza was a "Marrano of reason" who used coded language to conceal his true meaning,[36] he retained theological language for a real purpose. His God does not act on the world from the outside, yet his immanent philosophy leads, in his view, to a surer "love of God" than does any traditional doctrine. As unorthodox as his philosophy was, it was nevertheless, to quote the Romantic poet Novalis, "God-intoxicated." Yet, in preaching the intellectual love of God, he was translating into philosophical terms that most traditional of Jewish virtues: *ahavat ha-shem* ("the love of God"). He revolted against the Jewish God but nevertheless ended up close to home. For all his radical break with the past and heretical rejection of the Jewish tradition, then, Spinoza cannot be understood without reference to that tradition: he was at once the first secular Jew and the last medieval heretic. In the felicitous phrase of Harry Wolfson, "we cannot get the full meaning of what Benedictus says unless we know what has passed through the mind of Baruch."[37]

Maimonides' Stepson

The European Enlightenment generally treated Spinoza, in the words of one writer, as "the supreme philosophical bogeyman of Early Enlightenment Europe."[38] For instance, Pierre Bayle (1647–1706), the French skeptic, denounced Spinoza's pantheism and labeled him an atheist but nevertheless did much to publicize his philosophy beyond the small circle of Spinoza's free-thinking friends. The German Enlightenment was also well aware of Spinoza. In 1785, the philosophical world was rocked by a pantheism controversy in which the critic of Enlightenment, Friedrich Heinrich Jacobi (1743–1819) attacked the philosopher Gotthold Lessing (1729–1781), after the latter's death, for having embraced Spinoza's pantheism.[39] The German Jewish philosopher Moses Mendelssohn (1729–1786) sprang to the defense of his friend Lessing. Pantheism was a dirty word in this intellectual milieu, and Spinoza's alleged association with it made him deeply suspect in the eyes of many. Even though Mendelssohn acknowledged his debt to Spinoza in his own philosophy, he argued strenuously (following Spinoza's contemporary Gottfried Wilhelm Leibniz) that there was more than one "substance" and therefore God and the world were not equivalent.

Despite his excommunication by the Sephardic community in Amsterdam, Spinoza was more of a scandalous figure in the non-Jewish world than in the Jewish. Yet, for Jews seeking Enlightenment, the path often led as much through Spinoza and his medieval predecessors as it did through Voltaire and Kant. Even if it was the general atmosphere of the times that catalyzed their rebellion against the religious tradition, they often searched out Jewish sources for their secularism.

If the first seeds of secularism germinated in the Sephardic diaspora, it was in the soil of Ashkenaz—the Jews of central and eastern Europe—that they struck root. By historical consensus, the place where the Ashkenazi Jews first began to enter the modern world was Berlin in the second half of the eighteenth century. During this period, the German Jews were generally impoverished, with as many as 10 percent (up to 25 percent in some places) eking out a living as vagrants and beggars (the so-called *Betteljuden*).[40] Berlin was an exception to this bleak picture. Its 3,500 or so Jews in the period in question constituted a much smaller urban population than did the Jewish communities of Hamburg or Frankfurt. Due to stringent residency laws, most of its members either belonged to a dozen very wealthy mercantile families or were gainfully employed, usually with some connection to these families. The Seven Years War (1756–1763) had produced the enormous wealth that turned this handful of families into patrons of Jewish intellectuals like Moses Mendelssohn in search of enlightenment.[41] This new wealth also made it possible for Berlin Jews to acculturate by adopting elements of German and general European culture. Indeed, Mendelssohn was the model example of such acculturation, winning the admiration of German philosophers like Lessing, who became his close friend. With this new social reality came a weakening of rabbinic and traditional authority, which in turn led to what has been labeled an "epidemic" of conversions to Christianity (epidemic is probably an exaggeration of a somewhat more modest process). To be sure, these trends did not appear suddenly in Berlin in the years after the Seven Years War. As the historians Azriel Shochat and Shmuel Feiner have shown, acculturation, materialism, and disregard of rabbinic authority could be found in the half century preceding the Jewish Enlightenment (Haskalah) period.[42] But in Berlin these developments combined in an explosive mixture that produced the movements of Enlightenment, Jewish salons, Reform, and apostasy.

It was this heady party that an uncouth Lithuanian Jew tried to crash in the late 1770s. Named Shlomo ben Joshua, but soon to be known as Salomon Maimon (1754–1800), this *Ostjude* (Eastern Jew) was initially turned away at the Rosenthaler Gate, the one entrance to Berlin allowed to the Jews. His stated desire to write a learned philosophical commentary on Maimonides' *Guide of the Perplexed* made no impression on the Jewish officials at the Gate, who were only interested in those with more gainful professions in mind. After repairing to Posen for a couple of years, Maimon returned to Berlin around 1781 or 1782. This time he was able to gain admission and subsequently made a brilliant impression on Mendelssohn and his circle. But within a few years, he had worn out his welcome, both for his dissolute lifestyle (he seems to have spent as much time in pubs as in philosophical salons) and for his radical ideas, such as his advocacy of the philosophy of Spinoza and his proud assertion that he was a "free thinker in-the-making."[43] In retrospect, he appears as what Ruth Gay has called Mendelssohn's "dark twin."[44] While Mendelssohn was deformed in his body (he was a hunchback), he was recognized for his noble spirit, but Maimon, despite his intellectual accomplishments, won few such laurels. The rest of his life was spent oscillating between brilliant philosophical

writings, including a commentary on Kant that the great Königsberg philosopher hailed as understanding him better than any of his critics, and
alienating one patron after another.

Maimon's importance for our purposes is twofold. First, as opposed to
the various intellectuals he engaged in Berlin, Maimon was a true radical, a
secularist in the mold of Spinoza, and indeed, his ideas about God are a kind
of extreme Spinozistic reading of Maimonides. The Berlin Haskalah (Jewish Enlightenment movement), and especially Mendelssohn, was initially
quite moderate in its views, espousing a religion of reason that did not contradict traditional Jewish practice. It later came to champion radical reform,
but even there, the context was religious. It might even be argued that the
lack of a true secular alternative was one reason that many Berlin Jews up to
1830 converted to Christianity. Maimon's heresy was with respect not only
to the orthodoxy of his day but also to the moderate Haskalah. As scandalous in his ideas as in his life, Maimon, like da Prado and Spinoza, was a
secular Jew before his time.

Second, Maimon wrote what many consider the first modern Jewish autobiography, one that virtually established the conventions of the genre,
at least for those like him who originated in the learned culture of eastern
Europe. Maimon's *Lebensgeschichte* (*Autobiography*) created a sensation when
it appeared in 1792, since it seemed to epitomize the way one might climb
up from the depths of superstition and ignorance to Enlightenment; and,
to make the story more dramatic, it was a Jew, emblematic of the darkest
medieval obscurantism, who was doing the climbing. As Abraham Socher
has shown in a brilliant analysis of the *Lebensgeschichte* and its relationship
to Maimon's philosophical writings, Maimon was engaged in a shrewd
invention of a persona in this work.[45] Although some information from
those who knew him corroborates his self-presentation,[46] we should still
take it less at face value than as evidence for how this Lithuanian *talmid
hakham* (talmudic student) wished to sell himself—and his book—to a
German audience.

As Socher astutely points out, Maimon remained in many ways thoroughly indebted to the culture he claimed to despise and used that culture
as the stepping-stone to Enlightenment. His philosophy was deeply rooted
in both the textuality of the Lithuanian yeshiva tradition and the Sephardic
philosophical tradition. It is of great significance that he took the name
Maimon (the name of Maimonides' father). It was a kind of adoption in

reverse: having abandoned his own Ashkenazi father both physically and in name, he now adopted as his intellectual father, not a figure out of the Western philosophical tradition, but the greatest Sephardic philosopher.

Maimon made an important intervention in the pantheism controversy a few years after it broke out. He noted that far from reducing God to the world, Spinoza's God actually swallowed up the world. In other words, Spinoza was not an atheist, since he denied not the existence of God but the existence of the world. Maimon labeled this view "acosmic" and argued that it is the diametric *opposite* of atheism.[47] For the atheist, unity (that is, God) is imaginary and only the multiplicity of the world is real; for Spinoza, unity is real and multiplicity (the world) imaginary. Maimon strikingly compared Spinoza's position to that of the Kabbalah's doctrine of contraction, whereby God created the world by contracting himself to create an empty space.[48] It is quite unlikely that Spinoza was deeply influenced by the Kabbalah, but both clearly agree that true reality lies with God and not with the world. It is also a view that partly echoes with Gnosticism, the philosophy from late antiquity that sought salvation not in the evil world but in a hidden God.

Like Spinoza, Maimon was not an atheist, at least not in the very specific sense that this discussion suggests.[49] He agreed with Spinoza, against those in the pantheism controversy, that there is only one substance. But also like Spinoza, he rejected the God of the Bible in favor of an abstract, philosophical God whose roots lie in the teachings of Maimonides. Indeed, in his autobiography, he embedded a lengthy discourse on Maimonides' philosophy that most translations have mistakenly eliminated as extraneous. The contrary is true: Maimon's philosophical indebtedness to Maimonides is essential to understanding the narration of his life.

Using a classically Maimonidean argument, Maimon claimed that the statement "God exists" is no more meaningful than the statement "God does not exist." In this world, we mean by existence something that could or will go out of existence. Such a meaning cannot be applied to God; it is a category mistake, like saying "the wall does not see" (an example from Maimonides). The existence of God is beyond rational proof since the very concept of existence cannot be predicated of God. Since both belief and disbelief in God's existence are self-contradictory, the philosopher cannot be an atheist.[50] But, by the same token, he or she cannot be a believer, at least not in the traditional sense of the word.

Maimon's God is the idea of perfection, the sum of all perfections, which, as Socher has shown, was the medieval idea of "the perfection of the soul" (*shelemut ha-nefesh*). Put differently—and in Maimonides' language—God represents the unity of the intellect and the object of thought. Our understanding can never be identical to that of God, but we can grasp what it means to unite our intellect with the object of thought through mathematics. When we think of three straight lines whose ends are connected to each other such that the sum of their angles is 180 degrees, our thought and the triangle we have constructed through our thought are one and the same. Thus, when thought is constructive in this sense, it resembles in a limited way the thought of God.

In doing so, we approach asymptotically, but do not ever reach, the infinite mind of God, a mind that does not exist in any worldly sense but instead exists as a regulative principle or a limiting concept. This language, drawn from the infinitesimal calculus of Leibniz and Newton, was one of Maimon's innovations, since he wished to apply the most recent mathematics to philosophical reasoning. When, at the end of the nineteenth century, the neo-Kantian Jewish philosopher Hermann Cohen used calculus as the model for his own highly abstract idea of God as a "principle of origin," he was reviving Maimon's philosophy, whether he knew it or not.[51]

In so far as this idea—minus the modern mathematics—goes back to Maimonides, we can trace a fascinating theological trail from Maimonides through Spinoza to Maimon and Cohen. Whether Maimonides would recognize anything of himself in these later thinkers, all of whom rejected the God of the Bible for a rarified methodological principle, he would have to admit that the logical arguments he pioneered had set in motion a train that could not easily be recalled to its station. Indeed, Hermann Cohen himself recoiled from his own secular theology at the end of his life by suggesting a new idea: a personal God in whom a suffering individual can find solace.[52] But this existentialist God—similar in a way to the God of the Bible—could only be embraced by throwing off nearly a millennium of rationalist philosophy.

Maimon's innovation over both Maimonides and Spinoza was in viewing God as a construct of our minds, a boundary toward which the mind strives. Against Maimonides, God is not a mysterious Other standing inaccessibly outside of ourselves. But against Spinoza, neither is God simply equivalent to the world. Maimon's idealism—that is, that our minds construct the world—

makes God himself a construct of the mind whose existence in the external world is no longer a question. In this sense, Maimon's idealist philosophy was even more radically antithetical to traditional theism than Spinoza's.

Maimon's ideas about miracles were equally radical. As with Spinoza, the world is thoroughly rational in the sense that the order and connection of ideas is the same as the order and connection of things. But this rationality is from the point of view of the infinite understanding, which, as we have now seen, can only be approached but never attained by our limited understanding. The rationality of the world is in the mind of God. For God, the world is like the triangle in our example above: when he thinks it, he simultaneously constructs it. Its reality is in his mind. From this point of view, what we call "matter" is a product of our limited understanding, since it only reflects one possibility, while God's mind encompasses all possibilities. From God's vantage point, there is no matter, only ideas. Thus, when we see something that seems to contradict the laws of nature, we are responding to our limited view of the world. Since we can never comprehend all the laws of nature—something only available to God—we can never determine whether a given event ought to be called a miracle. This agnosticism with respect to miracles parallels Maimon's agnosticism about God's existence. But its net effect is to make the whole question of miracles moot, a brilliant move in light of the long history of debate on the issue.

Maimon's philosophy therefore reached backward to Spinoza and Maimonides. But he also pointed forward. His idealism anticipated Fichte and Hegel, and also Hermann Cohen. He argued that the world is a creation of our minds, with God serving as the limiting case for such construction. If both Spinoza and Maimon assimilated the world into God, theirs was a very peculiar form of secularism (remembering that the original meaning of the word was "of the world"). Yet, in both cases, they freed philosophy from biblical theology, since, while retaining the language of the divine, they emptied it of its theistic meanings and turned it into a product of the human mind.

Spinoza Resurrected

While Spinoza was largely contraband for both Jews and non-Jews during the German Enlightenment, his name being enough to provoke philosophical fireworks, he became a kind of cult hero to Jews during the first half of the nineteenth century, the period often called that of Romanticism.[53] Berthold Auerbach (1812–1882) wrote a highly popular biographical novel about Spinoza, which was first published in 1837 and republished at least four times later in the century. Moses Hess, whom we will consider in detail in a later chapter, signed his first book in 1837 "a disciple of Spinoza" (*einem Jünger Spinoza's*), possibly in contrast to the contemporaneous "young Hegelians" (*Jung Hegelianer*).[54] Hess's *Holy History of Mankind* divides world history into the Hegelian three stages, but he starts with Moses, proceeds to Jesus, and ends with Spinoza, the thinker who for him ushers in the modern age. Later, the American Jewish poet Emma Lazarus (1849–1887) countered the new wave of nineteenth-century anti-Semitism by contrasting Spinoza and Shylock.[55] The former stood for all that was noble in the Jewish people, a reflection no doubt of Lazarus's own secularism and detachment from organized Jewish life.

Spinoza also had a renaissance in eastern Europe. The Russian *maskil* (follower of the Haskalah) and later Zionist Moses Leib Lilienblum describes in his autobiography how he agonized between the God of Israel and the "god of Spinoza," finally choosing Spinoza.[56] But like other incipient secularists trained in the Eastern European yeshiva, Lilienblum arrived at his heretical beliefs through the traditional Jewish library. Attacked by the rabbi of Wilkomir for organizing a Haskalah reading circle and his books confiscated, Lilienblum confesses to having read Judah Halevi's twelfth-century *Kuzari*. On the other hand, he refuses to admit that he has also been reading Maimonides' *Guide of the Perplexed*.[57] Indeed, as an indication of how heretical Maimonides' great book had come to be perceived, at least by Orthodox Jews in eastern Europe, Lilienblum confesses at an earlier point that he was afraid to even start reading the *Guide*, since it might lead him to *apikorsut* (heresy).[58] Note again, the forbidden authors—from Judah Halevi and Maimonides to Spinoza—are all Sephardim, since the philosophical investigations that later Ashkenazi authorities, facing modernity, found so subversive originated in medieval Spain.

Another nineteenth-century admirer of Spinoza, as well as Emma Lazarus's inspiration, was Heinrich Heine (1797–1856). One of Germany's greatest poets, essayists, and critics of the Romantic age, Heine converted to Christianity in 1825 but famously denigrated his conversion as a mere "entrance card" to European society. In this respect, he represented those other German Jews—Marx's father was one—who converted to Christianity but not out of faith. The Jews of Heine's day—converted or not—celebrated the German Enlightenment ideal of *Bildung*, a hard-to-translate term combining reason, education, and culture. It has been suggested that, when other Germans turned to Romantic nationalism, only the Jews continued to believe in *Bildung*, thus creating a kind of German Jewish subculture. *Bildung* served as a shorthand substitute for religion, a secular belief system founded on German culture, but with a peculiarly Jewish twist.[59]

Consonant with his mordant criticisms of German nationalism, Heine was one of the key proponents of this secular, universalist ideal and indeed served as its exemplar for future generations of German and other European Jews. Despite his conversion, he never lost his interest in Jewish matters and wrote a number of historical poems and essays on Jewish subjects, many of which subversively celebrated the lives and customs of the folk as opposed to the rabbinic establishment. He had been briefly active in the Society for the Culture and Science of Judaism, which founded the historical study of Judaism and Jewish history. Heine also took a radical stance on the role of the Jews in European history. In an essay from 1836, "The Romantic School," he argued that the Jews had influenced Europe in three ways: through their suffering, through Christianity as a product of Judaism, and through Jewish thinkers, such as Spinoza and Moses Mendelssohn. Taken together, Heine's writings on the Jews constitute the first coherent statement of Jewish secularism in a language that clearly resonated with his contemporaries.[60]

Where pantheism was a dirty word in the period of Enlightenment, it became the religion of the Romantic age. Heine was one of its most fervent believers. In his essay, "Religion and Philosophy in Germany" (1835), he wrote:

> The immediate end of all our most recent reforms is the rehabilitation of matter—the restoration of its proper dignity, its moral recognition, its religioussanctification, its reconciliation with spirit. . . . God is identical with the world. . . . [H]e manifests himself in man, who both feels and thinks. . . . In man divinity attains self-consciousness—and the latter in turn is revealed through man.[61]

Heine then injected Spinoza with a dose of Hegel: this pantheistic God is the hero of world history, a category that is totally absent in Spinoza.

Heine's celebration of the material world against denatured spirit comes through clearly in his poetry. One of the more famous stanzas in his early poem, "Germany: A Winter's Tale," reads:

Yes, sugar peas for every man
As soon as their pods break.
We leave the heavens
To the angels and the sparrows.[62]

It was in the material needs of human beings—"sugar peas"—that Heine found true spirit.

In "Religion and Philosophy in Germany," Heine wrote a short passage on Spinoza that makes clear his debt to his seventeenth-century forebear as a major source for his own pantheism: "When we read Spinoza, we have the feeling that we are looking at all-powerful Nature in liveliest repose—a forest of thoughts, high as heaven, with green tops ever in motion, while below the immovable trunks are deeply rooted in the eternal earth." [63] He sees in Spinoza a descendant of the Hebrew prophets and labels his life "as blameless, pure and spotless as that of his divine cousin, Jesus Christ." He then appends one of the best one-paragraph summaries of Spinoza's philosophy, concluding that "only stupidity and malice could term this doctrine 'atheism.'" Echoing Maimon's interpretation of Spinoza, he sees this philosophy as the most pristine affirmation of God.

At the end of his life, when he came to embrace an idiosyncratic personal God, Heine reflected on whether in his earlier writings he had "torn the curtain from the German heaven and revealed the fact that all the gods of the old faith had departed from it, and that only an old spinster with leaden hands and a heart full of sorrow still sits there—Necessity."[64] He confesses sorrowfully that this is indeed what he had done, and as a result the "monks of atheism" now trumpet their heresy with unappetizing fanaticism. The only God left was necessity, the God of Spinoza. Moreover, Heine had embraced Spinoza's God out of his own historical analysis of the fate of the Jewish God:

> Our heart is full of a terrible pity. It is old Jehovah himself who is preparing for his death. We have known him so well from his cradle onwards, in Egypt, where he was brought up among divine calves. . . . We saw him say farewell to the playfellows of his childhood . . . in order to become a little god-king in Palestine to a tribe of poor shepherds. . . . We watched him emigrate to Rome, where he renounced all his national prejudices. . . . We watched him becoming yet more spiritualized. . . . [H]e became a loving Father, a friend of humanity . . . but nothing could save him. Do you hear the passing bell? Kneel down—they are bringing the sacrament to a dying God.[65]

The Jewish God thus has the same history as the Jewish people, at least, up to the rise of Christianity. With Christianity, he loses his connection to the material, becoming more and more spiritual and thus increasingly senescent. With the Enlightenment, this now-ethereal deity has reached the end of his long life, having played out his role on the stage of history. In an amusing version of this *Gotterdämmerung*, Heine has Spinoza administer the coup de grâce, as he wrote to his friend, Moses Moser in 1823:

> Perhaps the old Baron of Mt. Sinai and Autocrat of Judea has also become enlightened, has cast off national sentiment and given up his claims and adherents in favor of some vague cosmopolitanism? I'm afraid the Old Gentleman has lost his head, and the *petit juif d'Amsterdam* [i.e., Spinoza] may with some reason whisper in his ear: "*Entre nous, Monsieur, vous n'existez pas*" [Between us, Sir, you don't exist].[66]

The "death" of the Jewish—and Christian—God, which by the end of his life, Heine had come to mourn, was therefore partly the result of a development within Jewish history: the philosophy of Spinoza.

The death of the Jewish God did not, however, mean for Heine the death of the Jews. As critical as he could be of contemporary Jewish life, he was not yet ready to give it a decent burial. On the contrary, the governments of Europe should both emancipate the Jews *and* fund their synagogues, provide them leather for their tefillin and flour for their matzoh.[67] The state should encourage not the baptism of the Jews—"for this is merely water and water dries easily"—but rather circumcision. Heine, who himself had taken the baptismal plunge, wants to preserve the Jewish religion not out of conventional religiosity but to show that "the people of God still exist." The Jewish people, whom he calls "this Swiss guard of deism," is implicitly closer to Spinoza's God than to that of the rabbis.

Heine was equally ironical about other gods. Neither the pagan gods, who enjoyed a revival in both the Enlightenment and Romanticism, nor Christ escaped his pen. One of his more amusing poems treats the god Apollo, who relates that many centuries before, he had been exiled from Greece to wander in Europe.[68] A nun in a cloister on the Rhine has fallen in love with him and escapes the nunnery to search for him:

> Have you seen the god Apollo?
> It's a scarlet cloak he wears;

> Sweetly sings and plays the lyre
> And he is my darling idol.

A disheveled traveler, marked by his beard and his gestures as a Jew, replies:

> If I've seen him? Sure I've seen him!
> Not just once, but many times;
> Back home up in Amsterdam
> At the German synagogue.

> For he was the cantor there,
> And his name was Rabbi Faibisch
> In High-German that means Apollo [i.e., Phoebus Apollo]
> But my idol he is not.

Punning on Phoebus Apollo, Heine turns the Greek god into an Ashkenazi Jew, Rabbi Faibisch. His mother "sells sour pickles in the market and decrepit trousers, too." Moreover, this Rabbi Faibisch has not even remained an Orthodox Jew:

> He is even a free-thinker,
> Eats swine and has lost his job;
> Now he roams about the country
> With a troupe of painted actors.

On one level, this poem takes the form of the hoary Jewish joke that deflates the ethereal culture of classical Greece by comparing it to the mundane reality of the Ashkenazi Jews. In the process, Heine manages to mock both cultures. But the poem is also a kind of allegory in which the marriage of classical Greece and European Christianity somehow goes astray as a result of the intervention of the Jews: the god Apollo becomes first a disreputable rabbi and then a dissolute free-thinker. It is the Jews, representing secular modernity, who disrupt this marriage: *their* story becomes the culmination of the history of the West.

Heine's iconoclastic treatment of both God and the gods was therefore explicitly in the tradition of Spinoza, but we might wonder if a deeper debt to the Jewish tradition was at work. Could it be that the relative weakness of Jewish theology created a space for Heine's comedic and ironic reflections on the divine? If Jewish theology reached its apogee with Maimonides' doctrine of negative attributes, then this transcendent—perhaps even absent—

deity could hardly be touched by the poet's "human language." And perhaps this theological black hole allowed for a host of modern expressions, from Heine's pantheism to Sigmund Freud's frank atheism and Albert Einstein's scientific Spinozism.

That Freud (1856–1939) stood within this tradition becomes evident from a brief passage in *The Future of an Illusion* (1927), his manifesto against supernatural religion. Partaking in the culture of *Bildung*, he argues for what he calls "education to reality," according to which people must withdraw "their expectations from the other world and (concentrate) all their liberated energies into their life on earth."[69] If they do so, then "with one of our fellow-unbelievers, they will be able to say without regret:

> We leave the heavens
> To the angels and the sparrows."

We immediately recognize the couplet as Heine's. What is less obvious is the term "fellow-unbeliever" (*Unglaubensgenossen*) which is a pun on the word for a fellow member—or coreligionist—of the (Jewish) faith. Heine himself is the source for this phrase as well, but he used it to refer to Spinoza.[70] Thus, in invoking both this term and the poem, Freud deliberately creates a "synagogue" of the unbelievers, whose members include Spinoza, Heine, and Freud himself.

Recent scholarship has demonstrated conclusively that Freud identified stubbornly as a Jew, not despite his atheism but, even more strikingly, *because* of it.[71] To his Christian disciple, the pastor Oskar Pfister, he wondered with bemusement why the invention of psychoanalysis had to await "a completely godless Jew?"[72] He clearly regarded this as no coincidence, noting, in a letter to the Vienna lodge of the B'nai B'rith, that because he did not belong to "the compact majority," he was freer to pursue an iconoclastic theory.[73]

Even though he does not mention Judaism explicitly in *The Future of an Illusion*, it makes an important, if cameo, appearance. In that essay, he describes the origins of religion in terms that parallel those of child development. The purpose of civilization, he insists here as well as in his provocative essay, "Civilization and Its Discontents" (1930), is to force us to renounce our instincts and thus defend us against nature, meaning our basest appetites.[74] So it is with a child: "For once before one has found oneself in a similar state of helplessness: as a small child, in relation to one's parents.

One had reason to fear them, and especially one's father; and yet one was sure of his protection against the dangers one knew."[75] In order to defend against the childlike fears of helplessness whose memory adults carry within them, they give the forces of nature "the character of a father" by turning them into gods. These gods defend them equally against both the dangers of nature and the threats within human society. In *Totem and Taboo* (1913), Freud gave a different account of the origin of religion in which the "primal horde" killed its leader and, then, out of guilt, turned him into a totemic god. Either way, the god was created out of a *projection* of an earthly authority figure onto the heavens.

In the next stage of religion, these many gods are consolidated into one:

> The people which first succeeded in thus concentrating the divine attributes was not a little proud of the advance. It had laid open to view the father who had all along been hidden behind every divine figure as its nucleus. . . . Now that God was a single person, man's relations to him could recover the intimacy and intensity of the child's relation to his father. But if one had done so much for one's father, one wanted to have a reward, or at least to be his only beloved child, his Chosen People."[76]

It was therefore the Jews—God's chosen people—who prepared the ground theologically for Freud's own achievement: they exposed the relationship to God as that of a father with his chosen son. From the point of view of psychoanalysis, this was the critical advance because it is not possible to overcome the father until one realizes that the object of one's struggles *is* the father. Without Judaism, no psychoanalysis. In the next chapter, we will return to Freud's application of this insight to the Bible.

Freud did not inherit his atheism directly from Spinoza, even as he recognized Heine's "little Jew of Amsterdam" as the founder of the congregation of Jewish unbelievers. Perhaps the most important twentieth-century heir to Spinoza was Albert Einstein (1879–1955). Unlike Freud, whose family still preserved some elements of tradition, Einstein was born into a nonreligious milieu.[77] His family did not attend synagogue or celebrate Jewish holidays. As an early adolescent, Einstein rebelled briefly by adopting Orthodox practices, but this quixotic gesture toward Judaism did not last to his bar mitzvah. The real affirmation of his Jewish identity would come later as a recuperation of something largely alien. In this respect, he stood for a phenomenon not uncommon for central European Jews of the fin de siècle: the return to an idiosyncratic, nonreligious Jewish identity not inherited directly from one's parents.

In the first decade of the twentieth century, still in his twenties, Einstein and two of his friends formed an intellectual reading circle, which they mockingly named the Olympia Academy, in Bern. It was in that setting that he became acquainted with a wide range of philosophical writings, including Spinoza's *Ethics*.[78] In the 1920s, he returned to studying Spinoza, even writing a poetic homage titled "On Spinoza's Ethics."[79] From the end of 1920s to 1940 was the period during which he gave the most repeated expressions of his views on religion. Perhaps the pithiest of these was in 1929, when an American rabbi, Herbert S. Goldstein, sent him a telegram asking: "Do you believe in God? Stop. Answer paid 50 words." Einstein saved the rabbi almost half of his money by replying in only thirty words: "I believe in Spinoza's God, Who reveals Himself in the lawful harmony of the world, not in a God Who concerns Himself with the fate and the doings of mankind."[80] Throughout history, Einstein says elsewhere, "it is precisely among the heretics of every age that we find men who are filled with this highest kind of religious feeling and were in many cases regarded by their contemporaries as atheists, sometimes also as saints. Looked at in this light, men like Democritus, Francis of Assisi, and Spinoza are closely akin to one another."[81] Like the German Jewish philosopher Ernst Bloch, Einstein found true religion among the heretics.[82]

For Einstein, the universe is constructed in such a way that we can discover its laws: the rationality of our minds mirrors the rationality of the universe (the "mind of God"), a position Spinoza would have found most congenial. The goal of science must be to understand this mind: "I want to know how God created this world. I'm not interested in this or that phenomenon, in the spectrum of this or that element. I want to know his thoughts, the rest are details."[83] And, in one of his most evocative aphorisms: "Subtle is the Lord, but malicious He is not." When asked by a colleague what he meant, he replied: "Nature hides her secret because of her essential loftiness, but not by means of a ruse."[84] If the universe was constructed by a "ruse," it might have been inaccessible and would therefore appear to function miraculously. Einstein's God does not use miracles but rather uses laws that, no matter how subtle, we can hope to decipher. Interestingly enough, Maimonides claims the opposite: that God used a "ruse" (*ormat ha-shem*) to wean the Israelites away from idolatry, but this ruse was a nonmiraculous historical process. Seemingly in agreement about the lawfulness of the world, Maimonides and Einstein described it using opposite language.

Einstein's most famous statement on God's laws of nature, often misquoted, was in the context of the debate over quantum mechanics, the theory that seemed to embed indeterminacy or chance in nature. As is well known, Einstein was quite hostile to this theory, although his own physics had done much to make it possible. While he did not entirely reject probability in understanding the universe and even used it himself, he was uncomfortable with the consequences of such theories as Werner Heisenberg's famous uncertainty principle. And so, in a letter to the physicist Max Born in 1926, Einstein wrote: "Quantum mechanics is certainly imposing. But an inner voice tells me it is not yet the real thing. The theory says a lot, but does not really bring us any closer to the secret of the Old One. I, at any rate, am convinced that He does not play dice."[85] Here, Einstein appears as a true Spinozist: nature must be throughout determined, not subject to the probability of a dice game.

As with Spinoza, Einstein used God language in an inverted sense: his God is anything but the personal God of the Bible who created the world and manages its affairs from his heavenly office. But we are still left with the question: who (or what) is this God? Did Einstein believe like Spinoza that God is simply equivalent to the universe (*deus sive natura*), or that God is somehow greater than the universe? Even Spinoza's position was not simply the pantheistic equivalence of God and the *physical* universe, since extension (physicality) is only one of God's attributes. Einstein, too, seemed to hold that the universe consists of mind as well as matter. In an exchange with Israel's prime minister, David Ben-Gurion, he allowed that there must be something behind the E (energy) of $E = mc^2$.[86] The energy of the universe was perhaps the expression of an intangible spiritual essence, or what Spinoza called thought. Such a position would not make Einstein a theist in any traditional sense, but neither would it make him a crude materialist.

Since Einstein held that God has nothing to do with human affairs, a moral realm opens up for human autonomy. People are responsible for their own moral judgments. It is ironically with this Kantian theory that he articulated his affinity to Judaism:

> The pursuit of knowledge for its own sake, an almost fanatical love of justice and the desire for personal independence—these are the features of the Jewish tradi-

tion which make me thank my stars that I belong to it. . . . In the philosophical sense, there is in my opinion, no specifically Jewish point of view. Judaism seems to me to be concerned almost exclusively with the moral attitude in life and to life. . . . Judaism is not a creed: the Jewish God is simply a negation of superstition, an imaginary result of its elimination. . . . It is clear also that "serving God" was equated with "serving the living." . . . Judaism is thus no transcendental religion.[87]

Although Einstein was not raised in the liberal Judaism of late-nineteenth-century Germany and was personally hostile to its bourgeois assimilationism, his reduction of Judaism to ethics echoes several generations of German Jewish preachers and scholars. At the end of the nineteenth century, Moritz Lazarus summed up this point of view in his *Ethics of Judaism*, where he argued that the ethical core of Judaism is to be found not in the laws of the Bible or the Talmud but in the customs and practices of the Jews themselves.[88] In drawing his own radical politics, and especially his pacifism, from his interpretation of Judaism, Einstein was participating in a project that would encompass a range of Jews, from bourgeois liberals to social revolutionaries, all of whom saw in Judaism primarily a set of ethical teachings, albeit consisting of different messages. But it was here that he definitively departed from Spinoza, who thought that he could derive an ethics from his rational description of the universe. For Einstein, physics and ethics remained utterly separate disciplines.

As with Freud, Einstein's rejection of traditional religiosity and embrace of an impersonal God was accompanied by a profound affirmation of Jewish identity. In a vivid metaphor, Einstein compared the relationship of Jewish identity to religion to a snail and its shell: "It is known that a snail can shed its shell without thereby ceasing to be a snail. A Jew who abandons his faith . . . is in a similar position. He remains a Jew."[89] He also suggested that Judaism teaches the "intoxicated joy and amazement at the beauty and grandeur of this world . . . from which true scientific research draws its spiritual sustenance." In this account, the essence of Judaism is not theistic but rather something close to Spinozism. By configuring Judaism as a celebration of this world, Einstein seemed to be arguing that it is no surprise that so many modern scientists are Jews. One need only translate these statements into a medieval language to arrive at Maimonides' evocation of the world as God's "attributes of action."

Einstein's interest in Spinoza coincided with a Spinoza revival in Germany of the 1920s. One Jewish thinker who came to maturity during the Weimar years and for whom Spinoza was crucial in constructing a secular Jewish identity was Leo Strauss (1899–1973). Influenced by the Spinoza revival, Strauss wrote one of his earliest works on *Spinoza's Critique of Religion* (1930). For Strauss, Spinoza posed the starkest challenge to revealed religion. As he wrote in a 1962 preface to the English translation of his book: "Orthodoxy could be returned to only if Spinoza was wrong in every respect."[90] What Spinoza demonstrated was that there could be no reconciliation of religion and reason. And although this was the project of a medieval philosopher like Maimonides, even he concealed heretical views within a seemingly orthodox text, as Strauss argued controversially in his later work, *Persecution and the Art of Writing* (1952).

Yet the face-off between revelation and reason could not be settled by reason. Spinoza's philosophy was itself a statement of faith that was not susceptible to proof. Although Strauss appears to have been an atheist, he was highly critical of dogmatic atheism for this very reason: atheism had no greater truth claim than belief, a position similar to Maimon's. Strauss therefore rejected the cult of Spinoza that had captured the imagination of certain Weimar thinkers, Jews and others. Spinoza, he insisted in the 1962 preface, did not provide the solution to Strauss's own "theological-political predicament" as a young Weimar Jew estranged from the traditionalism of his upbringing.

Nevertheless, as Benjamin Lazier has shown, Strauss's own philosophy completed the circle back to Spinoza.[91] In his lectures from 1949, later published as *Natural Right and History*, Strauss leveled a devastating attack on historicism for relativizing truth. Historicism was the product of modern ideas of natural right, which had collapsed in a crisis of its own making (interestingly enough, Strauss only mentions Spinoza in passing in discussing modern natural right theory). This crisis was due to the fact that modern thinkers had opposed right to nature. The solution, for Strauss, was to return to classical natural right in which truth and morality were grounded in nature (*physis*) rather than human artifice (*nomos*). Nature thus took the place of God as the source of truth, just as it did for Spinoza. As Lazier notes, Strauss was an antinomian in two senses: in opposing *physis* to *nomos* and in rejecting God's law for one grounded in nature. But since, for Spinoza, nature *is* God, Strauss appeared to end up as a kind of twentieth-century

Spinozist, perhaps against his own original intention. In this reading, Spinoza, the quintessentially modern philosopher, became the unintentional midwife for the rebirth of the ancient Greeks. Athens conquered Jerusalem by way of Jerusalem's most wayward sons.

Maimon, Heine, Freud, Einstein, and Strauss all represent different versions of Jewish Spinozism. Whether God was a limit case, the equivalent of nature, or nature a realm without divinity, the legacy of Spinoza's attack on theistic religion resonated profoundly. And each of these thinkers wished to construct a Spinozistic world with a place for the Jews. In Maimon's case, it was a place for the Jewish textual tradition—Maimonides modernized. For Heine and Einstein, it was Judaism as an ethical critique of European values. For Freud, it was Judaism as the ground for psychoanalysis. All of this would surely have confounded Spinoza himself. But as these Jewish thinkers and others appropriated and transformed their seventeenth-century forebear, they turned him from a secular man into the first secular Jew. And even if they did not quote the premodern tradition directly, as had Maimon, by embracing Spinoza as their Moses, they inherited that tradition through him.

Secular Kabbalists

Spinoza did not represent the only path to a heretical God for secular Jews. Another path lay open for those steeped even more deeply in the textual tradition, rebels against the tradition whose rebellion was phrased in the tradition's own language. These thinkers turned not to the philosophical tradition represented by Maimonides but rather to the Kabbalah, medieval Jewish mysticism. On the face of it, the Kabbalah was a far less promising source than Maimonides, since it was grounded in mythic symbols seemingly beyond the ken of reason. In fact, Kabbalah emerged in thirteenth-century Spain at least partly in reaction against Maimonides' austere God. Where the great philosopher had stripped the divine of any human attributes, banishing him even beyond the reach of human language, the Kabbalists painted God's anatomy in shockingly carnal colors. For those who longed to resurrect the personal God of the Bible after the philosophers had vanquished him, the Kabbalah offered a myth of the divine more intimate than anything in the Bible.

So, how might Kabbalah, of all disciplines, have furnished modern secular thought? The answer lies in the dialectical theology of the mystics. They postulated a God with ten emanations or powers, the so-called *sefirot*. These *sefirot* also corresponded to different parts of God's anatomy (including his genitals). But above and beyond this divine *anthropos* was the Infinite, called in Hebrew *ein sof* ("without end"). It was this Infinite God who lay beyond language, thus corresponding to Maimonides' God. About the *ein sof*, the Kabbalists said very little. But playing on the particle *ein*, they equated this aspect of God with *ayin* or nothingness (the two words are the same, the first a preposition, the second a noun).[92] In some thirteenth-century texts, the highest *sefira* (*keter* or "crown") is called *ayin*, while in others, it is the Infinite itself that is so defined. In the sixteenth-century Kabbalah, associated with Isaac Luria, when God begins to create the world, he contracts himself away from a central point, leaving an empty space (*halal ha-panui*).[93] Without this realm devoid of God, the world could not exist. The nothingness of the thirteenth-century Kabbalist now gave way to the very physical sense of separation from the divine. In all these formulations, the Kabbalists paved the way for a radical secular identification of God with nothingness or even death. Needless to say, they would have been appalled to the learn that their meditations had been turned in this kind of a direction, but such is the fate of ideas uprooted from their context and transplanted into alien soil.

An outstanding example of one such secular Kabbalist was the "national poet" of the Hebrew renaissance, Hayim Nahman Bialik (1873–1934). Like Salomon Maimon a century earlier, Bialik was steeped in the Lithuanian talmudic tradition. He had been a student in the great Lithuanian yeshiva at Volozhin, which he famously called the "schoolhouse of the nation." It was there, with others of his generation, that he discovered enlightenment in contraband books passed from one hand to another. In 1891, at age eighteen, he left for Odessa, the "new city" that was the capital of the burgeoning Jewish national revival. But, like many of his age, he retained a powerful nostalgia for the old *bet midrash*, which he eulogized in several of his most important poems. This generation of east European secular Jews came directly out of the yeshiva, and their secularism was inextricably grounded in the textual tradition they rejected.

Rather than reconstruct Bialik's secular sensibility through his poetry, we will instead examine one of his most profound and complex essays, "Revelation and Concealment in Language" (1915), a work that addresses even more directly the absence of God.[94] Written just as Bialik was entering into a long period of poetic silence, it represents the poet's own struggle with the futility of language. As we shall see, the essay concludes with a meditation on the language of poetry. Indeed, as Ariel Hirschfeld has pointed out, the role of the poet in the essay is a translation into Hebrew of European Romantic notions of the poet as a solitary genius.[95] Such Western sources appear more important than Jewish sources, which are never even mentioned overtly.[96] Yet, despite the seeming universalism of the essay, its subtext is the dialectic between the Jewish religious tradition and secularism.

Bialik starts by observing the fate of language: words that "flashed like lightning to illuminate," that captured a whole philosophical system in one expression, that "deposed kings from their thrones, shook the foundations of heaven and earth"; all these powerful words have become nothing but idle chatter. This is the way of the world: "words rise to greatness, and, falling, turn profane." Our everyday language—our *secular* language— may have its origins in profound, earth-shattering events. But this powerful language, linked to a religious experience, quickly becomes mundane and meaningless.

For Bialik, the deterioration of language from the profound to the profane is like an exile from the realm of divine meaning to the realm of the secular. He uses explicitly Kabbalistic language to describe this descent: "their core is consumed and their spiritual strength fades or is hidden, and only their husks, cast out from the private domain to the public, still persist in language."[97] This is the idiom of the Lurianic Kabbalah in which the shattering of the divine vessels leaves only the husks—or *klippot*—in exile from God. Bialik embraces this mystical doctrine for a secular account of the fate of language.

Distanced from its divine origins, we inherit language in its profane state in which only the husks remain, emptied of their original content. This is the conventional language of social interaction. It is also the language of mathematics, the domain of logic. Here, one cannot help thinking of Spinoza's very different use of mathematical language. Where, for Spinoza, geometric proofs were the only language adequate to describe God, for Bialik, this language is by definition empty of all meaning beyond the conventional. Against a whole philosophical tradition that included Spinoza and Maimon, Bialik undercuts the claim of mathematics to convey necessary truth.

Yet perhaps this state of affairs is not so negative, because, as Bialik puts it, "an empty vessel can hold matter, while a full vessel cannot: if the empty word enslaves, how much more is this true of the full word?" For the writer today, a degraded or secular language offers more creative freedom than one already filled with content, a content that, in the Jewish context, must be religious. Bialik is not, however, satisfied with leaving us in such a happy state of linguistic freedom. The words we fill with our own meaning create only the illusion of security. We walk on them as if "across an iron bridge" but we are unaware of how shaky that bridge is, "how deep and dark the abyss that opens at their feet."

The words "abyss" (*tehom*), as well as "nothingness" (*blimah*) and "void" (*tohu*), are central to Bialik's vocabulary in the essay. This seemingly modernist vocabulary has its roots in traditional Judaism, starting, of course, with the Bible, but even more in the Kabbalah. No one steeped in traditional Judaism can avoid the association of the void with Luria's doctrine of the empty space, the primordial vacuum. The image of the iron bridge resonates as well with a famous homily of Nahman of Bratslav (1772–1810), the Hasidic master whose teachings are often compared to those of the Christian religious existentialist Søren Kierkegaard.

In a discussion of the verse where God hardens Pharaoh's heart, Nahman takes Luria's empty space and turned it into a theological paradox: how can Pharaoh be evil if God hardens his heart?[98] For Nahman, the contradictions inherent in faith are a void into which only a true Zaddik (a righteous Hasidic leader and also Nahman's way of referring to himself) can enter and return alive. By immersing himself in the void, the true Zaddik makes it possible for the rest of Israel to cross a bridge over the void to safety.

Bialik argues that language cannot reveal the essence of things, but "on the contrary, language itself stands as a barrier before them." What is this essence? The answer is: the void (*tohu*—the word is the one used in Genesis to describe the world before creation). "'For man shall not look on me and live,' says the void." This sentence is a daring paraphrase of God's statement to Moses, but here the void takes the place of God; the void *is* God. This divine void, this negative reality appears to be death. It is, Bialik says, "the very eternal darkness that is so fearsome—that darkness that from the time of Creation has always secretly drawn man's heart to it." In another place in the essay, he is even more explicit: he speaks of language as "the covering stone . . . sealed over the dead."

Language diverts us from confrontation with the void and denies the reality of death. Language is a barrier, not a vehicle. As Bialik puts it, once again, borrowing from but rewriting the Bible: "Your desire shall be for the void and speech shall rule over you." This is a reference to God's curse of Eve: "your desire shall be for your husband, and he shall rule over you." For Bialik, human beings all suffer under the curse of Eve, but it is now a curse emptied of sexuality and filled with language. The curse of language is that it blocks access to the very source that gives it life in the first place.

According to Bialik, we are caught in an unending cycle of concealing speech. Philosophical systems that claim to reveal turn out in the end only to conceal. And then these systems are replaced by new systems, which make equal promises, also ending in disillusionment. Yet between these systems, there are rare moments when the void is visible, when language briefly fails to conceal. Most human beings pass over these moments unaware. But there are others, whom Bialik compares to the priests of the Bible, who look into the void and live.

These are the poets, Bialik's own enterprise. He contrasts them to the writers of prose. The prose writers are like those who cross a frozen river. If it is frozen hard enough, they can cross without paying attention to the waters flowing darkly beneath. But the poets are precisely those for whom the river is not frozen hard. In order to cross, they must jump from one block of ice to the next, risking death in the void between. While the writers of prose treat language as inert and certain, for the poets, language can never be stable: "the words writhe in their hands; they are extinguished and lit again, flash on and off like the engravings of the signet in the stones of the High Priest's breastplate." This is an astonishing metaphor since this breastplate, the *urim ve-tumim*, which was probably an ancient Israelite oracle, now becomes the language of the poet. Once again, Bialik secularizes biblical language: the poet empties words of old meanings and fills them with new. Or, as he says in a phrase that applies to this essay itself: "the profane turns sacred and the sacred profane."

Thus, after expressing infinite despair at the possibility of language, Bialik nevertheless returns to poetry. But as if to offer another avenue of hope, he suggests in the final paragraph of the essay the possibility of a language without words: "song, tears and laughter." Here, too, we hear echoes of Nahman of Bratslav, whose homily on the paradox of Pharaoh also finds meaning in wordless song. These languages without words begin where words leave off. Instead of concealing, they reveal. Indeed, "they rise from the void. They are the rising up of the void." These nonverbal languages are the real source of creativity, because they come from the void. The void is not so silent, after all. It too is the source of a certain kind of nonconventional—dare we say divine?—language.

Bialik concludes with an affirmation of these messages from the void: "Every creation of the spirit which lacks an echo of one of these three languages is not really alive, and it were best that it had never come into the world." If the void is death, it is nevertheless the paradoxical source of creativity and life. Not the divine revelation at Sinai, but the negative revelation of the void becomes the voice to which the poet harkens. Only in the hands of the poet can the linguistic originality of the first human being be recaptured. Only in poetry, not in religion, can one find redemption.

Azzan Yadin has pointed out how close Bialik's essay is to Friedrich Nietzsche's "On Truth and Lie in a Non-Moral Sense."[99] Although Bialik is often considered to belong to the "anti-Nietzschean" party in Hebrew letters from the beginning of the twentieth century (a subject to which we will return), it appears that in the case of this essay, at least, he found Nietzsche's positions on language, truth, and God to be highly attractive. As the philosopher who proclaimed the "death of God," Nietzsche was a figure impossible to avoid in the early twentieth century.[100] What Bialik does with Nietzsche, though, is more than just "Judaize" him. By taking over the rich resonances of words from the religious tradition and turning their meanings inside out, Bialik was able to administer a different kind of death to God than had Nietzsche. The very resources of the Hebrew language became the spades with which he buried the religious tradition—and then resurrected it anew in secular form.

This process and its dangers found an important echo in a letter written in 1926 by the historian of Jewish mysticism Gershom Scholem (1897–1981) to the German Jewish philosopher Franz Rosenzweig.[101] Scholem, who had emigrated from Germany to Palestine three years earlier, warned of the dangers of creating a secular nationalist culture out of religious building blocks. The problem facing Zionism was not so much the Arabs, as many thought, but rather the apocalyptic dangers inherent in the revival of Hebrew. In this letter, Scholem proves himself to be, above all, a linguistic nationalist: the revival of Hebrew, with all its attendant culture, was perhaps *the* foremost accomplishment of Zionism. But there could be no such thing as the creation of a secular Hebrew divorced from the powerful religious undertones of its linguistic tradition. He writes:

> A language is composed of names. The power of the language is bound up in the name and its abyss is sealed within the name. Having conjured up the ancient names day after day, we can no longer suppress their potencies. We roused them, and they will manifest themselves, for we have conjured them up with very great power.

The word "abyss" reminds us immediately of Bialik's essay, which was likely in Scholem's mind when he wrote to Rosenzweig. And, like Bialik, he also drew his terminology from the Kabbalah, which was his scholarly discipline.

For the medieval Kabbalists, the core of the Hebrew language is divine names, and the core of that core is the four-letter name of God, the essential divine name. The Torah read mystically, according to the Kabbalists, is nothing but one very long name of God. Moreover, this name is God himself. So, there is no real distinction between God and the Torah, for the letters of the Hebrew alphabet are God's own limbs, the divine anatomy. The Hebrew language has an ontological status that is far different from all other, conventional human languages. In fact, the Kabbalists' linguistic theology is the diametric opposite of that of Maimonides, for whom the Torah was written in the lowly language of men (*leshon beney Adam*). As opposed to Maimonides, the Kabbalists endowed the language of the Bible with a holy status far beyond what the rabbis meant when they called Hebrew *leshon kodesh* ("holy tongue").

Given the idea that Hebrew is God's own language, to fashion a secular culture out of this language involved an extraordinarily risky challenge. As Scholem suggests, the apocalyptic potencies contained in the divine language might be aroused precisely by introducing Hebrew into the everyday world. With it came all the mystical and messianic baggage that had attached itself to the language throughout history. Was a purely secular language, devoid of its religious connotations, possible for a language like Hebrew? Scholem believed not. With Zionism, the inner dialectic of Judaism was in danger of exploding outward into the realm of the political. Religious forces would themselves be transformed into the apocalyptic by the actions of their secular opponents. Scholem's letter thus demonstrates how the religious and secular dimensions of a language like Hebrew could not be easily separated.

Like Einstein, Scholem was born into a nonreligious, acculturated family. His path back to Judaism was highly idiosyncratic and singular, yet he also took part in the larger renaissance of Jewish culture in Weimar Germany.[102] As an adolescent, he rebelled by learning Hebrew and embracing Zionism. In his diaries from the period, there is evidence that he followed a quasi-Orthodox practice for a period and also entertained mystical and messianic ideas, but there is little evidence of such religiosity from later in his life.[103] He was resolutely secular in his daily practice, yet, as a scholar of Jewish mysticism, he found deep spiritual significance in the sources he studied. He did not identify with a secularism that denied all transcendent meaning, but his God, like the *ein sof* of the Kabbalists, remained hidden behind a void. Scholem's own theological position thus represented an attempt to connect the religious and the secular dialectically, to preserve their opposition to each other but nevertheless show how the one generated the other.

Since most of Scholem's writings are historical studies of the Kabbalah, his own views on theology are not always easy to discern. The earliest statement of his position, which remains available only in an obscure German Jewish newspaper, was an attack on a work of theology by Hans Joachim Schoeps, a German Jewish historian of religion who held far right-wing German nationalist views.[104] Schoeps was strongly influenced by the Protestant existentialist theologian, Karl Barth, and his book was an attempt to transpose Barthian theology into a Jewish key. He argued for an antihistorical and antirationalist theology: to be a Jew for Schoeps was to bypass the historical tradition in favor of an immediate experience of God, an experience that lay beyond reason.

Scholem attacked Schoeps head-on but, in the process, also managed to give short shrift to other, less-radical Jewish existentialists such as Martin Buber. Scholem rejected out of hand the possibility of a direct revelation from God, arguing instead that only the literary tradition is accessible to us:

> Revelation is, despite its uniqueness, still a *medium*. It is [the] absolute, meaning-bestowing, but itself meaningless that becomes explicable only through the relation to time, to the Tradition. . . . Nothing in historical time requires concretization more than the "absolute concreteness" of the word of revelation. . . . The voice we perceive is the medium in which we live, and where it is not [the medium], it becomes hollow. . . . The residue of the voice, as that which in Judaism is the tradition in its creative development, cannot be separate from it [i.e., the voice].[105]

In a formulation that would have pleased Maimonides, Scholem asserts that there is no such thing as an unmediated "concrete" word of God: God does not speak in any human sense. God's revelation is abstract and infinite, but because it linguistically "bestows meaning," it can be concretized by human beings. The interpretive tradition has its source in revelation, but without the tradition, revelation is incomprehensible. Schoeps had reduced Judaism to an ahistorical faith because he failed to understand the essential function of tradition and the impossibility of pure, immediate communication with God. Against Schoeps's theology, which had certain similarities to Buber's *I and Thou*, Scholem calls for a return to historical consciousness, a theme we will explore in a later chapter. Only through the historical tradition, the literary products created by human beings, can we discern a "residue" of the divine voice.

Although Scholem was far from dismissing God as an illusion or projection, his philosophy is epistemologically similar. We cannot know anything of the divine, but only of the human responses to what is believed to be the divine voice. And even those responses can only be responses to responses and never direct evidence of the voice itself. God may speak Hebrew, but the Hebrew language of his people contains only a vanishing trace of that original divine language. The apocalyptic dangers of which Scholem warned in his letter to Rosenzweig are therefore the result not of using a divine language in history but of invoking a human language that its speakers *think* is grounded in revelation. The Jewish tradition, founded on revelation, is therefore paradoxically an entirely secular, or human, creation, but one whose practitioners believe has its source in an unknowable, incomprehensible God. Scholem's secular theology of the historical tradition may be seen as a historian's version of what Bialik expressed more poetically, since, in both cases, the divine void remains lurking beyond sight as the source of all human creativity.

The consequence of this theology, at once Kabbalistic and modern, is to grant to human beings extraordinary freedom to interpret both revelation and tradition. In one formulation of this argument, Scholem writes:

> [T]he sign of true Revelation is no longer the weight of the statements that attain communication in it, but the infinite number of interpretations to which it is open. The character of the absolute [word of God] is recognizable by its infinite number of possible interpretations. . . . Without giving up the fundamentalist

thesis of the divine character of the Scriptures, such mystical theses nevertheless achieve an astounding loosening of the concept of Revelation. Here the authority of Revelation also constitutes the basis of the freedom in its application and interpretation.[106]

It is the very word of God, itself meaningless, that produces dialectically an infinity of interpretations and the autonomy of its interpreters. In this version of the secular, human freedom derives not from man himself but from what the Gnostics called the *deus absconditus* (the hidden God).

In 1937, Scholem wrote a birthday letter to the German Jewish publisher and philanthropist Salman Schocken, in which he described in similar terms the challenge of a secular historian studying the Kabbalah.[107] Using language again reminiscent of Bialik, he speaks of venturing out into an abyss, to try to penetrate the "wall of history." The wall of history appears as a mist that hangs around the "mountain of facts," an obvious allusion to Mount Sinai. These facts, like Kant's "thing-in-itself," are impossible to grasp and thus "history may seem to be fundamentally an illusion, but an illusion without which in temporal reality no insight into the essence of things is possible. . . . Today, as at the very beginning, my work lives in this paradox, in the hope of a true communication from the mountain." The mountain will never speak, and so the historian is left only with history, with those sources that hang like a fog around the mountain.

At the beginning of the letter, Scholem confesses that during his adolescence, he entertained

> mystical theses which walked the fine line between religion and nihilism. I later [found in Franz Kafka] the most perfect and unsurpassed expression of this fine line, an expression which, as a secular statement of the Kabbalistic world-feeling in a modern spirit, seemed to me to wrap Kafka's writings in the halo of the canonical.

It was in Kafka that Scholem discovered a kind of heretical, secular Kabbalah, a literature paradoxically at once canonical *and* nihilistic. With Max Brod and Walter Benjamin, Scholem saw in Kafka a deeply Jewish writer, whose protagonists' continual but futile attempts to gain access to the "castle" or "the law" are metaphors for the modern search for God.[108] While many different readings of the famously enigmatic Kafka are possible, this theological one became especially compelling to those, like Scholem, who searched for a secular, even consciously heretical, gate through which to enter the Jewish tradition.

Kafka's parable, "Before the Law," provides a pithy summary of this paradox.[109] Although, characteristically, it contains no overt Jewish symbols, "Before the Law" certainly looks more Jewish than anything else, resonating as it does with the Kabbalistic idea that the Torah (or Law) and God are one and the same. The "man from the country" comes and asks to be admitted to the Law, but the doorkeeper, a terrifying figure with a "big sharp nose and long, thin black Tartar beard," informs him that if he should enter without permission, he will encounter progressively more fearsome doorkeepers at the inner doors. The man from the country decides to remain at the outer door and gradually parts with all of his possessions in vain attempts to bribe the doorkeeper. Finally, at the end of his life, he asks the doorkeeper: "Everyone strives to reach the Law, so how does it happen that all these many years no one but myself has ever begged for admittance?" The doorkeeper responds: "No one else could ever be admitted here, since this gate was made only for you. I am now going to shut it."

Kafka's parable, consciously or not, inverts the ancient "palace" (*hekhalot*) literature in which the mystic journeys through heavenly palaces in search of God.[110] Here, the seeker doesn't get through the first door. Rarely has there been such a pessimistic account of man's attempt to gain divine knowledge. Does the Law (or God) even exist inside the palace or is it merely a figment of the traveler's imagination? All of life, suggests Kafka, is a vain quest for divine knowledge, but in the end, we do not progress beyond the beginning of the journey. If it is modernity that has barred the way to the Law, then it has also rendered the very attempt to enter the Law a solitary and individual struggle: each person has his or her own gate.

Pagan Gods

Our exploration of secular Jewish ideas about God has progressed from the Spinozistic doctrine that God is the same as the universe to the negation of a transcendent being as a human projection and illusion, and concluded with a modern version of the Gnostic *deus absconditus*, except that this "hidden God" remains forever barred from view. There is a final type of Jewish secular theology, one that accompanied the Zionist return to the land: the resurrection of the ancient pagan gods, both Greek and Canaanite. If Spinoza and his children turned to the medieval philosophical tradition and Bialik, Scholem, and Kafka drew upon the Kabbalistic, the turn toward paganism as a source of the secular was more radical still: an assault on the God of Israel by recourse to his ancient enemies.

Already at the end of the nineteenth century, a number of writers, notably Micha Yosef Berdichevsky (who will play a major role in later chapters), revolted against the God of the Bible and the Talmud by seeking other gods whose voices had been suppressed by centuries of prophets and rabbis. Much later, in the 1960s, the Reconstructionist theologian Richard Rubenstein, disillusioned by the Holocaust with the biblical God of history, found inspiration instead in the Zionist return to the land and to the pagan gods of nature worshipped by the ancient Canaanites.[111]

One of the earliest voices to articulate this pagan vision of God, and with whom we shall conclude this chapter, was the poet Saul Tchernikhovsky (1875–1943). Tchernikhovsky is often paired with Bialik as the two poetic giants of the Hebrew national renaissance. Where Bialik was grounded in the world of the yeshiva, against which he rebelled but for which he still retained great nostalgia, Tchernikhovsky came from a more acculturated background. His parents were traditional but were also followers of the Haskalah and, in addition to an education in Bible and Hebrew language, he attended a Russian school from age ten. As a result, his poetry was open to a variety of cultural influences, including notably the Hellenic idea of beauty.

In 1899, the young Tchernikhovsky wrote a poem, "Facing the Statue of Apollo," that expresses the deep inner conflict of a Jew who straddled two worlds, the Jewish and the pagan.[112] Just as Heine saw Apollo as the god with whom the Jews must wrestle, so Tchernikhovsky finds the challenge to contemporary Jews in the image of the same Greek god. The poet comes in front of the statue of the god who has been "forgotten by the world." This is the god of power and vitality, a transposition of Nietzsche's Dionysian to its ostensible opposite:

> I come to you, forgotten god of the ages,
> god of ancient times and other days
> ruling the tempests of vigorous men,
> the breakers of their strength in youth's plenty!
>
> . . . .

I come to you—do you know me still?
I am the Jew: your adversary of old!

....

I bow to all precious things—robbed now
by human corpses and the rotten seed of man,
who rebel against the life bestowed by God, the Almighty
the God of mysterious wildernesses,
the God of the conquerors of Canaan in a whirlwind—
who then bound Him with the straps of *tefillin*.

By the end of the poem, the god Apollo appears conflated with the God of the Hebrews. Once upon a time, the Hebrews, too, had a God as vital as Apollo, but they "bound Him with the straps of *tefillin*," that is, with the religion of Judaism. Far from binding the Jew to his God, the tefillin here imprison God and render him impotent. Where Heine turned Apollo into a freethinking Ashkenazi Jew and thus a parody of European classicism, Tchernikhovsky's Apollo, who is also the Almighty God of the Bible, has been defeated by his people. For Tchernikhovsky, the path to national renaissance required liberating this God from religion, which meant liberating the Jews from the sacred bonds that they had imposed on themselves. By appropriating those gods against whom ancient Judaism warred, the secular nationalist might defeat the God in whose name priests and rabbis had enslaved Israel.

Each of these three types of Jewish secularism revolted against the Jewish God in favor of a different conception of the divine: nature, the void, and paganism. To be sure, not all secularists struggled in this way with the tradition. For some, the simple negation of God sufficed. But the influence of Spinoza was so great that many of the most articulate and enduring of Jewish secular thinkers became equally God-intoxicated. Their alternative to the God of the Bible may have been Maimonidean, Spinozistic, Kabbalistic, or pagan, but each of these choices reinterpreted traditional theology so as to bring the divine down to earth. And in order to do so, to declare that their Judaism was "not in the heavens," it was first necessary to subject to a secular reinterpretation the scripture on which that religion rests.

Chapter 2

Torah: The Secular Jewish Bible

In his 1883 iconoclastic diatribe, *The Conventional Lies of Our Civilization*, the Jewish physician, writer, and later Zionist Max Nordau devoted a chapter to a wholesale attack on religion as a form of primitive thinking. Among his many targets, Nordau also took on the Bible, about which he had this to say:

> We detect in this wasteland (*Wust*) the superstitious beliefs of the ancient inhabitants of Palestine, dim echoes of Indian and Persian fables, mistaken imitations of Egyptian teachings and practices, historical chronicles as dry as they are unreliable and poems, some typically human, erotic as well as Jewish nationalist-patriotic, all of which are rarely distinguished by beauties of the highest order, but more frequently by excess, crudity, bad taste and real Oriental sensuality. As a literary monument the Bible is of much later origin than the Vedas . . . ; as a work of literary value it is surpassed by everything written in the last two thousand years by authors even of the second rank . . . ; its conception of the universe is childish, and its morality . . . shocking.[1]

Expressing views no doubt common to other Jews bent on escaping the burdens of the Jewish religion for a cosmopolitan European identity, Nordau found nothing redeemable in the Book of Books: its ideas are unoriginal, its literary value next-to-worthless, and its ideas either laughable or revolting.

As this quotation from Nordau suggests, if the Bible is the source of Judaism, Jewish secularists might find it de rigueur to attack its relevance to modern life. In fact, Spinoza's opening salvo in his war on revealed religion was just such an attack. Yet we should not be too hasty in assuming that secularism must discard scripture. One could deny divine authorship but retain the Bible as a work of history or literature and, thus, as the source of an avowedly secular tradition. This is a process that Jonathan Sheehan has demonstrated for Germany and England in the seventeenth and eighteenth centuries. Far from negating religion altogether, Enlighteners from these countries recuperated it under new terms, turning the Bible from a text of salvation into a cultural monument.[2]

As Jews modernized, they also reappropriated the Bible as a cultural, historical, or nationalist text. The Jewish Enlightenment Bible, to adopt Sheehan's term, was distinctly different from the European Enlightenment Bible since it was pressed into service at once as the vehicle for the integration of the Jews and as the fount for a new, nonreligious identity. This Bible assumed many different forms, such as the setting for the first Hebrew novel, Avraham Mapu's *Ahavat Zion* (1853), in which the romantic freedom of biblical times contrasted implicitly with rabbinic repression in Jewish eastern Europe. Richard Cohen has demonstrated how, from Moses Mendelssohn to the artist Ephraim Moses Lilien, Jewish intellectuals tried to repossess the Bible, which Christian scholarship had claimed for its own, for the Jews.[3] Some of these efforts were quite traditional, such as Mendelssohn's *Bi'ur* (Commentary) that accompanied his translation of the Bible into German in Hebrew characters. Mendelssohn drew heavily on the canonical medieval commentators to create an enlightened Jewish reader. On the other hand, Lilien's art nouveau illustrated Bible featured scandalously naked figures, including an image of Theodor Herzl as the angel expelling Adam and Eve from the Garden of Eden and Haman as Christ on the cross.

In this chapter, we will examine some of the more radical of these Jewish Enlightenment Bibles, those that departed from traditional religious or ethical readings of Torah. Spinoza, and not Mendelssohn, is the founding father of this secular Jewish Bible. After examining precursors to Spinoza's secular reading of scripture, we will turn to a series of his radical disciples: Heinrich Heine, Sigmund Freud, Ahad Ha'am, Micha Yosef Berdichevsky, David Ben-Gurion, and Joseph Hayim Brenner. By reading the Bible against its religious grain, these writers used it as the building blocks for their own contemporary secularism.

In the rabbinic vocabulary, the term "Torah" is not limited only to the written law but includes the oral law that the rabbis held was also revealed to Moses at Sinai. From this point of view, the status of the Bible was only the starting point for a secular version of Torah. Radical, secular critiques had to take aim at all of Jewish history and rewrite it devoid of supernatural providence. The new, secular Torah was therefore the product of the modern discipline of history, which turned the history of the Jews from the Bible onward into a human story. In the last chapter of this book, we will return to history as a source for Jewish secularism.

Precursors

As did the subject of God, so too the secular Jewish Bible had important precursors in the premodern religious tradition. In the previous chapter, I suggested that the Bible contains the seeds of its own subversion. If the word "Torah" was meant to convey the word of God, some of its books disrupted this theological consistency. Clearly the editors of the Bible did not impose upon it the harmonious views that might have satisfied later theologians. But the biblical redactors were not alone in tolerating great diversity in scripture. The rabbis who succeeded them developed the extraordinarily subtle method of midrash, which exploited inconsistencies and contradictions in the text. Most of these midrashim, of course, can no more be called secular than the story of Rabbi Eliezer discussed in the introduction to this book. But insofar as the rabbis used the Bible as a platform for literary artifice, they, like Rabbi Eliezer's opponents, brought the Torah from the heavens down to earth.

Perhaps the most striking use of the Bible for purely secular, literary purposes can be found in the poetry of al-Andalus (Muslim Spain). The Song of Songs was often the inspiration for these poets. The Song resonated in the Middle Ages in two contradictory ways. On the one hand, it became a central text for the thirteenth-century Kabbalists, for whom the eroticism of the poem was an allegory for the erotic relations between the male and female potencies (*sefirot*) of God. They took Rabbi Akiva's reading of the Song to another level altogether by restoring the text's sensuality but displacing it from the human to the divine realm.

On the other hand, medieval Hebrew poets in the Iberian Peninsula used the Song as a model for the opposite purpose: to write secular, erotic poetry. Inspired by the secular Arabic poetry of the age, these Jews wished to show that Hebrew, a language to which they began to turn in the twelfth century, had as many artistic possibilities as Arabic.[4] If Arabs could write love poems, so could Jews, since, after all, the Hebrew Bible had the greatest love poem of them all. Like the Kabbalists, these writers restored the Song of Songs to its original eroticism, but now for purely secular purposes. Many of them also wrote religious poetry, for which the Song continued to provide inspiration, but it is the sudden and startling emergence of a secular poetry that seizes our attention. Here, as Robert Alter has argued, was an appropriation of the Bible as a canonical work for secular literature.[5]

Consider an example from the poetry of the Spanish Jew Solomon Ibn Gabirol (1021–1058). Since Ibn Gabirol was a Neoplatonist, it is entirely possible that his poetry should be read as a philosophical allegory, perhaps about the Messiah (see the last line below). But it can as easily be read as a love poem, pure and simple, just as the Song of Songs, which is its model, appears to have been originally a secular, erotic work:

> The gate that was shut—arise and open it
> And the gazelle that ran away—send him to me!
> At daybreak, when you come to me to lie between my breasts
> There your good fragrance will rest upon me
>
> What shape has your beloved, most beautiful bride
> That you say to me: "Send for him and bring him?"
> Is he bright-eyed, ruddy and handsome?
> My beloved, my dear one—rise up and anoint him![6]

While poets like Ibn Gabirol cannot be considered secular in any modern sense of the word, they nonetheless turned the Torah into the source of a thoroughly earthly poetry.

Another such poet and philosopher was Abraham Ibn Ezra (1092/3–1167), whose biblical commentary eventually became canonical. That it did owed much to its focus on a literal and grammatical reading of the biblical text, but it was these factors that also caused Ibn Ezra to flirt with heresies of his own, heresies that Baruch Spinoza adopted and expanded into a full-blown secular exegesis of the Bible. The best known of Ibn Ezra's subversive ideas are marked by expressions such as "those who understand will understand" or "the enlightened will understand." Thus, without explicitly saying what he meant, he hinted broadly that he harbored at a minimum some unconventional thoughts.

For example, on the phrase from Genesis 12:6 "and the Canaanite was *then* in the land," he suggests two possible interpretations. The verse might refer to a relationship between *past* and *distant past: before* Canaan conquered the land of Canaan, there were other inhabitants in the land. Or, "there is a great mystery and the wise will remain silent." The mysterious second interpretation is not difficult to guess: the passage might refer to a relation between *present* and *past*. In this reading, the author wrote the verse *after* the Canaanites had been expelled from the land, namely after the death of Moses. Since the textual evidence in Genesis 10 implies that Canaan was the first to inhabit the land, Ibn Ezra clearly believed that the verse was written after the death of Moses. The verse is an *interpolation* (a text inserted by another hand) by someone other than Moses, the assumed author, according to tradition, of the whole Torah. In his commentary to Deuteronomy 1:1–3, Ibn Ezra lists a number of other passages that would appear to be similar interpolations.

Nevertheless, Ibn Ezra was hardly prepared to reject Moses's authorship of the whole of the Torah based on these scattered verses. He directs scathing remarks at a Rabbi Isaac who thought that the verse "and these are the kings who reigned in the land of Edom" (Genesis 36:31) was written during the reign of King Jehoshaphat, concluding that his blasphemous book ought to be burned. And he condemns the views of Hiwi al-Balkhi with a pun on his name as Hiwi *ha-kalbi* ("Hiwi the dog").[7]

Hiwi, who is only known to us from others' denunciations of him, was a ninth-century Persian Jew who was perhaps the first to be deeply influenced by rationalist Arabic philosophy. He evidently came to the conclusion that the Bible's God is unjust, is not omniscient or omnipotent, changes his mind, and likes blood and sacrifices. The Bible is full of anthropomorphisms and contains many contradictions. Following one school of Muslim philosophy, since everything is predestined, biblical miracles are impossible. Hiwi's position was therefore much more thoroughgoing than merely a critical reading of the Bible. Rather, the Bible—and therefore the Jewish religion—stands at odds with everything taught by reason. By transmitting Hiwi's views, as well as those of other, lesser-known radicals, if only to reject them, Ibn Ezra gives us a window into the surprising range of opinions in the Jewish world of his time.

Ibn Ezra's radicalism does not rest only on his discovery of non-Mosaic interpolations in the Bible. The interpolations were rather the product of a wider theory of literal exegesis, namely, his attempt to understand the text *immanently.* Taking a stand against the craze for philosophy that swept Jewish intellectuals, he rejected the kind of allegorizing of the text that had become standard practice since the tenth century, a practice that resulted from the desire to harmonize the Bible with medieval science and philosophy. In Ibn Ezra's view, such allegories often demonstrate poor knowledge of both the biblical text and medieval science.

So, for example, in his desire to show agreement between the biblical story of Creation and Ptolemaic astronomy, a certain Spanish exegete distorted both the literal meaning of the text and astronomic science. Ibn Ezra does not merely oppose inserting scientific ideas into the Bible but also objects to distorting the text by misinterpreting science to fit the text. He levels the same charge against Saadia Gaon, the founder of medieval Jewish philosophy: "and in this path rose Saadia Gaon of the Exile and in the commentary on 'let there be lights,' he inserted opinions contradicting the knowledge of astronomy according to the astronomers." Against those like Saadia who would fit the text to their philosophical preconceptions, "we will not search along the wall like blind men in order to pull out things according to our needs. And why should we turn the obvious into the hidden?"

The first task of exegesis is to discover the literal meaning of the text. This literal meaning may involve allegories, but they are allegories immanent to the language of the Bible. Moreover, this biblical language is not philosophical but colloquial: "the Bible speaks the language of human beings." As a result, the Bible contains all kinds of figures of speech that suggest, for example, that God has a body or emotions. These statements are to be taken neither literally nor allegorically. Instead, they are simply everyday, human ways of speaking about God: one should infer no philosophical truths from them.

The dictum that "the Bible speaks the language of human beings" not only is a linguistic position for Ibn Ezra, as radical as that might be, but is linked to a larger issue. The purpose of the Bible's author was pedagogical, not philosophical, and he therefore accommodated his work to the language and understanding of common people. The perspective from which the Bible observes the world is also human. The creation of the world must be understood from an earthly point of view: the heavens in the creation story are the heavens that we see, and not the supralunar "heavens above the heavens." The Bible is concerned only with the sublunar world, which is the world observable by human beings, not the supralunar found in the books of the astronomers. Since the Bible not only speaks the language of human beings but does so from the perspective of human beings, it does not contain philosophical or astronomical knowledge, a specialized, scientific knowledge found in other books.

By arguing that the Bible speaks only from the perspective of human beings, Ibn Ezra boldly asserted that the Bible does not contain all knowledge.

To be sure, the subject matter of the Bible is holy, but its means of communication is worldly: the status of Hebrew is no different from any other human language. Since language is purely instrumental, no philosophical—or other—conclusions can be drawn from minor word variations, as long as the essential meaning is preserved. In this way, Ibn Ezra threw grave doubt on the whole discipline of midrash, which often bases its interpretations on just such repetitions and variations in the language of the text. All of the "knowledge" that derives from such interpretations is bogus in his eyes: the Bible may be the beginning of all knowledge, but it is not in itself all knowledge. This literal reading of the Bible would be embraced by modern biblical critics from Spinoza to Abraham Geiger, one of the founders of Reform Judaism.[8]

By limiting the knowledge that can be obtained from the Bible, Ibn Ezra made the study of nature—or, at least, the supralunar world—a subject independent of the Bible.[9] Indeed, as we noted in chapter 1, the study of nature, which one might call the realm of secular knowledge, was an enterprise embraced by a wide range of medieval Jewish thinkers, such as Abraham bar Hiyya, Moses Maimonides, Levi ben Gershon (Gersonides), and Hasdai Crescas.[10] But rather than reconciling science with revelation, which was the project of so many medieval Jewish, Christian, and Muslim philosophers, Ibn Ezra chose to separate them, thus rendering nature a realm autonomous from religion.

This radical stance confronted him with some serious challenges. For example, he believed strongly in astrology, as did most natural philosophers of his day, blaming his own ill fortune on the constellations present the day of his birth.[11] But if one's fate was thoroughly determined by the stars, what role did God have in the world? Commenting on the rabbinic dictum "Israel has no constellation (*mazal*)," Ibn Ezra struggled to show that belief in God could suspend the dictates of astrology. His solution to this conundrum involved a quasi-pantheistic theology. Following the Arabic Neoplatonists, he held that God not only was transcendent but also was present throughout the world. Overriding the determinism of the stars involved activating this divine immanence. This pantheism—or, more precisely, *panentheism* (that is, that God is everywhere in the world, but is also transcendent)—made Ibn Ezra a precursor of such modern thinkers as Spinoza and the nineteenth-century Enlightener Nahman Krochmal.[12] While he was far from denying the existence of the God of the Bible, Ibn Ezra's theology equated God with nature in a way that might be appropriated by more radical deniers of biblical providence.

As opposed to Ibn Ezra, Moses Maimonides had no difficulty in giving what he calls "figurative" interpretations when the teachings of science contradicted the Bible.[13] He used this method most famously with respect to verses in the Bible that attribute a body to God. Since, like all other Jewish, Muslim, and Christian philosophers, he held that God does not have a body—or any human or other earthly attributes—the Bible must conceal some other meaning beneath its repeated anthropomorphisms. It is that other meaning that he discovers through "figurative"—or allegorical—exegesis. Only where science does not manifestly contradict the Bible, as in the question of whether the world is eternal or created in time, should the philosopher avoid figurative interpretations of the text.[14]

Why, then, did Moses, who Maimonides believed was a cross between a prophet and a philosopher, resort to anthropomorphic descriptions of God when he wrote the Bible? The answer is similar to Ibn Ezra's: "the Bible speaks in the language of human beings." Invoking this talmudic saying was Maimonides' way of arguing that the common people, who have no knowledge of philosophy, needed to be taught in terms they could understand. This principle of "accommodation" (that the Bible "accommodates" itself to the understanding of the *vulgus*) was shared by many medieval philosophers.[15] But there is a major difference in the ways Ibn Ezra and Maimonides use the idea: For Ibn Ezra, the Bible only contains one meaning, the one expressed in human language. Where it contradicts science, it is because it is not a scientific text. For Maimonides, the Bible contains multiple meanings, especially where there seems to be a contradiction between revelation and science.

In what way, then, does Maimonides' exegesis anticipate a secular reading of the Bible? As we shall see, Spinoza would use Maimonides as a foil for the *wrong* way to read the Bible. But perhaps Spinoza was too hasty, or, rather, perhaps he owed more to Maimonides than he wanted to admit. By forcing the Bible into a confrontation with science, Maimonides set up a contest that the Bible would ultimately lose. It is science that ultimately decides what is true, and only where science has not established the truth can the Bible be taken literally. Once one admits that the literal meaning of biblical stories is unphilosophical and is accommodated to the faulty, childish understanding of the uneducated, the Bible loses credibility and prestige; it can only be saved by allegories. But the allegorical method only works as long as one accepts a priori the ultimate truth of the Bible. Once the Bible (*The* Book) becomes a book like any other, allegorizing problematic passages loses its meaning. Thus, although Maimonides' method, on the face of it, looks quintessentially medieval, it sows the seeds of its own destruction.

Maimonides also anticipated modernity in his historical explanation for the commandments.[16] In the Talmud, the rabbis already attempted to give "reasons" for the commandments, that is, to explain why a commandment took the particular form that it did. The rise of Jewish philosophy, starting with Saadia Gaon in the tenth century, vastly expanded this enterprise as part of the larger project of reconciling reason with revelation.[17]

Maimonides argued that certain of the commandments, especially the sacrificial laws, have the particular form that they do because they are specifically aimed at countering the pagan religion that surrounded the ancient Israelites. He was much enamored of an early medieval ethnographic work called *The Nabatean Agriculture* that purported to describe a group called the Sabeans who had lived in the ancient Near East. It was the pagan Sabean religion, Maimonides believed, that explains Israelite customs. God designed the laws of sacrifice to resemble those of the Sabeans, but with the object of worship the true God instead of their false deities. In this way, he might gradually wean the Israelites away from idolatry to the true religion. By the time the Temple was destroyed, the Israelites no longer needed sacrifice, since they had sufficiently given up idolatry and could now serve God with prayer.

Maimonides seems to hold that God designed the sacrificial system with a built-in mechanism to destroy itself. In other words, the sacrifices were merely instruments for a higher goal, and once that goal was reached, they became obsolete. Maimonides speaks of God's "divine cunning" (*'ormat ha-shem u-tevunato*), meaning that he operates indirectly, allowing the sacrifices to perform their educational function on their own. True to his argument about miracles, this form of divine intervention takes place within the realm of the possible, the realm of history.

The radical import of Maimonides' argument has preoccupied generations of scholars. Did he mean that the destruction of the Temple was a positive event, a result of the religious maturation of the Jews? How did he reconcile his commitment in his code of Jewish law (*Mishneh Torah*) to the reestablishment of the sacrifices in messianic times with the historical evolution propounded in the *Guide*? And if sacrifices became obsolete, couldn't the same happen to prayer, especially since prayer often involves conceiving of God in human terms? If the true worship of God is by philosophical meditation, then perhaps messianic times might mean, at least for philosophers, ignoring portions of the law.

Maimonides himself never articulated such conclusions and his insistence that all the commandments were also given to instill obedience means that he did not think that the reasons for the commandments had practical implications. The author of the first comprehensive code of Jewish law hardly intended to lead an antinomian movement! Nevertheless, Maimonides' historical explanation of the commandments is an extraordinary precursor of modern historical investigations of Judaism. And just as a historical-critical approach to ancient sources fed modern Reform's abandonment of the law, so Maimonides' recourse to a historical argument, long before the rise of modern historicism, provided a medieval source for those modern secularists wishing to use history to overthrow tradition.

While it is true, as Yosef Hayim Yerushalmi argues,[18] that after Josephus Flavius, Jews generally did not write history, there are nevertheless important exceptions to this rule. Writers such as Joseph ha-Kohen, David Gans, and Solomon Usque all attempted in various ways to understand the history of the Jews in the context of world history, even if their focus remained theological and Judeocentric. Most striking was Solomon ibn Verga's *Shevet Yehudah*, which attempted to reconstruct the reasons for the expulsion of the Jews from Spain. Although he remained wedded to the traditional idea that exile is the result of God's punishment, ibn Verga situated this theology in a sociological account of the Jews' place in Spain and why it led to their expulsion. This was not yet modern historiography, but it contained elements of the modern.[19]

Azariah dei Rossi (1511–1588), the author of *Me'or Einayim* (1573), was the first to apply Renaissance hermeneutics to Jewish sources with his historical-critical interpretations of aggadot, or rabbinic legends. By demolishing the historicity of some of these legends, he cleared the way for a more modern historiography. But the most important implication of dei Rossi's book was his refusal to privilege the ancients over the moderns. Where the sayings of the rabbis contradicted modern science, dei Rossi opted for science. Although dei Rossi can hardly be called a secularist, there is nothing more fundamental to a secular point of view than denying that we are dwarfs standing on the shoulders of giants. As Lester Segal has put it, dei Rossi believed paradoxically that we may be dwarfs, but we see farthest standing on our own two feet.[20]

These Renaissance historical writers may have anticipated modern historiography, but they did not apply their insights to the Bible, which remained a sacred history. They were less radical, in a way, than Abraham Ibn Ezra, although he, too, was far from a modern historical reading to the Bible. That innovation, one of the hallmarks of Jewish secularism, would have to await Baruch Spinoza.

Spinoza's Bible

In chapter 1, I argued that Spinoza was at once the last medieval heretic and the first modern secularist. His pantheistic theology was thoroughly grounded in medieval categories, even as he overturned them. The same is true of his reading of the Bible. Spinoza seized upon Ibn Ezra's arguments to deny Moses's authorship of the Torah and give the honor instead to Ezra the Scribe from the period after the return of the Jews from Babylonia (post–538 BCE). In doing so, he shifted the Torah from a work of prophecy to a work of history, written long after the fact of Israel's early theocracy. Instead of its author channeling the word of God, he was a historian who reconstructed its ancient past. Spinoza demolished the Bible's theology and reduced its message to one of only quaint historical curiosity. He also borrowed from Ibn Ezra the assertion that the Bible does not contain all knowledge. Where Ibn Ezra thought it contained knowledge only of the sublunar world, Spinoza restricted its knowledge only to the history of ancient Israel. Yet, far from consigning the Bible to permanent irrelevance, Spinoza unintentionally laid the groundwork for its later recuperation. It was his method that made it possible for those who wanted to salvage a nonreligious message from between its lines.

That Spinoza should reject much of the Bible comes as no surprise, in light of what we learned of his naturalistic philosophy in chapter 1. After abolishing belief in prophecy and miracles, little might seem left of the Bible's cardinal claims. Why, though, was Spinoza impelled to attack the Bible on these grounds?[21] Many commentators have seen the *Theological-Political Treatise*, first published in 1670, as revenge for his treatment at the hands of the Amsterdam Sephardic community. Yet it is equally possible that Spinoza already held these views when he was excommunicated and that the *herem* was a reaction to his unwillingness to suppress them. If Spinoza's views on prophecy, miracles, and the divine authorship of the Bible predated his excommunication—and the sources are too meager to know for sure—the frame in which he set them in the *Treatise* had a grander purpose.

⌐ Spinoza's goal was to create a state safe for philosophers.[22] The Bible had served as a tool for religious authorities—Christian and Jewish—to squash rebellious ideas. A state constructed on fear needed superstitious ideas, such as those in the Bible, to instill obedience.[23] Spinoza's political theory sought a state based on reason, not fear, and only in a state where opinion was free might philosophy flourish. Safeguarding philosophers meant liberating speech and opinion from political control, a position so familiar to us that we forget how bold Spinoza was in pioneering it. In order to achieve this desired end, Spinoza needed to show that the Bible contained no philosophical truths and therefore could not be brought to bear on philosophical debates. Spinoza thus liberated philosophy from religion. This was an extraordinary achievement, since all of medieval philosophy—Jewish, Christian, and Muslim—had devoted itself to harmonizing scripture with reason. Now, in one stroke, Spinoza abolished this whole discipline that had occupied the efforts of the best minds of all three monotheistic religions for a millennium.⌐

Spinoza did not, however, thoroughly separate church (or synagogue) and state; that modern achievement would have to await John Locke. In the republic he preached, religion would be subordinate to the state and would be used to teach moral virtue. The need for this civic religion came from the inherent irrationality of the masses, an elitism Spinoza shared with medieval philosophers like Maimonides and which made him, at least on this issue, more medieval than modern. To be sure, this religion would not advocate superstitious beliefs, such as in miracles or in Gods who become men, but it is hard to understand what claim it would have on people's imaginations without such devices. At times, Spinoza seems to hold that the Bible, properly sanitized of irrational beliefs, could serve this purpose, since he admitted that it did teach moral truths. But the exact mechanism by which religion, biblical or otherwise, would shore up the obedience of the irrational masses remains unclear. Indeed, the *Theological-Political Treatise* sometimes reads like two books in one: the first part a wholesale attack on the Bible and the second part an effort to harness it to a modern republic.[24] Spinoza's attack on the Bible went beyond the mere critique of its outlandish beliefs, however. Instead, he subjected it to an entirely new reading. In effect, he reduced the Bible to just another book on the shelves of the library, one that should be read like any other book and its claims of truth subjected to the same scrutiny. Even more: "I hold that the method of interpreting Scripture is no different from the method of interpreting Nature, and is in fact in complete accord with it. For the method of interpreting Nature consists essentially in composing a detailed study of Nature from which, as being the source of our assured data, we can deduce the definitions of the things of Nature."[25] The Bible should be interpreted the way we interpret nature for the simple reason that it is not supernatural but a part of nature.

The method we use in studying nature is immanent: nature provides the data for its own study, and we are not allowed to import anything from outside it, such as theological speculations not grounded in the world. So, too, we can only understand the Bible from the Bible. Of course, in the case of a book, there are many things outside it that could shed light on its meaning, such as the history of the period or archaeology; Spinoza's immanent hermeneutics is therefore quite far from contemporary biblical studies. Yet he was adamant that we can only decipher the Bible with the data it supplies us, since otherwise, we might be tempted to apply philosophy to it and thus end up stuck in the quagmire of medieval religious thought.

What did Spinoza mean by reading the Bible from the Bible? If we want to understand a particular word or phrase in the Bible, we need to assemble all its usages and conclude from this inductive method what it means in the particular context in which we find it. Although this method is, in a sense, literalist, it is not entirely so. Spinoza recognizes that every language uses metaphors, so that at times the Bible may be speaking metaphorically. For example, when the Bible says that "God is a fire," we must first determine whether this statement contradicts principles stated within the Bible, regardless of whether the statement contradicts philosophical reason. Now, Moses states in a number of places that God cannot be compared to anything in the physical world. Therefore, the phrase "God is a fire" must be understood metaphorically.[26] By examining other instances of the word "fire," we see that it can also mean jealousy or anger. Since the Bible nowhere says that God is without emotions, "God is a fire" must mean that God is jealous.

For those who know Spinoza's *Ethics*, it is immediately apparent that the Bible teaches the exact *opposite* of his philosophy: whereas Spinoza's God has a body (i.e., extension) but no emotions, the Bible's God—or, at least, Spinoza's rather skewed version of the Bible's God—has the reverse, emotions but no body. The Bible thus appears to be the inverse of a philosophical text, since its notion of God is the opposite of a philosophical one (read: Spinoza's).

Excellent knowledge of Hebrew is therefore necessary to understand the Bible following this immanent method. Here, Spinoza, who wrote a small Hebrew grammar, claimed superiority over other biblical interpreters, a subtle suggestion, given his attack on the doctrine of the chosen people, that the Jews have certain special qualities, after all. But he insisted that Hebrew was no different from any other language. Adopting the talmudic phrase beloved of Ibn Ezra and Maimonides, "the Bible speaks the language of human beings," Spinoza gave it his own meaning. We recall that Maimonides had used the phrase to explain why the Bible's plain meaning contradicted philosophy, yet even if it spoke the language of human beings, it still taught philosophical truths in allegorical form. Ibn Ezra, on the other hand, used the phrase as a way to argue for a literalist hermeneutics: the Bible does not teach philosophical truths and should be understood to speak in a language accessible to all people. It was this latter usage that Spinoza borrowed quite explicitly. Since the Bible speaks the language of human beings, it could not possibly contain philosophical truth, which for Spinoza could only be conveyed *more geometrico*, that is, in a technical language like mathematics

In his historical and philological critique of the Bible, Spinoza was not entirely alone. Other seventeenth-century biblical interpreters made similar arguments, albeit in less radical and less uncompromising tones. Thomas Hobbes had preceded Spinoza in questioning Moses's authorship and Isaac La Peyrère (who may have also come from a Marrano background) held that the Bible only recounted the history of ancient Israel, which originated with Adam and Eve, who were, however, preceded by a "pre-Adamite" race unrelated to the Jews.[27] Many biblical scholars in the sixteenth and seventeenth centuries had either learned Hebrew or availed themselves of Jewish informants, so Spinoza's claim to uniqueness was hardly credible.

But where all of these scholars agreed that the Bible, no matter how reinterpreted, was still the word of God, Spinoza struck out on his own in denying this centuries-old belief. For Spinoza, the word of God had to be a timeless, universal truth. The Bible instead taught only the history of ancient Israel and was therefore at once historically contingent and limited to a particular nation. As such, it had no value as a philosophical text. It did, however, have value as a historical text, although Spinoza's philosophy left no place for history. In this way, Spinoza's historical interpretation inadvertently created a role for the Bible once history achieved, by the nineteenth century, pride of place in the human sciences.

Spinoza's purpose was to show that the Bible no longer had any relevance. In order to do so, he had to identify in what sense the ancient Israelites were "chosen." We learned in chapter 1 that God has no volition and cannot, therefore, "choose" any people in the sense that the Bible means.[28] But instead of discarding this language, Spinoza translates it into his own terms. Everything in the world exists by necessity. The character of the ancient Israelites is therefore by necessity what it is, and only in that sense can one say that they are chosen. By the same token, every nation is chosen by virtue of its essential character.

A sociological or historical examination of ancient Israel yields the conclusion that what characterized this nation the most, surprisingly enough, was not religious or moral ideas, as one might have expected, but politics: "The Hebrew nation was chosen by God before all others not by reason of its understanding nor of its spiritual qualities, but by reason of its social organization and the good fortune whereby it achieved supremacy and retained it for so many years. ... Their election and vocation consisted only in the material success and prosperity of their state."[29] The proof of this "election" lay not in biblical doctrines but in biblical history: the Bible attests to the longevity and success of the Hebrew state. Here, too, as with the language of the Bible, one must decipher the character of ancient Israel from the Bible—and only from the Bible. For Spinoza, the quintessence of this state was the theocracy that flourished at the time of Moses, Joshua, and the Judges. The institution of the monarchy already weakened this state, which finally went into decline with the rule of the priests in the Second Temple period.[30]

Yet, if the Bible was anything but the word of God, at least as a philosopher might understand that term, neither could Spinoza deny that it had some connection to the divine.[31] Since everything that exists is a mode of God, then the Bible, too, must partake in that divine substance. It was, to be sure, the product of the imaginations of the prophets, and not of reason, but even imagination represents an idea of God, no matter how unclear or inadequate. For the Bible teaches eternal moral truths, even if it does not teach metaphysics. Reducing the Bible to one book in the library about the long-passed history of a faraway, small group of people might neuter its contemporary power, but it did not rob it altogether of meaning. On the contrary, as the source of moral teachings, it could be pressed into the service of a liberal republic. And, as the source for the secular history of the Jewish people, the Bible might once again become relevant to later thinkers intent on transforming it into a cultural monument.

Heine's Portable Religion

In Heinrich Heine, one finds a modern reader deeply indebted to Spinoza, who sought to recuperate the Bible for his own idiosyncratically secular project. The Bible, Heine memorably wrote in 1840, was the Jews' portable country: "a book is their fatherland, their possession, their ruler, their fortune and misfortune. They live within its peaceful precincts. Here they exercise their inalienable civil rights. From here they cannot be driven out."[32] The Jews "clung to the Law, to the abstract idea," while Greeks and Romans "clung to the soil," a formulation that anticipates in some ways Franz Rosenzweig's existentialist philosophy of Judaism nearly a century later. In identifying a spiritual book as the Jews' fatherland, Heine contrasted it implicitly with the bellicose and intolerant German fatherland that was the target of some of his most barbed writings.

Since the biblical fatherland was the first nonterritorial religion, Heine holds somewhat paradoxically that the modern idea of cosmopolitanism "has sprung almost completely from Judea's soil."[33] The Jews "bore within them the modern principles which are only now visibly unfolding among the nations of Europe." The Bible fundamentally shaped the culture of the West no less than did the literature of ancient Greece. In an era when others saw in the Jews an Oriental people, Heine argued the opposite. Desiring to write the Jews back into the history of Western civilization, he asserted that "Judea has always seemed to me a fragment of the West which has somehow gotten lost in the East."[34] How ironic then, that "the very people who had given the world a God, and whose whole life was inspired by devotion to God, were stigmatized as deicides."[35] Yet, if the West was ungrateful to the Jews for having rescued the Bible and its God from the conflagration of the Temple, it had nevertheless adopted through Protestantism the fundamental principles of Judaism. As Heine says of the Scottish Protestants: "Are they not Hebrews, whose names are even biblical ... and whose religion is merely pork-eating Judaism?"[36] The fundamental principle of Judaism that this Christianity absorbed was morality: "one needs neither palm trees nor camels to be good; and goodness is better than beauty."[37]

With these words, written at the end of his life when he had returned to his own version of religion, Heine decisively broke with the Hellenism of his youth. But the Bible with which he identified was a document of social revolution, not religion. The socialism he had long espoused was already taught by Moses.[38] In Heine's reading, Moses looms larger than God; indeed, at one juncture, he sees God as nothing but the Bible's projection of Moses onto the heavens: "How small Sinai appears when Moses stands upon it. ... Sometimes it would seem to me as if this Mosaic God were only the reflected brightness of Moses himself to whom he appears so similar, in anger and in love."[39] As Freud would argue nearly a century later, Heine suggests that the religion of Israel was really the creation of Moses and not of the mysterious spirit with whom he claimed to commune on Sinai.

The most uncompromising advocate of the Mosaic religion was Jesus, of whom Heine said in terms more provocative today than ever: "No socialist was more of a terrorist than our Lord and Savior."[40] But Moses himself, no less a socialist, took a more pragmatic position: instead of decreeing the abolition of private property, he "sought its moral transformation" through the law of the Jubilee Year. Similarly, Moses could not abolish slavery, but he demonstrated his hatred of it with the law according to which a slave who refused manumission has his ear nailed to the doorpost of his master's house. Inspired by this image, Heine cries out: "Oh, Moses, our teacher! Moshe Rabbenu, august warrior against slavery, give me hammer and nails that I may nail to the Brandenburg Gate by their long ears our complacent slaves in liveries of black, red and gold!"[41] Thus did Heine transform "Moshe Rabbenu" into "Moses Our Revolutionary," the author of social justice and cosmopolitanism for the modern world. Heine's Bible was thus a political document, a call to arms.

Freud's Bible

Heine's appropriation of the Bible for political purposes demonstrates the way the Jewish secular Bible became a malleable document, although perhaps no more malleable than it was in the hands of rabbis, philosophers, or Kabbalists. Yet Heine's reading of the Bible had great resonance in the nineteenth and twentieth centuries, when Reformers and others sought in scripture ethical teachings rather than religious commandments. Sigmund Freud's *Moses and Monotheism* represents a much more idiosyncratic reading of the Bible, but in his claim for the Bible as an ethical text, he was not far from Heine, with whom, as we already saw in chapter 1, he had great affinity. As the capstone book of his long career, *Moses and Monotheism* was both Freud's application of psychoanalysis to the Bible and his singular pledge of allegiance to the Jewish people.[42]

As singular—even peculiar—as the book may be, it nevertheless reveals a great deal not only about Freud himself but also about how secular Jews more generally might interpret scripture. Although hardly a biblical scholar, Freud appropriated—some might say "misappropriated"—biblical scholarship for his purposes. This scholarship, which had its origins in Spinoza's *Theological-Political Treatise*, was accustomed to reading the Bible against the grain, that is, in arguing that the real biblical history was quite different from, if not the opposite of, what the Bible itself claimed.

For Freud, reading the Bible was much like treating a patient on the couch. As he says of the biblical text, but as he might equally have said of psychoanalysis: "Striking omissions, disturbing repetitions, palpable contradictions, signs of things the communication of which was never intended" are all clues to a truth that lies hidden beneath appearances.[43] This is also the method of biblical criticism generally, which finds in textual aberrations traces of the real history of ancient Israel. Freud takes this method even further, arguing that "the distortion of a text is not unlike a murder."[44] The writer, like the murderer, has more trouble covering up his traces than in committing the crime. But, of course, Freud was also hinting at the actual murder of Moses that he claimed to find between the lines of the text, for he argues that the Israelites, chafing at the religion Moses imposed on them, murdered him in the desert. Thus, the Bible's silences and distortions really did conceal a murder, at least as Freud saw it.

Freud famously argued that the real Moses was a priest in the service of the Pharaoh Akhenaten from whom he got the idea of monotheism. After the end of Akhenaten's reign, Moses fled, taking a slave group with him whom he turned into a nation with the belief in one God. It was not God but Moses who created the Jews (hence the resonance of the German title that Freud chose for his book: *Der Mann Moses und der Monotheismus*), and their leader and religion were not native but foreign. Rather than God choosing the Jews, it was Moses who chose them, making them "his" people.[45] The concept of the chosen people is therefore a result of projection: the Israelites displaced the one who had chosen them onto the heavens. Here was an interpretation that might well have found favor with Spinoza.

Freud thus denied to the Jews not only their founder but also the indigenous origins of their religion. If turning Moses into an Egyptian can be considered the "murder" of the founder of the Jewish nation, Freud was recapitulating the Israelites' murder of Moses in the desert. But, on the other hand, if Freud identified with Moses, a supposition for which there is considerable evidence, perhaps he saw himself as crossing the opposite boundary, from the Jewish to the non-Jewish world, to bring his revelation of psychoanalysis.

In the third and longest part of his book, which Freud withheld from publication until after he was forced to flee to England in 1938, he went much further. If he had metaphorically murdered the Hebrew Moses in the earlier essays, he resurrects him in part 3 and, in the process, celebrates the Jews in much more positive terms than in the earlier parts. The problem of the first two sections of the book was whether Moses was an Egyptian, and in so concluding, Freud remained well within the universe of modern biblical scholarship, even if he stretched the evidence more than was warranted. In part 3, though, he shifts to a different problem: who are the Jews, and why are they hated?

In his introduction to this part of the book, written before he left Austria in June 1938, Freud rather strangely launches into a sarcastic critique of Soviet Russia, Fascist Italy, and Nazi Germany for the purpose of showing how barbarism has been linked to progress, at least in the case of the first two.[46] Thus, the Soviet Union had abolished religion and encouraged sexual freedom—both moves which Freud approves—but it had done so through enormous coercion. The Italians had also used barbaric means to instill order, while the Nazis had done the same without any "progressive idea." Why did Freud feel these banal observations were necessary? The answer lies in the conclusion of part 3: the Jews had long ago discovered how to achieve spiritual progress without external coercion, and Judaism thus emerges as the real alternative to these modern nightmares.

The burden of part 3 is to show how the history of ancient Israel recapitulates the origin of religions that he had described twenty-five years earlier in *Totem and Taboo*. In that work, Freud argued that the "primal horde" of prehistory revolted against its patriarchal leader, killed him, but then, out of guilt over the murder, created a totemic god in his stead. So, too, with the murder of Moses. But Freud adds another theory from his studies of child development. The latency period in the sexual maturation of boys now explains what happens to the Mosaic religion after the murder of its founder. Just as the repression of early childhood sexuality is necessary for the emergence of mature sexuality, so the memory of Moses's murder was repressed by the Israelites for a long latency period. Later in the nation's history, that which had been repressed "returned"—or was resurrected—in the form of the religion of the prophets. The murder of Moses was therefore necessary to perpetuate the religion of Akhenaten, since it was the process of repression and the return of the repressed that caused the Israelites to internalize it.

Moreover, it was not only Egyptian monotheism but even more the act of repression born of guilt that taught the Jews the "renunciation of the instincts," which, for Freud, was necessary for civilization:

> The religion that began with the prohibition against making an image of its God has developed in the course of centuries more and more into a religion of instinctual renunciation. Not that it demands sexual abstinence: it is content with a considerable restriction of sexual freedom. God, however, becomes completely withdrawn from sexuality and raised to an ideal of ethical perfection. Ethics, however, means restriction of instinctual gratification.[47]

This instinctual renunciation had profound consequences for the Jews. It is proof of their "special psychical fitness" that the Jews have produced so many leaders who could carry on the work of Moses.[48] The religion that emerged caused them to disdain magic and mysticism and encouraged them to "progress in spirituality and sublimations. The people, happy in their conviction of possessing truth, overcome by the consciousness of being the chosen, came to value highly all intellectual and ethical achievements."[49]

Note that spiritual, intellectual, and ethical achievements are all of a piece and are the product of "sublimations."

As a result of their intellectual and spiritual character (the word *Geistigkeit* can mean either in German), the Jews renounced the athleticism of the Greeks in favor of "what is culturally more important."[50] With this last pronouncement, Freud, who for much of his life had held Greek culture in awe, now, like Heine also at the end of his life, took the side of Jerusalem over Athens. Even Islam, which seemed similar to Judaism, "lacked the profundity which in the Jewish religion resulted from the murder of its founder."[51] In the final analysis, the murder of Moses was the event necessary to raise the Jews above all other civilizations.

Freud argues that this unique spiritual achievement was passed on genetically from one generation to another: "there probably exists in the mental life of the individual not only what he has experienced himself, but also what he brought with him at birth, fragments of phylogenetic origin, an archaic heritage."[52] This is one of the most vexed questions to arise from Freud's last book. He explicitly adopted a version of Lamarckism, the discredited theory that acquired characteristics might be genetically inherited. Freud was well aware that biological research had rejected this idea, but he nevertheless forged ahead, arguing that even if acquired *physical* characteristics were not inherited, "memory traces" could be passed on from generation to generation.[53]

As a result of latency and the return of the repressed, the Jews had embedded such memory traces deep in their genome, and this was the key to their longevity as a people. Already in 1930, when he wrote a preface to a Hebrew translation of *Totem and Taboo*, Freud made clear his view that neither the "religion of his fathers" nor "nationalist ideals" constituted his Jewish identity. If asked in what way he continued to believe that "he is in his essential nature a Jew and …has no desire to alter that nature," he would answer "'a very great deal, and probably its essence.' "[54] This was an essence he could not, he says, express in words but "some day, no doubt, it will become accessible to the scientific mind." While *Totem and Taboo* did not deal with Judaism and "makes no exceptions in favour of Jewry," Freud clearly holds out the hope that science "cannot remain a stranger to the spirit of the new Jewry."

With *Moses and Monotheism*, Freud believed that he met the challenge he had posed to himself in 1930. Now he had an answer to the "essence" of

Jewishness. It was an essence transmitted genetically, but being well aware of the seemingly similar doctrine propounded by the Nazis, he insists that "admixture of blood made little difference, since what kept [the Jews] together was something ideal—the possession they had in common of certain intellectual and emotional values."[55] It was almost as if, in order to refute Nazi propaganda about the inferiority of the Jews, Freud had to adopt a different kind of racial theory to argue for their superiority.

The Mosaic religion—the teachings of Moses, followed by the religion constructed in the wake of his murder, the repression of the murder, and the return of the repressed—taught three things: (1) the new conception of God, (2) the doctrine of the chosen people and, (3) the forcing upon the people of "a progress in spirituality which ... further opened the way to respect for intellectual work and to further instinctual renunciations."[56]

The last point is the most important: Freud hints broadly that his own intellectual work owed its origins and impetus to the instinctual renunciations he had inherited as a Jew. Anxious early in his career that psychoanalysis not be seen as a "Jewish science," Freud now came to embrace it as exactly that. Where, three decades earlier, he had welcomed Carl Jung into his fold of disciples as a Christian who might put a non-Jewish face on the movement, now, having long broken with Jung, he found no reason to hide his work's true identity. Indeed, the sharp attack on Christianity as a religion that had resurrected the myth and magic of ancient Egypt may be seen as a covert attack on Jung who had made myth central to his theory of the collective unconscious. Oddly enough, Freud's psychological Lamarckism looks suspiciously like Jung's views, but he insists that in the case of the Jews, the memory traces were not of myth but of its very opposite: intellectuality.

For the dying Freud, then, the intellectual spirit that created psychoanalysis was at bottom the heritage of biblical Judaism. What Yosef Hayim Yerushalmi, following Philip Rieff, felicitously called "the psychological Jew"[57] was the product of a long tradition of "special psychic fitness." With psychoanalysis, the process that began with the murder of Moses could finally become self-conscious and its neurosis overcome. Moreover, this process was one of gradual secularization already present in a nutshell in the Bible itself: "And even the [prophets'] exhortation to believe in God seems to recede in comparison with the seriousness of ...ethical demands."[58] No wonder, then, that it was the Jewish science of psychoanalysis that had first revealed the great "illusion" of religion, since the religion of the Bible was really the teachings of *der Mann Moses*—and not of God.

The Zionist Bible

In the introduction to the Hebrew edition of *Totem and Taboo*, Freud confessed his ambivalence over Jewish nationalism. While he distanced himself personally from Zionism, he also admitted his admiration for the project of recreating the Jewish nation. In *Moses and Monotheism*, he does not mention Zionism, but his pride in what might be called the secular Jewish heritage was certainly of a piece with the motivation that brought other secular Jews into the movement's orbit. For just as Freud reinterpreted the Bible as the foundational text for a psychological Judaism, so did many Zionists find in scripture the fount for secular nationalism.

In the so-called Zionist passage of his *Theological-Political Treatise*, Spinoza suggested the possibility that the Jews might regain their sovereignty and thus their identity, which was based on their ancient state. What Spinoza would have thought of the Zionist movement and the state it created we can never know, but he likely would have found the secularism of its founders to be highly sympathetic. If the ancient Israelite state drew its strength from theocracy, that strength also ultimately led to the weakness that brought it down in the form of priestly rule. A modern state of the Jews, like Spinoza's ideal republic, would have to rest on a secular basis, using religion at most to inculcate morality and obedience.

As we shall see in the next chapter, Spinoza's political reading of the Bible provided a model for Jewish nationalists at the end of the nineteenth century, who, following other European nationalist movements, sought to appropriate their ancient text as the foundation stone for the new nation-state. Even before the rise of Zionism, Hebrew writers of the eastern European Haskalah, such as Abraham Mapu, returned to the Bible as the model for an enlightened Jewish people. But which Bible might one adopt for a national credo? The conquests of Joshua? The ethical teachings of Jeremiah? Or, perhaps, the universalism of Amos and the Second Isaiah? The Bible, of course, does not speak in one voice. In addition, if one was committed to a secular reading of the Bible, what should one do with the evident religiosity of the text?

⌈Ahad Ha'am (the pen name of Asher Ginzberg, 1856–1927) was the ideological leader of "cultural Zionism," the strand of Jewish nationalism that saw in Zionism primarily a movement of cultural renewal rooted in a spiritual center in Palestine. As opposed to more radical Zionists, who preached a decisive break between the new Israel and the Jewish Diaspora, Ahad Ha'am envisioned a continuity between the two in which the center of secular Hebrew culture in Palestine would emanate rays of renewal to the Diaspora. Sometimes called the "secular rabbi" of Zionism, Ahad Ha'am sought a nonreligious foundation for the Jewish national spirit⌉

This foundation he found in the Bible and, more specifically, in the prophets, starting with Moses.[59] The biblical prophet, he argues, is a man with an uncompromising sense of justice, an ethical reading of the Bible that is reminiscent of Heine and Freud. But justice of this sort could not by itself sustain a society. The priests, who counterbalanced the prophets, were necessary as agents of compromise and institutionalization. Moses, as the first prophet, sets the pattern. Ahad Ha'am argues that whether or not Moses actually existed is immaterial. As with Heine and other modern Jews, Ahad Ha'am sees the figure of Moses as archetypical and the way the Bible tells his story as the model for all subsequent Jewish history.[60] Indeed, Ahad Ha'am retells the Moses story as a virtual allegory for his own times. Like the cosmopolitan Jews of the modern era, Moses first sought to establish justice in Egyptian society, but when he came to realize the injustice perpetrated on the Jews, he committed himself to their cause. Thus was born the first Zionist.

The prophets made ethics the core value of ancient Israel. This was the era in which the "Torah of the heart" prevailed, that is, an inner moral sense that required no written text.[61] In "Transvaluation of Values," an attack on the Jewish followers of Nietzsche, Ahad Ha'am adopted Nietzsche's slogan (*Umwertung alles Werten*) and turned it against him. The Jews, he argues, anticipated the doctrine of the *Übermensch* with their own identity as a "Supernation" (*ha-am ha-eliyon*), defined by their commitment to morality.[62] So was Nietzsche's attack on biblical ethics stood on its head! But this inner morality gave way gradually to a fossilized written doctrine, starting with the priests and continuing with the rabbis of the Talmud. The phrase "people of the book" is a pejorative one for Ahad Ha'am since the "book" means a set of external laws that enslaves the people and anesthetizes their inner vitality. This book is therefore not "The Book," since the Bible taken by itself is not an instrument of enslavement, which is rather the later legal tradition and what it does to the Bible. The recovery of the ethical spirit of the Bible is what cultural Zionism comes to accomplish

In this attack on the postbiblical tradition, Ahad Ha'am was responding to the Jewish education prevalent among the intellectual elite of eastern Europe. While primary education might involve reading the Bible with the eleventh-century exegesis of Rashi, the later years of education spent in the yeshiva were devoted exclusively to Talmud and medieval codes, the core texts of the rabbinic tradition. Biblical verses only served as proof texts, and thus knowledge of the Bible (especially the Prophets and Writings) was refracted through the talmudic use of these texts. In short, the Bible as a coherent book was relegated to the nursery school and ignored later. The return to the Bible characteristic of both the Haskalah and later nationalists like Ahad Ha'am, Hayim Nahman Bialik, and Micha Yosef Berdichevsky (to whom we will turn in a moment) was itself a rebellion against the rabbinic curriculum.

Following the German Romantic philosopher Herder, who invented the term *Volksgeist* ("spirit of the people"), Ahad Ha'am frequently used the phrase "national spirit" or "national morality" to substitute for God. It is the spirit of the nation rather than God that he seeks to recuperate, ethics rather than law. This national spirit is to be found first and foremost in the Bible. It sometimes hides in the guise of religion, but it is in fact prior to and autonomous from religion.[63] This spirit was suppressed during the centuries of exile but never lost. Surprisingly, though, Ahad Ha'am utterly rejected nineteenth-century Reform Judaism, which had tried to reestablish Judaism on a biblical basis, a goal seemingly the same as his. In one of his earliest essays, from 1891, he denounced their position as "slavery in freedom," assimilation rather than national awakening.[64] Having renounced the idea of a Jewish people, they had abandoned the national spirit that animates it and had thus betrayed the Bible in the bargain. Only Zionism as a cultural movement might return the Jews to the essence of their scripture

Ahad Ha'am's position, as critical as it was of Diaspora assimilation, nevertheless excited a radical rejection by a younger generation of Hebrew writers not content with what they viewed as his compromising positions. Led by Micha Yosef Berdichevsky (1865–1921), these writers had fallen under the influence of the German philosopher Friedrich Nietzsche and the Hebrew translation of phrase "transvaluation of values" (*shinui arakhim*) became their battle cry.[65]

Berdichevsky was the most profound and influential of these radicals. He adopted Nietzsche's attack on biblical ethics (and it was primarily against him that Ahad Ha'am wrote his "Nietzschean" essay).[66] Priests and prophets had emasculated the ancient Hebrews by turning their vital religion of nature into an abstract, spiritualized doctrine called Judaism. As a result, Judaism took priority over the Jews, that is, the vital needs of the people.[67] In an early essay titled "On the Book" (1899), Berdichevsky celebrated the religion of Israel before Sinai:

> At the time when we worshiped many gods and burned incense to them on the mountains and the hills, erecting altars to the queen of heaven [i.e., the Canaanite goddess Asherah], then we danced like rams and rejoiced in the light and in the servants of the light. ... The blood of male goats, of sheep and goats connect man to nature. The priest came before the prophet and the first born before the priest. [68]

The original religion of the Hebrews was polytheistic and pagan. As opposed to the religion of the prophets, it reveled in blood. But then the God of Sinai, the monotheistic God "came, from Seir or from Faran, and gave us a book for the generations, a book with chapters and verses ... and we sank in it and returned and sank again." Although biblical religion was also based on sacrifice, it robbed the people of their lifeblood:

> A fire burnt on the eternal altar and a priest came and stuck a ritual knife into our belly. And the blood flowed and was mingled with the sacrificial fire. The worshipers fell on their faces and cried out to God ... "save us from the cloud that rises and covers everything." And God answers: "You are my children. I have molded you in an iron kiln. You cannot die and yet your life is not life. You are a nation of history and I gave you books.[69]

Biblical religion enacts a kind of quasi-murder of the people. But like a grotesque zombie, the people cannot die a merciful death; they continue to limp along, enslaved to their stultifying books, in a "life that is not life."

Berdichevsky followed Ahad Ha'am in condemning enslavement to the written word, but where Ahad Ha'am found in the prophets a living religion, Berdichevsky finds the same enslavement.[70] A revolutionary break from the past is necessary to create a new future. But Berdichevsky nevertheless believed that history contained a model for this future. The true vitality of the Jews lay not in the Bible's master narrative but in a tradition that competed with the revelation at Sinai and that was never entirely suppressed by it. In his last book, *Sinai und Gerizim*, written in German, Berdichevsky argued that two traditions coexisted in the Bible, with a religion of nature and martial vitality preceding Moses's antinatural Torah. He claimed that evidence of this pre-Sinaitic law could be found in the blessings and curses, mentioned in Deuteronomy 27 and 28, that were to be pronounced on Mount Gerizim and Mount Ebal after the conquest of the land:

> The revelation on Gerizim and Ebal, which is generally thought to be the final seal on the various revelations of law in [the Bible—starting with Sinai], was actually the first; the covenant of Gerizim was the most ancient and its value for the religion of Israel was and is greater than the value of all the other covenants, despite the fact that it was suppressed.[71]

The curses, he believed, corresponded in a rough way to the Ten Commandments but were concerned with the political process of governing the nation, such as "cursed be he who removes his neighbor's landmark."[72] These blessings and curses were associated with Joshua since they were to be pronounced in the land. Joshua's political "Torah" was therefore a nationalist counterpart to Moses' ethical Torah. In Berdichevsky's hands, Joshua became a leader of the same stature as Moses, a legislator of his own tradition that actually predated that of Moses

Reinterpreting for his own purposes a talmudic saying that "the sword and the book descended from the heaven coupled together,"[73] Berdichevsky associates the sword with the Torah of Gerizim and Ebal and the book with Sinai. The two continued to struggle with each other throughout the biblical period and into the postbiblical. Rather than arguing, as many did, that Athens stood for physical strength and beauty while Jerusalem stood for ethics, Berdichevsky saw all of these qualities as indigenous to ancient Israel. The culture celebrating nature and strength struggled with—and ultimately lost out to—a religion of ethics and law. Jewish history is the record of this battle of "Judaism" against "the Jews." In chapter 4, we will return to Berdichevsky's interpretation of Jewish history as the battle between tradition and countertradition.

Since the book had predominated over the sword since the destruction of the Second Temple, it was now time to redress this imbalance. Translating Nietzsche's slogan "in order to build a house, one must first destroy a house" into Hebrew yielded the far more pointed conclusion: "in order to destroy a temple [*bayit* = house or temple], it is first necessary to destroy a temple."[74] The temple of the book—based on the Torah of Moses, the prophets, the priests, and the rabbis—must be destroyed to make way for a new temple of the sword, that of Joshua and his heirs.

Berdichevsky famously proclaimed: "To be or not to be! To be the last Jews or the first Hebrews."[75] This cry was taken up by Zionists of various ideological stripes in the slogan "negation of the exile" (*shelilat ha-golah*). For many, to reject the exile meant to reject the religion of exile in the belief that it was the religion itself that had created the exile. That is, as Berdichevsky had argued, the turn in biblical times from militant nationalism to prophetic ethics weakened the national spirit and led to defeat and exile. For later Jewish nationalists, the return to a vitalistic ethos entailed at once a revolt against biblical religion but equally the recovery of the Bible's militant nationalism. Where Heine's Bible was the diasporic "portable religion" of Israel, the Zionist Bible became the warrant for possession of the land

It is now generally acknowledged that modern nationalisms invent traditions to establish their legitimacy.[76] Needless to say, these traditions are not actually invented in the sense of fabricated out of whole cloth. They are instead, as with the Bible, long-standing folk or mythic traditions that nationalists mobilize and reshape for their own purposes. If modern Jews in general reinterpreted the Bible according to their lights, so too did Jewish nationalists, for the Bible was, of course, a book about the very land that the Zionists wished to reclaim. To appropriate the Bible as a nationalist text involved a great deal of invention, but in ways that the text itself often seemed to invite. Moreover, the exclusive focus on the Bible as the only Jewish text relevant to Zionism was itself a radical statement about all other texts, whether or not written in the Land of Israel.

Israel's first prime minister, David Ben-Gurion, played a major role in the elevation of the Bible to the status of national myth. In the new State of Israel, a kind of "bibliomania" became the order of the day, with Bible competitions and archaeology serving as national sports.[77] Ben-Gurion convened a biweekly Bible study group in his house and issued pronouncements on a variety of biblical themes. Perhaps the most controversial of his biblical readings came in 1959 when he delivered an address to his study group of scholars and politicians on the antiquity of Israel.[78] He argued, based on a close reading of the text, that the Hebrews were already a settled people in the land in the time of the patriarchs.

Ben-Gurion even suggests that Abraham migrated to Canaan in order to join this people. The Canaanites who were then in the land (Genesis 12:6) were the same as Hebrews, or, rather, the name "Canaanite" had both a specific and general meaning. These people already believed in a "High God" (Genesis 14:18–19), which may have been another reason why Abraham, also already a believer in one God, was attracted to them. The Hebrews therefore predated Abraham, in much the same way as claimed by the "Canaanite" writers, a fringe literary movement of the 1940s and '50s that wanted to reconstruct a prebiblical (read: pre-Jewish) Near Eastern identity for the new Hebrews.[79] But where they wanted to sever any relationship between the Hebrews and the later diasporic Jews, Ben-Gurion drew the opposite conclusion: since the Bible contains many stories of exile and return (including the Egypt story), Diaspora is part of biblical identity.

According to Ben-Gurion, only a small portion of this people, the wealthy family of Joseph, went to Egypt where, instead of staying for 430 years, as the Bible says, they remained at most two or three generations. At the end of this abbreviated stay, a group of some six hundred (and not 600,000 as in the Bible's account) left and journeyed through the desert. This was the group that received the Torah given by Moses. When this small group entered the land under Joshua, they already found their kinsmen there. Hence, the town of Shechem was not destroyed because it was already occupied by Hebrews. Ben-Gurion insists that these Israelites, as they came to be called, were a united people throughout this period, even though one small group had separated itself by going to Egypt.

Who was Moses and why did he become the leader of the group of Hebrews in Egypt? Ben-Gurion's position is ambiguous. Moses was reared in Pharaoh's house (Exodus 2:5–10) and therefore absorbed all the rich Egyptian culture of that day. He was consequently able to rise above all his brethren, reject their slavery, and take them out of the land of Egypt. Ben-Gurion was certainly not inclined to go as far as Freud and turn Moses into an Egyptian. Still, it was Egyptian culture that gave him the initiative to transform Hebrew monotheism into a doctrine of political liberation. If Ben-Gurion saw in the story an allegory of modern Jewish history, he was implying that cosmopolitan culture was the necessary precondition for Zionism; the Jewish religion by itself would not suffice.

Ben-Gurion's interpretation engendered very considerable controversy at the time, since it overturned the Bible's master narrative of the Exodus.[80] One of the religious parties even tabled a no-confidence motion in the Knesset in 1960 following his lecture on the Exodus, on the grounds that he had offended the beliefs of the observant. On the other hand, a secular opposition member of the Knesset objected on the grounds that Ben-Gurion was acting like other modern dictators in rewriting history.

But while his views may have seemed offensive to his political opponents, Ben-Gurion actually anticipated a line of contemporary biblical criticism that has become something of a consensus: most of the Israelites were indigenous to the land, and the Exodus either did not happen at all or happened to only a very small group. While some today use this interpretation to throw doubt on the Bible as the source of Jewish national identity, Ben-Gurion drew the exact opposite message: the land belonged to the Jews because they had never entirely left it and, in fact, were there long before the Bible's chronology.

Ben-Gurion's opponents were correct, though, in identifying his interpretation of the Bible as militantly secular. As opposed to the Orthodox tradition, he wanted to privilege the Bible above all later literature, a stance reflected in the curriculum of Israel's secular school system. While not disparaging rabbinic midrash, he rejected its application to the Bible. The Song of Songs, for example, is a secular love poem that can compete with Greek and Latin love poetry, while the midrashic understanding of the Song as the love between God and Israel is a fallacious reading.[81] All later commentaries, such as the canonical commentary of Rashi, are only commentaries: "The Bible is illuminated by its own light."[82] This formulation comes very close to that of Spinoza and, given Ben-Gurion's call to repeal the *herem* on Spinoza, he may well have had in mind his seventeenth-century predecessor in literal interpretation, although he did not mention him in this context. He did, however, invoke Spinoza's own predecessor Maimonides, quoting the dictum that "the Torah speaks in the language of human beings."[83] While the authors of the Bible, lacking Maimonides' philosophical profundity, may have believed that God actually speaks, Ben-Gurion himself sided with Maimonides—or, better, with his interpretation of Maimonides, that the Bible in the form we have it is the creation of human beings.

Ben-Gurion's secular reading of the Bible was explicitly political, even military. While conceding that the Torah of Moses was based on a monotheistic religion, he parted company with the dean of Israel's bible scholars, Yehezkel Kaufman, and insisted, like Spinoza, that the Bible was primarily a *nationalist* book. That is, the Bible was a document that gave a political identity to the ancient nation of Israel, an identity that transcended mere religion. Ben-Gurion therefore unsurprisingly reads the book through the eyes of the political founder of latter-day Israel. He says that after Israel's War of Independence, he now understands the Bible from the point of view of the new political, military, and geographical questions that war awakened. The Bible proves that the Jews never disparaged military might since they never embraced a solely spiritual view of the world.[84] At times, he reads the experience of the Israeli army back into biblical times: the tribes in the time of Joshua, for example, were like the brigades of the Israeli army, which could be dissolved and reintegrated into other units.[85] This seemingly banal observation is actually rooted in Ben-Gurion's controversial decision to disband independent militias on the both the Right and the Left. If the tribes of Israel were artificial units subordinate to the overarching nation (a historically doubtful claim), so, too, in modern times, the state's army superseded all pre-state armed groups. At other times, he takes lessons from the Bible, such as the way King Uziah integrated settlement of the land and irrigation projects with military activities, much as the modern Israeli army combined agricultural settlement with national defense.[86]

The Bible would serve the new State of Israel as the model for creating the nation, since it demonstrated that the earliest history of the nation was rooted in the land itself:

> The admixture of people which flows in from foreign exiles will be cleansed, refined and purified from harmful, foreign dross in the melting pot of Jewish brotherhood and through military discipline. The barriers between communities will be torn down, and true unity of a new nation reviving its youth will be forged which will draw from an ancient past saturated with struggle.[87]

If the Bible itself suggested that this "melting pot" had actually been in Egypt (Deuteronomy 4:20) as well as in the Sinai desert, for Ben-Gurion, the real nation of Israel was already forged in the land before the Bible's own history. It was this image of the Jews as the indigenous people of the land that would serve the latter-day task of forging them anew

The Labor Zionist movement, which Ben-Gurion led, often read the Bible not only as the template for modern Jewish nationalism but also as a socialist manifesto. Biblical laws such as the Jubilee, which seemed to undercut private property by returning it to God every forty-nine years, might be seen as the basis for a Hebrew socialism. This was a nationalist version of Heine's revolutionary reading of the Bible, even though Heine himself would have been highly suspicious of any harnessing of socialism to nationalism.⏋

But the Bible was also a book available to other ideologies. Vladimir Jabotinsky (1880–1940), the founder of right-wing Revisionist Zionism, found in the Bible a model for a Jewish nationalism that put nation and not class at the center. While Jabotinsky's reading of the Bible did not turn the ancient Israelites into unfettered capitalists, it extolled the small landholders and farmers as representing the opposite of socialist ideals.[88]

Unlike Ben-Gurion, Jabotinsky was raised in a quite acculturated environment in the Russian city of Odessa. Although he learned some Hebrew in his youth, his primary original language was Russian. Later, he became infatuated with Italian culture. When, after becoming a Zionist, he turned to writing in Hebrew, his impressive command of the language still lacked much biblical resonance. This distance from the Bible is also evident in his fascinating novel, *Samson*, written in Russian and published in 1927.[89] The biblical Samson becomes something of a hybrid between the Israelites and the Philistines, whom Jabotinsky portrays as models of both national pride and sexual health. In one astonishing passage describing a Philistine mass ceremony, the Philistine women are provocatively bare-breasted, their nudity evidently a sign of their vigor. The novel is devoid of any divine presence, and Samson comes to convey the culture of the virile Philistines to the still-stunted Israelites. His intermarriages with Philistine women represent Israel breaking the chains of sexual bondage in favor of a new, liberated national life. Such a positive view of the Philistines clearly contradicts the Bible's overt message and suggests that for a nationalist like Jabotinsky, a contrarian reading of the text was at times more compelling than a literal one

While many Zionists read the Bible, as did Ben-Gurion and Jabotinsky, in search of the sources of modern nationalism, not all did so. Like Max Nordau, with whom we began this chapter, there were those who adamantly rejected Scripture as relevant to modern life. One such radical was the Hebrew writer Joseph Hayim Brenner (1881–1921). Brenner went further than Berdichevsky, for where the latter found a countertradition to rescue from between the lines of the Bible, Brenner found nothing redeemable.

To make matters even more incendiary, he broached his views in a 1911 essay in which he professed to having no problem with the wave of Jewish conversions to Russian Orthodoxy. From his secular point of view, there was no difference between the Old Testament and the New. In order to indicate this alienation from the Bible, he adopted deliberately foreign lo-cutions in Hebrew. He calls the Bible *biblia* (from the Greek) and biblical Judaism *yahadut biblit*, as opposed to the more traditional *yahadut tanakhit* (from Tanakh, the traditional way of referring to the Bible as a whole). Even more provocatively, he refers to the book as *brit yeshanah* (Old Testament), the Christian term for the Hebrew Bible.[90] Many of the virtues he finds in the Old Testament he also finds in the New, which, he says defiantly, is "our book, bone of our bone, flesh of our flesh."[91] Moreover:

> They come to frighten us that the New Testament is about to defeat the sons of the Old Testament. But I, a free Hebrew, answer this fear as follows: as far as I am concerned, the Old Testament, that everyone yells is "holy scripture," the "book of books," the "eternal book," has the same value [as the New]. I liberated myself from the hypnosis of the twenty-four books of the Bible (*biblia*) a long time ago. Many secular books from much more recent times are more dear, greater and more profound, to me."[92]

Taking to heart Spinoza's teaching, Brenner reduces the Bible to *biblia*, books like any other—and not necessarily the best of them. For Brenner, the new Hebrew culture he struggled to create had to be founded on the modern condition of the Jews and not on their ancient literature. In chapter 4, we will return to Brenner and see how this view played out in his defini-tion of secular Jewish culture.

The historical approach to the Bible pioneered by Spinoza, who stood on the shoulders of Abraham Ibn Ezra and Moses Maimonides, became the immanent method by which later secular readers understood the text, even as they found in it ancient versions of their own philosophies. The secular Torah of Spinoza, Heine, Freud, Ahad Ha'am, Berdichevsky, Ben-Gurion, and Jabotinsky (to mention only those treated in this chapter) became the fount for a Jewish collectivity and culture that might replace or supersede the Jewish religion. It is this construction of Israel as a nation—a political and cultural community—that serves as a bridge to our next chapter.

Chapter 3

Israel: Race, Nation, or State

The premodern definition of Judaism—God, Torah, and Israel—presumed that theology and scripture were meaningless without a people to believe in and enact them. Biblical Israel was constituted through a covenant between God and the descendents of Jacob. Israel thus presupposed Torah, which in turn presupposed God. After biblical times, Israel was understood by the Jews themselves as well as by others to be both the follower of a scriptural religion—a "people of the book" to use the Muslim phrase—and a nation that had lost its land. With the modern age, the unified meaning of Judaism came unglued, and its component parts competed with each other to claim the mantle of *verus Israel.* The early German Reform movement developed a purely religious self-definition, "German citizens of the Mosaic persuasion." The Reformers also reduced Torah to just the Bible, criticizing and in some cases discarding postbiblical rabbinic literature.

In reaction against this religious definition of Israel and also to the demographic explosion of the Jewish population in eastern Europe, there emerged new political and cultural definitions of the Jews, defined by some historically as a "community of fate" and by others, more racially, as a "community of descent." In this chapter, we will examine how secular thinkers replaced the traditional category of Israel with various biological and political definitions—racial, national, and statist—and in the next chapter, we will turn to cultural definitions of Israel. Since racial definitions of the Jews are sometimes associated with Zionists or proto-Zionists, like Moses Hess, it is important to emphasize that they were by no means limited only to Jewish nationalists but instead reflected the more general emphasis on race in late-nineteenth- and early-twentieth-century European and American thought, before the Nazis rendered such language taboo. Nationalist (or national) definitions of the Jews were, of course, not only racial, as the cases of Emma Lazarus and Theodor Herzl will demonstrate. And neither were all national definitions cut from the same cloth, as Herzl's critics Bernard Lazare and Hannah Arendt suggest, for these critics leavened their nationalism with utopian universalism. Finally, the advent of the State of Israel narrowed

Israel as a nation to a specific state, expressed perhaps in its purest form by Israel's first prime minister, David Ben-Gurion.

Spinoza will once again be a key figure in this story since he was the first to suggest a political definition of Israel divorced from God. We will also find some crucial groundwork in Moses Mendelssohn, who, even though a religious thinker, argued that Judaism already at its origins separated synagogue from state, thus foreshadowing secular modernity. As we have done in the previous two chapters, we begin by examining the premodern roots of secular Jewish politics and identity.

Precursors

The features of a secular, political definition of Israel that we will discuss in this chapter—race, nation and state—can be found in *nuce* in the Bible itself. Since the Bible claims that this nation was grounded in a family, it shares certain biological characteristics with the nineteenth-century idea of race, although tribes, as opposed to races, allow for intermarriage. The Bible tells the story of the gradual development of the nation from this single family to twelve tribes and finally a unified state under the Davidic monarchy (a state that lasted only two generations until it split in two). But since this state was repeatedly subjected to destruction and exile, Israel thus developed an identity of a nation that could exist without its state. While the modern notions of race, nation, and state are related, each can exist without the other, just as one could say that they did in ancient Israel.

We shall see in a moment how Spinoza and Mendelssohn both insisted that the Jews have lacked all political power since the destruction of their ancient state. However, both had to have been well aware that the Jews continued to function as a quasi-political community in their own time.[1] Spinoza's own fate at the hands of the Portuguese "nation" of Amsterdam can only be explained in political terms, since a purely religious community would not have had the capacity to ban him. The *herem* was a political act by a community possessing certain coercive powers, even if these powers were far less than those of a sovereign state. So, Spinoza's argument that the Jews no longer acted politically because they no longer had a state was belied by his own experience. Perhaps the *Theological-Political Treatise* might be seen as more prescriptive than descriptive in this regard, reflecting Spinoza's (unconscious?) wish that the Jews had vanished with their ancient state.

In fact, however, Spinoza's secular, political definition of Israel and Mendelssohn's claim that Judaism was first to separate religion and state both had significant premodern precursors that assumed that the Jews continued to function as a political community in Diaspora. With the destruction of the Second Temple in 70 CE, the Jews lost political sovereignty. Over the many centuries, though, the rabbis gradually established themselves as non-state authorities, at times competing with lay leaders for communal power.[2] Many theorists grounded this community in the covenant between God and Israel, an argument that might be called religious. According to the political theory derived from revelation, the rabbis were surrogate kings, legitimated by the biblical institution of monarchy and derived their authority from Moses. Yet, side by side with the language of divine covenant, starting in rabbinic literature, one can find quasi-secular theories of the Jewish polis. A secular theory of Jewish politics might find its legitimacy outside of divine sanction, either in popular consent or some form of contract.

Although we don't know whether the rabbinic academies of the Talmud actually functioned as courts, by the Middle Ages, rabbinic courts were the central legal authorities in most Jewish communities. These courts had the right to enforce their decisions by fining those against whom they ruled. This procedure was called *hefker bet-din* ("judicial expropriation"). Rabbinic political theory extended this power to the community as a whole. That is, they argued that the community as a whole was like a rabbinic court and could therefore expropriate the property of its members. This expropriation, originally a means of punishment, became here the authority to levy taxes. Thus, if we consider a rabbinic court to be ecclesiastical—a debatable assumption—the extension of its powers to the community might be considered a definite move toward secularization. What is also important for our purposes is that this last doctrine is not grounded in revelation. It is a distinctly secular theory of the power of the community.

Along the same lines, the rabbis also held that the community's authority came from an implied contract between all its members.[3] This contract gives the community the right to compel individuals within the town, for example, to share in the cost of building the door to a courtyard around which they live. Similarly, the community can compel its members to participate in building or repairing the wall of a town since they all receive protection from it. Later rabbinic law extended this principle to the point of allowing the townspeople to bind their members to pay for any common projects, in other words, to tax them. Medieval Jewish theorists preferred this contractual language, which was also common in non-Jewish political theory, rather than arguing that the communal authority was grounded in the covenant at Sinai. By using the language of contract, Jewish political theory in the Middle Ages distanced itself from its biblical roots and created the possibility of a secular communal government.

The existence of these two different types of political theory—religious and secular—became the source of conflict in the Middle Ages between rabbis and lay leaders. The rabbis might embrace the theory of the community as a court since, of course, they themselves constituted the real courts. The lay leaders could argue that they were what the Talmud calls the "select men of the town" (*berurim*) and their power had precedence over that of the rabbis. Maimonides, who was himself a rabbinical judge, argued that the talmudic law governing the townspeople only applied when there was no rabbi (the term Maimonides uses is "wise man" or *hakham*). He thus seemed to take a position on the "religious" end of the spectrum.

Despite Maimonides' predictable preference for rabbis over lay leaders, he laid the basis in his code of Jewish law for a secular political theory. As Menachem Lorberbaum has shown, Maimonides articulated both an ideal political theory and a realistic one.[4] The king possesses powers to enforce obedience that exceed those stated in the Torah, such as executing anyone who rebels against him.[5] In addition, the distinction he makes between the Davidic kings and the kings of Israel looks like a distinction between constitutional and absolutist monarchy: the former can be judged by the Sanhedrin, the latter not.[6] Although Maimonides clearly preferred a king who is bound by law, as a realist, he recognized that "secular" kings—including non-biblical Jewish kings like the Hasmoneans—might exercise unlimited power.

Maimonides' realism also extended to his messianic theory. Although the messianic kingdom might seem the framework for an idealist political theory, in fact, Maimonides describes the Messiah in realistic, political terms.[7] Borrowing a talmudic saying that "the only difference between our days and the days of the Messiah is subjugation to the nations [i.e., lack of political sovereignty],"[8] Maimonides states:

> King Messiah will arise and restore the kingdom of David to its former state and original sovereignty. He will rebuild the sanctuary and gather the dispersed

of Israel. All the ancient laws will be reinstated in his days. . . . Let no one think that in the days of the Messiah any of the laws of nature will be set aside or any innovation be introduced into creation. The world will follow its normal course. . . . Israel will live securely among the wicked of the heathens who are likened to wolves and leopards.[9]

Maimonides thus took the miraculous out of the messianic, rendering it purely political.

Although Maimonides was reluctant to apply a secular political theory to existing communal authorities, he did codify the practice of emergency decrees, literally "requirements of the hour" (*hora'at sha'ah*):

> Even as a physician will amputate the hand or the foot of a patient in order to save his life, so the court may advocate, when an emergency arises, the temporary disregard of some of the commandments that the commandments as a whole may be preserved.[10]

What follows from this concept is that the rabbis were empowered to impose "floggings for rebelliousness" (*malkot mardut*) when legally stipulated punishments did not apply. To quote one talmudic example that justified this extraordinary extension of legal power: "a man had intercourse with his wife under a fig tree and he was brought before the court and flogged, not because he [legally] deserved such a penalty but because 'the requirements of the hour' demanded it."[11] This idea of emergency powers looks like a medieval version of the idea of the twentieth-century conservative German political theorist, Carl Schmitt, that sovereign power is defined by the "state of exception," that is, the ability to suspend the law in states of emergency.[12]

Maimonides therefore laid the groundwork for a secular politics based on exigency and power rather than divine commandment. Although he preferred rabbis to exercise this power, a thirteenth-century school of Spanish thinkers, located originally in Barcelona, applied the notion of an autonomous politics to lay leaders, thus secularizing Jewish politics much further. As described by Lorberbaum, Moses Nahmanides, Solomon ibn Adret, and Nissim Gerondi were the main innovators of this secular politics.[13] Perhaps under the influence of Ashkenazi legal traditions, Nahmanides recognized the validity of local custom and communal ordinances that were enacted outside of the framework of Torah law. Adret went further, allowing the use of force in order to "preserve society" (*tikkun ha-medinah*), even when it is forbidden by the Torah. Gerondi completed this process by stating that the laws to "preserve society" are not temporary emergency regulations but are a legal system complementary to that of the Torah (this dual system of laws may be compared very roughly to the courts of equity and law in the English legal system). Where Maimonides had recognized the extraordinary power of monarchs, he still insisted that there was only one law, that of the Torah. For Gerondi (and his contemporary in Southern France, Menachem Meiri), the power of the king—or any government, for that matter—is grounded in what we would call secular law, which exists side by side with the law of God. Torah law may be perfect, but it is perhaps *too* perfect for governing a state. Hence the need for a secular or political law whose sources of authority are human rather than divine

As halakhic authorities, none of these medieval Jewish writers can be called secular. All were writing within the framework of the legal system that they believed to be divinely revealed. But their recognition of an autonomous realm of politics and law resembles in many ways Christian doctrines of religious and secular spheres, the first that of the church, the second that of the king. Just as the existence of this secular sphere in the Middle Ages provided a necessary precursor for modern secular politics, so, too, medieval Jewish political thought carved out a secular political realm that, even if not directly quoted, formed the backdrop for ideologies of secular Jewish politics in the modern world.

Spinoza and Mendelssohn: Religion and the State

Spinoza was the first to define the Jews in purely political terms. It was in their ancient theocratic state that they were "chosen" by God, which, in Spinoza's language, meant that they expressed their essential nature. Theocracy meant that the ancient Israelites believed that God himself was their ruler, a belief that contradicts the elementary teachings of philosophy. A secular reading of the Bible thus convinced Spinoza that the founding scripture of ancient Israel taught nothing about philosophical truth; the Bible was rather a historical handbook of politics.

Γ Spinoza states explicitly that the Bible cannot serve as a model for contemporary politics, a view made pressing by the contrary opinion of Reformers like John Calvin that it could do exactly that. Spinoza argues that since God no longer makes written covenants with human beings but instead inscribes such covenants in their hearts—a position he arrives at by a secular interpretation of Christian theology—a theocracy like that of the Bible is no longer possible.[14] In other words, he uses an ostensible Christian teaching against those Christians who would construct a latter-day theocracy. If God now makes spiritual covenants only in people's hearts, then the only kind of political covenants possible after the Bible are those between people, which is to say, a monarchy or a republic.

Yet, while such an argument would seem to relegate the Bible to irrelevance, a closer reading of Spinoza's account of the ancient Israelite theocracy contains some surprises. Although a theocracy, this state actually bears sufficient similarities to a republic—Spinoza's preferred form of government—so that examples from the Bible, which Spinoza brings in profusion, can serve to illuminate contemporary political theory.[15] The creation of the Israelite polity followed the same course as the formation of a democracy.[16] The members of the community made a social contract in which they ceded some of their rights to the sovereign. In this analysis of the Israelite covenant as a social contract, Spinoza anticipated twentieth-century studies that showed how the biblical covenant was modeled on suzerainty treaties in the ancient Near East.[17] In the case of ancient Israel, that sovereign was God, but this transfer was "notional rather than practical," by which Spinoza means that philosophically speaking, God was a fictional sovereign, a placeholder for the real sovereign, which was the people themselves.[18] Indeed, God cannot serve as a sovereign, except through the agency of human beings.[19]

As in a true democracy, "no man served his equal."[20] All possessions were shared equally—a reference here to the biblical Jubilee—and this created social solidarity. The ceremonial laws turned life into a long training in obedience, yet for the Israelites, obedience was not bondage but freedom.[21] These formulations sound very close to Spinoza's own philosophy (although he did not preach socialism): while the Israelites mistakenly understood eternal necessities as divine commandments, they rightly concluded that freedom lies in acquiescing to necessity.

On the other hand, Spinoza caustically criticizes the ancient Israelite state for its insularity. Since the Israelites' patriotism was equivalent to religious piety, they conceived a hatred for all other peoples, which, in turn, caused other nations to hate them with equal ferocity.[22] Clearly, Spinoza did not recommend such xenophobia for a modern republic.

The Israelite state was also not a model because of its inherent weakness, which was that, out of fear, the Israelites ceded their sovereignty first to Moses and later to kings. It was at Sinai that the people, in terror at the presence of God, made Moses their absolute leader, a precursor of a king. In the preface to the *Theological-Political Treatise*, Spinoza holds that superstition arises from fear of the unknown and that this superstition results in tyranny. The Israelites embodied this fear, and for Spinoza, their belief in God was but an irrational superstition. Thus, the absolute rule of Moses comes to replace a proto-democracy. Nevertheless, after Moses' death, sovereignty once again reverted to the people, since Moses did not create a hereditary monarchy. That would only come later, after the period of the Judges.

The second weakness of the Israelite state was the elevation of the Levites as a priestly class with temporal power. The emergence of this potentially independent class dates back to the golden calf and is thus a birth defect within the body politic. As the history of Israel continued, the priests repeatedly challenged secular authority. The inner conflicts of the state, which go back to its origins, eventually brought about its downfall. Here, Spinoza draws a cautionary lesson about the importance of always subordinating religious authority to the secular.

But the Bible itself, says Spinoza, should not be taken as the source for granting separate political power to churches, despite the way the biblical priests assumed such power. The priests originally received their power from Moses, that is, from a secular sovereign (secular in the sense that, in Spinoza's account, it was the people who empowered him).[23] The Hebrews never doubted that the sovereign retains absolute power over religion. That is why the Jewish religion necessarily lost the force of law once the Jews lost their state.

It was only Christianity that injected this doubt into its political theology: an autonomous Church is a Christian artifact. This was because Christianity was invented by those without power, while Judaism was in essence a state religion. Therefore, ancient Israel provides a model, even if one not realized in practice after the time of Moses, of the proper subordination of religion to state. In this sense, Judaism is closer to a modern religion, in Spinoza's terms, than Christianity. Stripped of belief in the fictitious God, the

Bible might serve after all as the inspiration for a republic in which religion provides only moral instruction and the affairs of state are left to the state. Just as the ancient Israelites formed a polity in which no one subjugated his equal, so a modern republic might be formed by a social compact between its freely acting members. With religion thus confined to the churches (and synagogues), philosophers might pursue truth without fear of theologians.

The assertion that the Jews were, above all, political geniuses was an astonishing claim to make in the seventeenth century. No other people appeared as politically feckless. By the same token, no one thought of the biblical Jews primarily in political terms but instead as religious precursors to Christianity. Thus, Spinoza turned the Bible, or at least the Bible as people understood it in his day, on its head: its contribution to world history was not in the realm of theology but in the realm of politics. The Jews are defined by their state. And since they had lost their state, they—and their book—had lost any reason for existence.

As is well known, though, Spinoza held out the possibility that since their nature is preeminently political, the Jews might become chosen again, meaning that they might regain their state.[24] To be sure, their religion, symbolized by the ritual of circumcision, discouraged "manliness," so that they might no longer have the martial prowess to attain statehood. But the very same circumcision was also the reason why they had continued to exist as a kind of ghost people without a state. That, and other religious rites, segregated them from the Gentiles, thus incurring hatred and persecution, which, in a kind of feedback loop, further segregated them. Thus, against Spinoza's intention, the Jewish religion actually did trump politics, for without it, the Jews should have gone the way of all other ancient peoples who disappeared into the dustbin of history.

It is possible that this so-called Zionist passage of Spinoza's *Treatise*, in which he raised the possibility of renewed Jewish sovereignty, was prompted by a tumultuous event that swept the Jewish world only five years before he wrote his book.[25] In 1665, a Turkish Jew named Shabbtai Zvi proclaimed himself the Messiah, and enthusiasts for his movement sprung up in far-flung locales, including Amsterdam. Spinoza was aware of the Sabbatian episode, since Henry Oldenburg, his English correspondent, asked him specifically about it.[26] Although much of the scholarship on Sabbatianism, pioneered by Gershom Scholem, focuses on the Kabbalistic theology of the movement, its political import may have attracted Spinoza's special attention. Shabbtai Zvi used royal titles and was so addressed by his followers. In addition to his supernatural and mystical pretensions, he also sought to reclaim Jewish sovereignty in the land of Israel from the Ottoman sultan. The possibility of renewed Jewish statehood in Spinoza's time was therefore not entirely theoretical.

As we have seen in detail, Spinoza did not advocate the separation of church and state but rather the subordination of the first to the second. Religion was to be the handmaiden of the state in teaching obedience to the many who could not arrive at such an understanding with their reason. By the time Moses Mendelssohn took up similar questions a century after Spinoza, the idea of fully privatizing religion, developed in the greatest detail by John Locke, had become much more widespread. Mendelssohn built upon Spinoza but went further in fully divorcing religion from temporal authority, and like Spinoza, he used the Jewish tradition as his model. Unlike Spinoza, though, Mendelssohn can hardly be considered secular in either his beliefs or practices; he remained a traditional Jew throughout his life. But his political theory made an important contribution, based on his interpretation of Judaism, to the secularization of the state.

Mendelssohn's *Jerusalem* (1783) bears the subtitle *On Religious Power and Judaism*. Although the term "Judaism" appears from time to time prior to Mendelssohn, he undoubtedly played a major role in identifying the beliefs and practices of the Jews with this reified concept.[27] Mendelssohn's particular way of defining this entity called Judaism was intended to mark it as the most modern of religions, that is, the most suitable for a modern state in which religion is relegated to the private sphere.

Jerusalem is divided into two parts. The first is a theoretical discussion of which rights can be alienated, that is, turned over by an individual to the state. By the time Mendelssohn took up this question, the modern social contract theory of the state was a century old, and it hinged on the idea that people in the state of nature voluntarily created the state by endowing it with some of the rights that they had previously held individually. Mendelssohn argues that human beings cannot alienate all of their natural rights, only those that pertain to their material existence. What they cannot alienate are their beliefs and opinions. Thus, the state, no matter how absolute, cannot legitimately control convictions.[28] While the state has an absolute right over the relations between its subjects, a right that gives it the power of coercion, the church, by Mendelssohn's definition, deals only with the relations between human beings and God.[29]

Religious institutions have no rights over material goods and therefore cannot coerce their members. The role of these institutions is to inculcate belief, but because belief cannot be coerced, they can only do so by education and persuasion. For this reason, Mendelssohn denies that churches have the right to excommunicate their members, that is, to use coercion to force belief (an argument he had already made a year earlier in a preface to a German edition of Menasseh ben Israel's plea for the readmission of the Jews to England). He adds, in what must be a veiled reference to Spinoza: "Reader! To whatever visible church, synagogue, or mosque you may belong! See if you do not find more truth in religion among the host of the excommunicated than among the far greater host of those who excommunicated them."[30]

In part 2 of *Jerusalem*, Mendelssohn demonstrates that it is Judaism that conforms most closely to his ideal definition of noncoercive religion. In part 1, he had argued that "the state prescribes laws, religion commandments."[31] But the anonymous author of the tract who prompted him to write *Jerusalem* had argued that the Mosaic religion enforced its commandments with physical punishments, such as stoning. Wasn't Mendelssohn's distinction between "laws" and "commandments" a distinction without a difference? In what sense, then, was Judaism a noncoercive religion?

Mendelssohn answers this potentially fatal challenge with a novel theory of the commandments. On the one hand, he associates himself with Spinoza's argument that the revelation at Sinai created the legislation that constituted the Hebrew commonwealth, which was initially a theocracy. As such, these laws were enforced like those of any state, with corporal punishments. But with the destruction of Israelite state, these punishments lapsed. Having followed Spinoza this far, Mendelssohn was now compelled to explain why one might continue to adhere to these laws absent a state and whether the laws carried with them any powers of enforcement. As an Orthodox Jew (the term, of course, is anachronistic for the late eighteenth century), Mendelssohn had to justify personally continuing to follow the law, especially since he had been challenged by several Christian writers to reconcile a religion of reason with Judaism.

Mendelssohn's distinction between laws and commandments lies at the heart of his answer to this challenge. While the commandments had the force of law under the Israelite state, they were essentially something different: "But [the commandments] are also [in addition to prescriptions for action] . . . to be regarded as a kind of script and they have significance and meaning as ceremonial laws. They guide the inquiring intelligence to divine truths."[32] The commandments themselves do not reveal divine truth, but they guide the mind in the direction of discovering it. They were therefore not limited in utility to the ancient polity but continue to serve philosophy.

Mendelssohn obviously recognized that the *herem*, the functional equivalent of excommunication, still operated in the Jewish world, but he insisted that the original intent of Judaism was otherwise. Judaism was not essentially a political religion, despite its origins as a theocracy. Here, he departed radically from Spinoza. With the destruction of the two Temples, Judaism might realize the essence of its revelation: a set of commandments designed to educate toward the religion of reason. Since such convictions can never be coerced, Judaism could reach its potential without a state (although Mendelssohn certainly did not negate the possibility of renewed sovereignty). While they were fulfilled in community, the commandments were directed toward the individual. Religion could best flourish in private, far from the power of the state.

Alexander Altmann has argued that Mendelssohn's original plan for *Jerusalem* called for shifting the blame for religious coercion to Christianity.[33] The final version does not contain such an explicit accusation, but one can still find hints of it between the lines. Thus: "Judaism knows of no revealed religion, but only revealed legislation"[34] Such a statement would become a virtual cliché in modern interfaith dialogue, with Judaism defined as "orthopraxis" versus Christianity's "Orthodoxy." While Judaism does not coerce belief, Christianity, replete with Inquisitions and excommunications, does exactly that. Since Mendelssohn's definition of the modern state requires that the church relinquish all its powers of coercion, Judaism emerges as the most modern of all religions, the most prepared for a world in which secular power is absolute and religion banished from the public square.

Mendelssohn and Spinoza therefore started with a similar premise about the political nature of ancient Judaism, but ended diametrically opposed: for Spinoza, there could be no reason for the existence of Jewish law after the destruction of the state, while for Mendelssohn, the law continued to function as a means of education without a state. Mendelssohn tried to construct a Jewish identity devoid of politics—that is, devoid of power and coercion—while Spinoza could not see a future for Jewish identity without politics, which, for him, meant a state. Both, for different reasons, denied that the Jews operated politically in Diaspora. While both sought a secular realm of politics, only Spinoza—perhaps unintentionally—opened the door to a future secular Jewish politics.

Spinoza and Mendelssohn either ignored or deliberately suppressed the premodern tradition that identified Israel as a political community even after the disappearance of the ancient Jewish state. Modern writers who revived this definition of Israel on a secular basis still had to determine what kind of political community they inhabited. Absent a religious identity, what united the Jews? The three broad answers to this question that we will examine here are (1) a race, (2) a nation, and (3) a state.

A Jewish Race? Moses Hess, Israel Zangwill, and Vladimir Jabotinsky

The first to attempt an answer was Moses Hess (1812–1875), who died largely forgotten, only to be resurrected more than a quarter century later as a prophet of Zionism. Profoundly influenced by Spinoza, Hess was a crucial transitional figure, whose life encompassed in compressed form many of the permutations the German Jews traversed during the nineteenth century. Raised in a traditional Jewish home where he received an Orthodox education from his rabbinic grandfather, he fell under the influence of the Young Hegelians in the late-1830s and became a minor figure in the history of German socialism. However, in the 1850s, disillusioned with socialism and alarmed by the rise of German anti-Semitism, Hess turned to a kind of quasi-racial Jewish nationalism, which, as we shall see, had a peculiar gender politics. Most German Jews were neither socialists nor Jewish nationalists, but in taking these various radical positions, Hess illuminates the polarities of his culture. Although he came to embrace what he called "the old synagogue," there was a strongly secular element to his thought encapsulated first by his lifelong embrace of Spinoza and second by his attempt to forge a Jewish identity based on ethnicity rather than religion

In his first publication in 1837, *The Holy History of Mankind,* Hess already established his debt to Spinoza by referring to himself anonymously as "a Spinoza disciple." Hess's use of Spinoza, as with almost everything else in this early, immature work, was totally idiosyncratic. It would appear that Spinoza provided him with the tools to rehabilitate Judaism by raising it dialectically to a higher—and secular—level. Where Hegel had discarded Judaism as a primitive religion superseded entirely by Christianity, Spinoza allowed Hess to retain much more of Judaism in his religion of reason

In the crucial passage in *The Holy History,* Hess says that Judaism appears spiritual when compared with paganism but materialist when compared with Christianity, a statement that is fully consonant with Hegel. But, for Hess, Judaism is much more positive than for Hegel: religion and politics were perfectly integrated, since Jewish law treated body and soul as part of the same organism, rather like Spinoza's account of the body and the mind. The Gospels, on the other hand, abandoned the exterior world, the world of politics, in favor of the inner, spiritual man. Nevertheless, belief in Christ persists only because it is a response to worldly suffering. This suffering will be conquered by a "third law" that will supersede not only the old Jewish law but the Christian as well. When the state becomes holy once again, a new Kingdom of God will appear.

And what will be basis of this new Kingdom? It will be "the old Law, whose body had been buried with Christ, [which] has been clarified and resurrected in Spinoza. The kernel of a new covenant resides in the Master's [i.e., Spinoza's] teaching of salvation."[35] Spinoza would no doubt have been mystified to discover that he had "resurrected" the old law. But in Hess's account, by uniting body and spirit, politics and religion, as had Jewish law, Spinoza brought to dialectical fruition both Judaism and Christianity, albeit with a greater emphasis on the Jewish, since Spinoza, like the old law, united inner and outer worlds.

When Hess developed his nationalist theory in *Rome and Jerusalem* (1862), he argued that the Jews themselves should now fulfill the Spinozistic idea of the state. His innovation was not only to call for renewed Jewish sovereignty but also to privilege the Jews as the quintessential nation. This argument revolved around claiming that the basis for Judaism is ethnicity, the continuity of the generations. The Jewish belief in immortality shared nothing with the Christian idea of individual salvation: "The source of the Jewish belief in immortality . . . is family love."[36] Judaism is communal or familial and therefore inherently anticapitalistic, since capitalism atomizes individuals and shreds their natural communities. In this way, Hess would harness the ethos of the Jewish family, with a special emphasis on the role of women in the family, to a messianic politics.

Indeed, in *Rome and Jerusalem*, Hess frequently refers to the family as the basic unit of the nation and extols in hyperbolic terms the Jewish family and maternal love:

> Such love which, like maternal love, flows out of the very life-blood and yet is as pure as the divine spirit; such infinite love for family can have its seat only in a Jewish heart. And this love is the natural source whence springs the higher, intellectual love of God, which, according to Spinoza, is the highest point to which the spirit can rise. Out of this inexhaustible fountain of family love have the redeemers of humanity drawn their inspiration.[37]

Spinoza might have been again surprised to learn that his *amor dei intellectualis* derived directly from the Jewish family (Spinoza never referred to his own family in any of his writings). For Hess, though, the intuited connection between the intellectual love of God and familial love allowed him to marry his love for Spinoza with Jewish nationalism.

This celebration of the family, reminiscent of a conventional trope of German Jewish preachers of the time, leads Hess to equally celebratory remarks about Jewish women, the guardians of the family: "Oh, how stupid are those who minimize the value of woman's influence upon the development of Judaism! Was it not said of the Jews, that they were redeemed from Egypt because of the merit of the pious women and that the future redemption will be brought about through them."[38] He also quotes approvingly the words of the French author Pierre Mercier in his *Essai sur la littérature juive*: "The Jews alone had the healthy sense to subordinate love of women to maternal love."[39] Rarely has the Jewish mother come in for such praise.

The Jewish religious genius owed its existence "to the fertility and resilience of the Jewish tribe (*Stammes*),"[40] an ironic statement since Hess himself had no children. And national redemption would be based on this fact: "Every Jew has within him the potentiality of a Messiah, and every Jewess that of a *Mater Dolorosa*."[41] So did Hess return the Virgin Mary to her people. But far from jealously hoarding this familial gene, Hess believed that the Jews would spread their family love universally "until all mankind has become a single family."[42] This statement reflects the paradoxical nature of

Hess's nationalism, which combined a virtually racial view of the Jews with expressions of humanitarian universalism.

By the 1860s, it was becoming increasingly common to use the language of blood and race to define a nation, although racial anti-Semitism was still in its infancy. By the time he wrote *Rome and Jerusalem*, Hess, the erstwhile socialist, had become convinced that the struggle of races took precedence over the class struggle: "Social life is, first of all, a product of the life of definite human races (*Menschenracen*), of originally different folk tribes (*Volksstämme*)."[43] It is clear from several passages in the book that Hess was moving toward a biological definition of Jewish identity. For example: "The Jewish race is an original (*ursprüngliche*) [race], which, despite climatic influences, reproduces [itself] in its integrity. The Jewish type is that which remains always the same throughout the course of the centuries."[44] As Kenneth Koltun-Fromm has shown, Hess believed in "polygeneticism," that is, that the human race originated from many races, rather than one.[45] Adam and Eve were the progenitors of the Jewish race and no other—a theme that unwittingly echoes some of the more chauvinist expressions of medieval Jewish mysticism.[46]

Since intermarriage, according to Hess, like climatic influences, does not erase racial types,[47] the Jews, as the most persistent of all races, do not lose their characteristics when they intermarry with "Indo-Germanic peoples."[48] On this score, Hess tells the story of a Russian nobleman of his acquaintance whose ancestry was partly Mongolian. However, his children, born of a union with a Polish Jewess, had characteristically Jewish features. In intermarriage, which Hess had advocated in his earlier writings, the Jew remains Jewish.[49] The Jews were thus a unique community of descent, what later nationalists would call a "blood community,"[50] a community from which one could not easily sue for divorce. On the other hand, typical of Hess's desire to balance this racial nationalism with universalism, he argues that his studies of racial science in the 1850s had convinced him of the inevitable disappearance of "any particular race dominance and the necessary regeneration of all oppressed peoples."[51]

Where does this leave religion in Hess's proto-Zionism? In one sense, he relativizes religion, making it subordinate to his racial concept of nationalism: "If Judaism owes its immortality to the remarkable religious productivity of the Jewish genius, this genius itself owes its existence to the fertility of the Jewish race."[52] But Hess nevertheless repeatedly invokes religious language in his argument. He parts company with Mendelssohn, who claimed that Judaism has no dogmas. Not so, Hess says, but the dogmas of Judaism, as opposed to those of Christianity, are open-ended, always developing and never completed: "on the wide, dogmatic basis of Judaism, many and various views of life were able to develop."[53] One might say that Hess's use of the word "dogma" is misleading, since what he has in mind is the exact opposite of dogma. Judaism allows for the freedom to philosophize, and that is why "Judaism never excluded philosophical thought or even condemned it. . . . Saadia and Maimonides, Spinoza and Mendelssohn did not become apostates, in spite of their progressive spirit, though there were many fanatics who wanted to exclude them from Judaism."[54] Spinoza would probably not subscribe to this description of himself; by all accounts, he was perfectly happy to play the role of the apostate. But this sentence is really about Hess establishing for himself an intellectual lineage. As a Spinozist, he saw himself at risk for excommunication by the "rationalists" (i.e., the Reformers), but as such, he found himself in a distinguished chain of tradition.

This is a peculiar, counterhistorical argument, to say the least, in which Spinoza, once again, stands for the true Judaism while all others—Reformers and contemporary Orthodox—renounce its pluralism in favor of their own narrow beliefs. Hess takes a vehement stand against both of these representatives of Jewish religion in nineteenth-century Germany: "Dissatisfied with reform and repulsed by the fanaticism of the Orthodox and heterodox, you ask me, with which religious faction should one affiliate with his family in these days?" Hess's answer: "I know only one religious fellowship, the old Synagogue, which is fortunately still in existence and will, I hope, exist until the national regeneration of world Jewry is complete."[55] Hess volunteers that if he had a family, he would join such a synagogue and observe all the feast and fast days. But, then, unable to restrain himself, he immediately begins to rearrange the furniture and reform this old synagogue, leveling criticisms at the cantors and choirs as "soulless singing machines" that look suspiciously like those of the Reformers he despised

Of course, Hess did not have a family, and this paean to the old-time religion looks more sentimental than essential to his philosophy. Once again, it is Spinoza who is pressed into service as Hess's standard bearer. In the epilogue to *Rome and Jerusalem*, he assails Samuel David Luzzato, the conservative Italian scholar, for impugning Spinoza's philosophy for its arid rationalism. On the contrary, says Hess: "In Spinoza, who developed out of the idea of God as the All a whole ethical, spiritual life and who represented knowledge of God as the highest and last result of this life, in this most recent revelation of the Jewish genius, all contradictions disappear."[56] Despite his use of the word "revelation," Hess means something more in the spirit of his seventeenth-century Dutch hero:

> The religious genius of the Jews was not only animated in antiquity by the holy spirit and divine revelations. The holy spirit always rests on Israel as long as it concerns itself with the life of humanity in a new great, world historical phase of development, with a new social creation.[57]

As Spinoza had already argued, the peculiar vocation of the Jews was politics, not religion. The contribution of the Jews to the future of humanity would therefore lie in this social sphere. By re-creating their national state, the Jews would bring salvation to mankind. The true manifestation of Spinoza's God would be the Jewish state.

The religious language of Hess's text should therefore not mislead us. In his embrace of Spinoza, which extended back to his earliest writing, Hess articulated a secular vision for the Jewish people. To be sure, this vision was based on the "old Law," but only as a point of departure, not the port of arrival at which the God of the philosophers would find his true expression in the renewed Jewish nation. And it was specifically women, as the guarantors of the fertility of the Jewish race, who would bring to fulfillment Spinoza's vision, albeit a vision that Heinrich Heine's *petit juif d'Amsterdam* would scarcely have recognized

The question of race emerged precisely at a time when a religious identity was no longer viable for many Jews, Zionist or not. Many thinkers would have welcomed Jewish assimilation, but those who recognized its impossibility were often led to racialized ways of defining the Jews. Regardless of which side of the nationalism debate they took, many assumed that one could only speak of the Jews in the secular language of racial science. Hess was one of the first defenders of the Jews to claim that the Jews are a nation with distinctive ethnic characteristics, for whom race trumps religion. Benjamin Disraeli was another, and—as we saw in the last chapter—so was Freud, who claimed that the psychological truth underlying the Jewish religion was passed on genetically. By the turn of the twentieth century, a full-blown debate had broken out over this question, with some Zionists claiming a racial identity, and Marxists and Jewish assimilationists frequently arguing the opposite.[58]

This is not the place to review this extensive literature, but one example, the writer and Jewish nationalist, Israel Zangwill (1864–1926), will demonstrate the ambiguities of the debate. Zangwill was, by turns, an assimilationist, a Zionist, and a territorialist—a chameleon who defied easy categorization. He often spoke in contradictory ways about Jews and race. In his celebrated—if hackneyed—play, *The Melting Pot*, which popularized that phrase, he appears to champion intermarriage and assimilation. He himself had excited great hostility among some of his fellow Zionists when he married a Gentile. But his actual position was much more complicated. Despite his prophecy of the "melting" of all prior ethnicities in the American crucible, it turns out that race is not so easily effaced. In a debate about whether the Russian pianist Anton Rubinstein was a Jew, since he was baptized shortly after birth, one character in the play asks: "And did the water outside change the blood within?"[59] Blood remains thicker than water, at least the water of baptism, which raises the question of whether blood is also stronger than the fires of the melting pot

In the afterword to the 1914 edition of the play, Zangwill expresses his ideas on race with puzzling ambiguity. He argues, on the one hand, that Jewish traits are racially "recessive" so that Jews should ultimately disappear as recognizable types in America. On the other hand, he also claims that the Jew is "the toughest of all the white elements that have been poured into the American crucible, the race having, by its unique experience of several thousand years of exposure to alien majorities, developed a salamandrine power of survival. And this asbestoid fibre is made even more fireproof by the anti-Semitism of American uncivilisation."[60] And then, as if conscious of the contradictions in his argument, he backs off from the miscegenistic message of the play by concluding that the "Jew may be Americanised and the American Judaised without any gamic interaction."[61] Since Zangwill's own politics oscillated among so many different positions, it is not surprising to find contradictory ideas about race in his writings. But although he was perhaps more mercurial than most, he was not that odd in a time when, in the felicitous analysis of Michael Stanislawski, a whole variety of thinkers inhabited a world at once cosmopolitan and nationalist.[62]

Another such cosmopolitan nationalist, whom we encountered in chapter 2, was Vladimir Jabotinsky, the founder of right-wing Revisionist Zionism. Although he was an acculturated Russian intellectual, the political conundrum of the Jews at the beginning of the twentieth century turned him to Zionism. Inspired by Italian nationalism, Jabotinsky brought to his new ideological commitment categories borrowed from secular European cultures, including positivism and social Darwinism. A related category was race. In 1913, Jabotinsky wrote an essay on the subject that reflected prevalent European ideas associating nations with distinct racial groups. Like Hess a half century earlier, Jabotinsky argued that "the bedrock of all that is national is race."[63] He allowed that all races are made up of the same ingredients, but the proportion of these ingredients differs as a result of climate, geography, and so forth. Against the Marxists, he claimed that race is a more fundamental substrate of society than economics: since each race produces different economic "conditions of production" based on geographical differences, there is no universal economic law. Although this essay scarcely mentions the Jews, Jabotinsky's purpose is clear. The Jews are a separate race/nation, whose claim to political sovereignty is like any other. Religion plays little role in this identity.

At the same time, Jabotinsky admitted that no pure nation or race actually exists, but he favored policies that would prevent the mixing of peoples, languages, and religions as much as possible. National cultures must be allowed to flourish in contiguous territories with a minimum of interference from minorities. Departing from Hess, who tempered his racial views with utopian universalism, Jabotinsky held that the unification of humanity into one people is illusory; cultural-racial differences will always exist. While he argued, in the dissertation he submitted for his law degree in 1912, for a legal system of autonomy for national minorities—a view clearly inspired by the contemporary European Jewish question—he would not apply this system later to the Arabs of the incipient Jewish state; the latter group must be separated by an "iron wall" from the Jewish majority.[64] In chapter 2, we looked at Jabotinsky's writings on the Bible and especially his novel *Samson*. In the novel, Jabotinsky seems to contradict his argument for preventing the mixing of races, at least with respect to ancient Philistines and Israelites. But his contemporary politics were unyielding on preserving the Jewish race in its own integral state.

The Politics of Secular Nationalism: Emma Lazarus and Theodor Herzl

Not all nationalists embraced a racial definition of the Jewish nation. One of the earliest American proponents of a return of the Jews to their ancestral home was Emma Lazarus (1849–1887), eventually the poet laureate of the Statue of Liberty. Lazarus did at times seem to hold to a racial definition of the Jews, but in an ironic sense: "Naturally a race whose members are unmistakably recognized at a glance, whatever be their color, complexion, costume or language, yet who dispute the cardinal fact as to whether they are a race, cannot easily be brought into unanimity upon more doubtful propositions."[65] Lazarus uses the term "race" in a broader sense than a biological group, since it includes cultural as well as physiological signs. She has in mind something like the definition of a nation. But even if the Jews have the superficial characteristics of a race, they don't behave like one. And, in any case, Lazarus, like Hess, wanted to inculcate a sense of solidarity among the Jews without segregating them from the outside world. She quotes Claude Montefiore approvingly when he says that the law forbidding taking interest from "brothers" may be understood universally since "by superior virtue we regard the stranger also as our brother and our neighbor."[66]

Lazarus was a thoroughly secular Jew, the scion of an old Sephardic American family who was largely alienated from her religious community. She thus anticipated in an American context the cosmopolitan Jewish nationalism of the fin de siècle, a stance inaccessible to most of the eastern European Jewish immigrants whom she championed. To prevent the collapse of nationalism into xenophobia, Lazarus constructed a definition of the nation largely divorced from religion: "But if our people persist in entrenching themselves behind a Chinese wall of petrified religious forms, the great modern stream of scientific philosophy will sweep past them."[67] And, more broadly:

> Not the teaching of the *Thora*, not the inculcation of the Talmud, not the preservation of the Hebrew tongue, not the maintenance of Synagogue worship, not even the circumcision of the flesh . . . should be our primary consideration. But holding fast to the most spiritualized form of our belief—the Unity of the Creative force, the necessity of the Moral Law,—we should adapt ourselves to the

practical requirements of the hour and make our race the fittest to survive, a paragon to all the nations of the earth.[68]

Although this program sounds superficially similar to nineteenth-century Reform, it was, in fact, already the view of "those shrewd old Ta-naites" (i.e., the rabbis of the Talmud).[69] It was they who prepared a philosophy singularly adaptive to modernity.

Rejecting Reform's call for the "denationalization of the Jewish religion," she argues, on the contrary, for "the *secularization* and spiritualizing of the Jewish nationality."[70] What she means by these terms is something rather different from the meaning we might assign to them. By "secularization" she means attending to the physical condition of the nation: strengthening the Jewish body and developing productive occupations (both were preoccupations of the Haskalah and of the later Zionist movement).[71] By "spiritualizing," she meant primarily ethical ideals rather than theology

For Lazarus, the Jews were highly suited for modernity, a view that echoes Mendelssohn: "The Jews are . . . most frequently the pioneers of progress. The simplicity of their creed enables them more readily and naturally to throw off the shackles of superstition and to enlarge the boundaries of free speculation than any other sect. Considering their religion from the highest standpoint, their creed today is at one with the latest doctrines of science, proclaiming the unity of the Creative force."[72] Note that this is Lazarus's preferred way of avoiding any overtly theological language. Even if the Jewish religion has succumbed to superstition and meaningless rituals, the Bible and the rabbis already long ago prepared the ground for a thoroughly modern belief system hospitable to contemporary science

Lazarus repeatedly invokes Spinoza in constructing a chain of tradition leading to modernity.[73] Attacking a critic who thought the Jews were lacking in great spiritual thinkers, she writes: "If Miss Cobbe had looked in Rabbinical literature before passing judgment upon its deficiencies, she would have found in Ibn Gabirol a poet whose hymns ring in harmony with the Psalms and the prophesies of old, whose philosophy contained in embryo that later philosophy of Spinoza which has given tone and direction to all modern metaphysical speculation."[74] This connection between Ibn Gabirol's Neoplatonism and Spinoza's pantheism is certainly plausible, but whether or not a causal relationship existed between these two thinkers separated by nearly half a millennium, it demonstrates that Lazarus wanted to construct a genealogy for modern secularism. Similarly, nothing in Maimonides contradicted what she found in the nineteenth-century philosopher Herbert Spencer.[75] The final figure who clearly played a central role in this genealogy was Heinrich Heine, whom Lazarus was one of the first to translate for an American audience and who served as a model for someone like herself, torn between Jewish and cosmopolitan identities.[76]

For Lazarus, as well as for many other Western Zionists, Jewish nationalism was a solution to the problem of Jewish suffering. But as Esther Schor has shown, she already thought of the Jews' return to "the fair sunrise land that gave them birth" long before the encounter with the Russian Jewish refugees in the early 1880s that turned her into a fervent nationalist.[77] This encounter led her to call for national unity, yet, for all that she championed the idea of a Jewish nation, she never entirely embraced the eastern European Jews who aroused her sympathy. Some of her statements about them reflect a deep ambivalence, even repulsion from the "wretched refuse's" barbaric ways. In this, Lazarus revealed the aristocratic Sephardic world of her upbringing and that her nationalism was born as much of noblesse oblige as of egalitarian sentiment. Moreover, she did not advocate that all Jews return to "the fair sunrise land." She was too much an American patriot for that. Europe should "give me your tired and poor, / your huddled masses yearning to breathe free," but she did not believe America could absorb them all. Palestine would be the refuge for the rest with the financial and political assistance, but not the presence, of their American Jewish brothers and sisters. As one of the first American Zionists, Lazarus set the stage for the vicarious nationalism that would characterize her political progeny.

A similar kind of noblesse oblige characterized Theodor Herzl (1860–1904), although he gave it a theoretical basis. Like Lazarus, Herzl came to define the Jews as a nation out of sympathy for their suffering. In *Der Judenstaat* (The Jews' State [1895]), he announced a discovery: "We are one people—our enemies have made us one whether we will it or not."[78] Herzl's analysis of anti-Semitism is therefore intimately tied to his definition of a Jewish political identity. The religiously motivated hatred of the Jews in the Middle Ages bears no relation to its modern successor, even if the latter borrowed certain rhetorical tropes from the former. In contrast to the religious hatred of the Jews in the Middle Ages, this new anti-Semitism is secular, an economic and political phenomenon to which the answer must be political.[79] It is the peculiar condition of modernity that transforms this people into a nation, since it is in the modern period that the religious overlay on anti-Semitism is stripped away, leaving a purely national and economic struggle. Emancipation thus produces anti-Semitism, which in turn produces Jewish nationalism.

Modern anti-Semitism is a product of competition between emancipated Jews and their host societies. The modern attempt by the Jews to assimilate, a product of the new secular definition of society, creates a confrontation with European society in ways inconceivable during the segregated Middle Ages. Every field of economic activity into which the Jews enter provokes new resentment, although Herzl, the journalist, reserves his greatest criticism for those closest to home, the "mediocre intellectuals" (*mittele Intellektualen*) who "present a danger to society just as great as our accumulating wealth."[80] To be sure, Herzl recognizes that the Jews were a people before modernity, possessing what he calls a "collective personality."[81] Here, too, it was oppression that created the people: "the enemy turns us into one against our wishes."[82] Religion apparently played no role in forming this identity, which was forced upon the unwilling Jews. Jewish collective identity is therefore not the result of positive factors, even though Herzl embraces it as a normative value: "it must not perish."[83] In general, Herzl's arguments for Zionism are deterministic—it is the inevitable result of historical processes—but perhaps recognizing that a national movement cannot be built only on the iron laws of history, at times he seeks to mobilize his readers to voluntaristic action.

This tension between inevitability and voluntarism was also the classic conundrum of Marxism: the economic laws of history were supposed to mechanically produce a revolution, yet Marx also saw the proletariat as an active agent in its own liberation. Could such an agent speed up the laws of history? This question was particularly pressing in the Russian Empire, where objective, economic conditions in the late nineteenth century were not ripe for a socialist revolution, since capitalism remained at primitive stage of development. Lenin famously argued that the Russian Social Democratic Party could act as the vanguard of the proletariat and force a revolution before objective conditions made it inevitable.

The same dilemma confronted the early Zionists. Objective conditions such as political persecution, economic crisis, and demographic explosion, especially in eastern Europe, were all conspiring to create a Jewish nation, yet the vast majority of that nation was not behaving as a political entity.

The Zionists—and other political actors—all diagnosed an emergency, but the nation itself was not yet prepared to act. In *Der Judenstaat*, Herzl proposed a novel theory, similar in intent to Lenin's doctrine, for why the Zionist movement could act on behalf of the nation, even without any formal mechanism empowering it to do so.

As the source for his doctrine, Herzl turned not to the Jewish tradition, of which he was largely ignorant, but instead to Roman law. The principle, known as *negotiorum gestio* ("agent of affairs") provides for an agent (gestor) to act on an emergency basis in place of the owner of a business—or other property—if that owner is not able to act on his own behalf.[84] For example, if someone has to take a sudden trip and is unable to appoint someone else to manage his affairs while he is absent, his neighbor may take action to save his business in case of, say, a flood or fire. Although no prior formal contract exists between the agent and the owner—and the owner may not even be aware of the agent's action—the agent may do so as a matter of expediency. As Herzl puts it, "his mission is given to him by a higher necessity."[85] The relationship between the *gestor* and owner is quasi-contractual, which means that the law empowers the *gestor* to act as if a contract with the owner existed

Herzl argues that the Zionist movement acts as a *gestor* on behalf of the Jewish people. The present condition of the Jews represents the same kind of emergency that justified the self-appointment of a *gestor* in Roman law. Herzl arrives at the *negotiorum gestio* by first rejecting out of hand the social contract theory of the state. He focuses his attack on Rousseau but, by implication, also overturns the arguments of Spinoza and Mendelssohn. Although he does not give a very clear account of what is wrong with social contract theory, Herzl seems to believe that it renders impossible any changes in a state's constitution.[86] Be that as it may, in the case of the Jews, he holds that the Roman principle is necessary because the Jews are not in a position to make a formal contract to create a state. They are like the owner of a house on fire. An agent must seize the initiative to save the house. In doing so, the Zionist movement, in the role of *gestor*, enters into an implied, quasi-contract with the Jewish people. It has responsibilities toward that people like those of a government

In the only gesture toward Jewish history or tradition in his pamphlet, Herzl compares the Society of Jews (his term for the Zionist movement) to Moses, the "old great *gestor* of the Jews in simple times."[87] Where Spinoza had seen Moses as empowered by the social contract at Sinai, Herzl portrays him rather as an agent who takes on himself the leadership of the Jews, deriving his legitimacy not from God, but from the "higher necessity" of his actions. Like Moses, the Zionists need no contract, no prior appointment. They will play the same role, but with the aid of modern technology.

Had Herzl known more about the medieval tradition of Jewish political thought, he might have recognized in the doctrine of emergency powers, as spelled out by Moses Maimonides and Nissim of Gerona, a indigenous basis for the Zionist movement as he conceived it. While the medieval thinkers did not have nationalism in mind, they nevertheless carved out a realm of secular law that allowed political authorities to break out of the bonds of tradition when the community was in danger. Without knowing it, Herzl replicated the medieval argument in modern terms,

Herzl's use of this principle from Roman law reveals not only how far he was from grounding Jewish politics in the historical and religious tradition but also how elitist was his vision of Zionism. Indeed, in the section of *Der Judenstaat* in which he takes up the constitution of the Jews' state, he argues against democracy, which "leads to idle talk in Parliament and to the ugly category of professional politicians."[88] Democracy requires the counterweight of monarchy, which provides stability and permanence. Since the political history of the Jews has been interrupted for such a long time, rendering monarchy moot, Herzl opts instead for "an aristocratic republic," along the lines of the Republic of Venice. What exactly he had in mind is hard to say, and even his utopian novel about the Jewish state, *Altneuland*, does not shed a great deal of light (if anything, it looks more like an collection of anarchist collectives than a nation-state). Despite his peculiar vision of an aristocratic republic, however, the Zionist Organization that Herzl founded operated on democratic principles.

One thing is clear, though. Herzl's imagined state would not be a theocracy: "No! Faith will hold us together, science makes us free. We will not even allow the theocratic inclinations of our spiritual leaders to raise their ugly heads. We will know how to keep them in their temples, just as we will know how to keep our professional army in the barracks."[89] Religion has no role in politics. In *Altneuland*, the Temple in Jerusalem has been rebuilt, but no one goes there. The state of the Jews will be secular, led not by priests and rabbis but by the lay aristocrats of the Zionist movement, acting as the *gestor* of the Jewish people.

Against Herzl: Bernard Lazare and Hannah Arendt

Herzl's vision of a secular Jewish politics served as the catalyst for renewed activism. While the Zionist idea—as well as the term "Zionism"—predated Herzl, it was he who gave it new energy and turned it into an international movement. But Herzl's emphasis on diplomacy and mobilizing Jewish wealth hardly went uncontested. Cultural Zionism as an alternative to Herzl's politics is a subject I will take up in the next chapter. Other political alternatives also emerged both immediately and in the longer term.[90] These alternatives included forms of socialism and autonomism. The first argued for mobilizing the Jewish working class as the agent of change (in either the land of Israel or the Diaspora), while the second saw the future of Jewish politics in the Diaspora rather than in a Jewish homeland (the two could, of course, be combined, as was the case for the Bund).

Rather than examine the many thinkers who contributed combinations and permutations of these alternatives to political Zionism, let us look at one whose trajectory led him from assimilationism and cultural anarchism through political Zionism to Jewish socialism and autonomism. Bernard Lazare (1865–1903), born into an acculturated Sephardic family in the south of France, played a leading role in defending Alfred Dreyfus during the famous Affair that was a watershed for Lazare—and many others—between assimilation and political self-assertion.[91] In his earliest writing on the Jews from before the Affair, Lazare distinguished between the Israelites, with whom he identified, and the Jews. The first were culturally French and only retained vestiges of the "Israelite" religion, while the latter, as immigrants, could never be considered French. Against the charge that his harsh criticism of these Jews was no different from contemporary anti-Semitism, he declared unconvincingly that he was *antijuif,* but not anti-Semitic, because he was an Israelite.

Lazare was famously on the margins of every political movement with which he associated. He first declared himself an anarchist, but rejected the so-called "revolution of facts" (i.e., terrorism) in favor of a "revolution of ideas." His was predominantly a literary anarchism: "long live free verse!" He broke ranks with other Dreyfusards whom he accused of using the Affair for political purposes instead of in the interest of pure justice. And he would also stake out a position as a dissenter and purist once he embraced Jewish nationalism.

Although it was the Dreyfus Affair that definitively turned Lazare toward a political solution to the Jewish Question, he, like Herzl, had already begun to be preoccupied with the Jews several years earlier.[92] His 1893 essay, "The Revolutionary Spirit in Judaism," demonstrated a desire, which he developed more later, to marry his anarchism with Jewish sources.[93] With no biblical belief in the afterlife, he contended, justice for the Jews had to be realized in this world. Moreover, the Jewish conception of God "led them to conceive the equality of men, it led them even to anarchy . . . for they never accepted with cheerful heart this government, whatever it was."[94] In 1894, Lazare visited Amsterdam and described in a later essay (where he may have projected his new Zionist sentiments onto the earlier Amsterdam visit) how his search for "the holy Spinoza" led him to the old Portuguese synagogue. After a long meditation inside, he went out to the courtyard where he found a group of poor Russian Jewish refugees, who put him in mind of the generations of Jewish suffering. These two images—the pariah heretic and the impoverished, oppressed refugees—merged in Lazare's consciousness as symbols of the common history that constituted the Jews, an amalgam that would have made sense to his namesake, Emma Lazarus.

With the shock of the Dreyfus Affair and the outbreak of anti-Semitic pogroms throughout France, Lazare came increasingly to identify with the *juifs* he had previously scorned. It was these Jews, and not the Israelites—the wealthy, acculturated, and assimilated—who desperately needed a new politics, based on the realization that the Jews are a nation. In a lecture delivered to a group of Russian Jewish students in Paris in 1897, Lazare dismissed the idea that the Jews are united only by a common religion.[95] A group of people characterized by atheists, pantheists, and deists—as well as the Orthodox—cannot be only a religious confession. As he says in his posthumous fragments, *Job's Dungheap*, it is the Christians who treat the Jews as having solely a religious history, since they believe that the Jews have only one function: to create Christianity.[96]

By the same token, neither were the Jews a race.[97] The wide variety of physical types among the Jews negated the position advanced a third of a century earlier by Moses Hess. Although there may be certain traits that suggest a common origin, this ostensibly "racial" genealogy cannot be the unifying factor for the Jews, since it remains remote and theoretical. Nor—against Herzl—can anti-Semitism, since anti-Semitism arises because the Jews are already a people, and not vice versa: "it is on account of our being bound together that these traits are attributed to us."[98] It is rather a common history, as well as common ideas and traditions, that constitutes the Jews as a nation.

For Lazare the anarchist, nationalism meant the desire for freedom: "A Jew who today may declare 'I am a nationalist' . . . will be saying, 'I want to be a man fully free, I want to enjoy the sunshine. I want to have a right to my dignity as a man. I want to escape oppression, to escape outrage, to escape the scorn with which men seek to overwhelm me.' At certain moments in history, nationalism is for human groups the manifestation of the spirit of freedom."[99]

Zionism seemed initially to promise just such a liberation for the Jewish nation. But this solution had to be revolutionary, that is, it had to come from the masses themselves, for only when they realized that salvation would not come from heaven or from powerful allies could they set about freeing themselves.[100] It was on this score that Lazare came to verbal blows with Herzl, whom he had previously supported. The catalyst for the break was Herzl's plan for a Jewish Colonial Bank. Dripping with socialist sarcasm, Lazare wrote: "a bank is never and never will be the instrument of national revival and what irony it is to make a bank the founder of the Jewish nation."[101] He accused Herzl of wanting to lead the Jewish masses "like a herd . . . an ignorant child, without inquiring as to its needs or aspirations, without taking account of its intellectual, economic and moral state."[102] As an anarchist, Lazare could not conceive of a hierarchical movement as being genuinely revolutionary.

The true Jews for Lazare are the poor, the proletariat, and the intellectuals. In ancient times, it was the poor who returned from Babylonia to the land of Israel, while the rich stayed behind: "They must remain there for it is the poor who make nations; the rich do not know how to create."[103] Reflecting the social reality of the fin de siècle, Lazare argues that since the Jews have more poor than any other nation, they are in a position to act as "the anarchist people among the nations."[104] But they are also in such a position because of Jewish history and Judaism. Against Marx's essay "On the Jewish Question," he argues that the Jews have never been primarily a mercantile or bourgeois people. The origins of capitalism were not with the Jews, for the ideal of both the Bible and Talmud is not commerce but agriculture and crafts. And this ideal is linked to a belief in social justice: usury is forbidden and egalitarianism endorsed.

To be sure, the rabbis of the Talmud "put to slumber [the Jews'] instincts of revolt. . . . It could be said that Israel could be vanquished only by himself."[105] But the tradition of social justice was kept alive specifically by those Jews who rejected rabbinic authority. It is for this reason, says Lazare, that Jews have been implicated in virtually every modern revolutionary movement: the true heirs to the biblical teachings of justice are secular Jewish anarchists and socialists, who retain the fundamental message of these teachings even if they are ignorant of the texts themselves. In this stance, Lazare articulates one of the key arguments of many secular Jews: since Judaism teaches social justice, it is entirely consonant with universalist progressive and revolutionary movements. The true Judaism is a tradition extending from the prophets and the psalmists to Marx and Lassalle.[106]

Lazare contrasts the Jewish idea of social justice with the Christian one. The Bible, in the Christian interpretation, resolves the problem of evil with the doctrine of original sin. Judaism believes by contrast that each person must pay for his or her sin. It is Job, for Lazare, who challenges conventional ideas of sin and evil with the ideal of justice.[107] In this way, Lazare intuits how iconoclastic the book of Job is in relation to the rest of the Bible, but he puts Job at the center of Judaism. For Judaism, in Lazare's reading, the problem of Job is moral, not metaphysical, and therefore Judaism is much more of a religion of justice than Christianity. Against Christian otherworldliness, Judaism is preeminently a teaching for this world, and that is another reason why the philosophy of Spinoza is quintessentially Jewish.[108] Moreover, because they do not believe in mysticism or metaphysics, the Jews have no problem reconciling their faith with science. Since the tradition is based on exegesis, which supposes a "minimum of faith," Spinoza, the rationalist exegete, still belongs to the tradition.[109]

By the time Lazare composed the fragments making up *Job's Dungheap*, he had come to the conclusion that the primary enemies of the Jewish people were as much the wealthy, assimilated Jews—the "parvenus"—as the anti-Semites. It was the rich Jews who would block a healthy nationalism, and it was they whom Herzl mistakenly sought out as his allies. Taking a position like the Marxist historian Raphael Mahler's, he held that Jewish history has always been the record of class struggle.[110] In contemporary times, Jewish politics means resisting not only external oppression but even more oppression from within. The modern Jobs sitting on their dung heaps are the poor and persecuted Jews, "receiving a dole from [the] rich and having rebelled only against persecution from without and not against oppression from within. Revolutionaries within the society of others, but not within their own."[111] The liberation of the Jews would come from an *internal* Jewish politics: "The Jews must free themselves as a people and within their own nation."[112]

Lazare, like other Jewish nationalists on the Left, was forced to answer the charge, leveled by both Jewish and non-Jewish socialists, that a nationalist agenda betrayed the ideals of internationalism. Lazare's answer to the internationalist challenge: "I find nothing in nationalism which would be contrary to socialist orthodoxy, and I, who am orthodox in nothing, do not hesitate for an instant in accepting nationalism alongside internationalism."[113] The reason he sees no contradiction is because of his own definition of humanity: "Nothing seems to me so needful for mankind as variety. . . . Human richness is built out of this variety. Thus, every human group is necessary, is useful to mankind; it contributes in bringing beauty into the world[;] it is a source of forms, of thoughts, of images. Why should we regiment the human species, why should we make it bow down before a single rule . . . ?"[114] Diversity is thus inherent to human nature, a position taken up later by Hannah Arendt and, later still, by the theoreticians of multiculturalism

Echoing Hess, Lazare argues that by working for the liberation of each nation, one contributes toward the liberation of humanity as a whole. In a striking metaphor, he writes that one should answer those who say "You should labor for humanity" as follows: "Yes, but our ambition is to work for mankind in other fashion than do those dung heaps which by their decay bring forth new flowers and new fruits. We are through with being eternally exploited by all peoples, a troop of cattle and of serfs, the butt of every lash."[115] The dung heap makes its contribution to the "new flowers and new fruits" by its own decomposition, an unconscious and unintended consequence. One can hardly avoid the association between this dung heap and that of Job, on which the Jewish proletariat now sit. Instead of vanishing out of existence and by that decomposition fructifying other nations, the poor and the oppressed of the Jewish people must take matters into their own hands and liberate themselves

Here, modernity can serve a positive purpose. Emancipation causes the oppressed Jews to become more conscious of their condition: "Out of a wretch sometimes benumbed by his wretchedness [emancipation] will make a sensitive being who will doubly feel every pin-prick and whose existence will consequently become a thousand times less tolerable. Out of an unconscious pariah it will make a conscious pariah."[116] Only the conscious pariah can arrive at the true solution, which is nationalism: "The pride at being a pariah and above all this pariah that is the Jew and whom one makes out to be the master of the world. Who desires to create nobility out of his infamy, royalty out of his degradation."[117] Only the pariah driven by political consciousness could fight for a "different emancipation, total, integral."[118]

For Lazare, though, this different kind of emancipation did not necessarily mean a state in Palestine or even in any other territory. In the last years of his life, he arrived at an ideology of autonomism, much like that of Simon Dubnow, although it does not appear that he knew the Russian Jewish historian's writings.[119] For Lazare, autonomism meant Jewish political and cultural autonomy, which could be realized in the countries in which the Jews lived. It meant agitation for Jewish rights, and it meant creating institutions of national education. Lazare did not reject colonization in Palestine, but his vision was closer to the cultural Zionism of Ahad Ha'am than to the diplomatic and political Zionism of Herzl.

In the end, as Philippe Oriol has suggested, Jerusalem for Lazare meant neither the "unforgettable historical fatherland" of Herzl nor even the spiritual center of Ahad Ha'am, but rather a utopian Arcadia: "I imagine that for those still groaning in the ghettos, like their ancestors of the Middle Ages, the words ['next year in Jerusalem'] mean: Next year we will be in a country of liberty, we will be human beings, we will be permitted to live under the bright sun, which belongs to everyone, except for us."[120] The Jewish utopia that Lazare envisioned was very much in line with the anarchism of his youth: small, autonomous, self-determining communities coexisting peacefully with other such communities. Here, there was no real place for the nation-state. Nor was there any place for wealth or inequality, for just as no ethnic community would oppress another, so no class within the *ethnos* would oppress another class. Only on this basis could Lazare embrace a Jewish politics.

Lazare represented a certain kind of socialist critic of Herzl's diplomatic and political Zionism during Herzl's lifetime (like Herzl, Lazare died young, at thirty-eight, one year before Herzl died). Hannah Arendt (1906–1975), while not exactly a socialist, took up Lazare's position in the era when the Zionist movement realized its dream of Jewish sovereignty. It is hard to overstate the degree to which Arendt was indebted, as she herself made clear, to Lazare's peculiar theory of secular Jewish politics. Not only did she borrow from him the terms "parvenu," "pariah," and "conscious pariah," which feature so prominently in her biography of the early-nineteenth-century salon Jewess Rahel Varnhagen and in her later essay "The Jew as Pariah: A Hidden Tradition," but even more, she embraced his critique of Herzl's politics in favor of a utopian vision beyond state nationalism.

Born into an assimilated family in which she claimed never to have heard the word "Jew" uttered,[121] Arendt was given a minimal Jewish education. When the local rabbi in Königsberg came to give her instruction, she announced that she did not believe in God; he responded cleverly, "And who asked you?"[122] In this highly Germanized family background she was not much different from her contemporary, Gershom Scholem (the two became friends in the 1930s but had a falling out in the early 1960s over Arendt's book on the Eichmann trial).[123] Arendt chose to study philosophy and wrote her doctoral dissertation on St. Augustine's concept of love.[124] This work takes up a theme that would preoccupy her in her later philosophy: how can man be "at home in the world" when knowledge of one's birth and death makes the world a contingent place. Freedom requires transcending this world. While Augustine proposed brotherly love based on faith in Christ—the City of God that walks in the world but is not of the world—Arendt's own philosophy became secular: through political action, human beings can create community and thus secure their freedom in this world. And this struggle was not only an abstract philosophical one but ultimately also a personal one: the young woman who became a stateless person after her flight from Nazi Germany sought her own path back to being at home in the world.

In response to the Nazis, Arendt came to identify as a Jew in purely political terms.[125] Not Judaism, the religion, but *Jewishness*, the identity into which one was irreducibly born, required a political response. That political response she found in Zionism, albeit a Zionism of a very particular sort. And out of her own experience as a stateless person in the 1930s, she developed a theory of how the modern nation-state, while proclaiming the universal rights of man, failed to extend these rights to its own minorities, by which Arendt meant the Jews. For Arendt, the Jews served as a paradigmatic case challenging modernity and demanding a different political theory.

Although Arendt is best known as the author of *Eichmann in Jerusalem*, she was primarily a political theorist, and the Eichmann book itself must be understood in light of her larger political position. Here is not the place to give a full account of her theory of politics.[126] In brief, modernity, in creating the sphere of society separate from the political, had undermined the arena where people might meet as equals and undertake action, as opposed to mere labor, which belonged only to society.[127] In this, she embraced Aristotle's understanding of human beings as political animals, and the polis as the site for the fulfillment of human nature (that most subjects of the polis were slaves, not equals, need not detain us).

In her magnum opus, *The Origins of Totalitarianism*, Arendt argued that the modern nation-state, as invented by the French Revolution, appeared to reestablish the political by making everyone citizens, but its notion of equality was deeply flawed because the nation was understood to be homogeneous: it could not tolerate diversity.[128] Because the nation-state is based on ethnic homogeneity, its promise of equality is abstract and formal. Universal equality in which everyone is equal as an individual fails to recognize that human beings are characterized by difference. Although people are born as particular individuals, with their own unique histories and identities, Arendt argues that it is through the group, which also has its own unique history and identity, that one should achieve equality in the political—as opposed to the private—sphere.[129] The realm of the political should ideally be where people meet and act in a context that respects both individual and group difference. It is the problem of the ethnic and cultural minority within the modern state that challenges the state's claim to equality. In this theory, Arendt was a multiculturalist *avant la lettre*.[130]

The contradictions in modern nationalism became especially evident after World War I with the abject failure of treaties supposedly guaranteeing minority rights. By expelling their minorities and creating large groups of stateless persons, modern nations—and particularly Nazi Germany, of course—arrived at the endpoint of modernity. Having tied human identity to the state, modern nationalism stripped groups of people of their humanity by stripping them of their citizenship. Arendt sees this deprivation of statehood as a crime worse than enslavement, a kind of hyperbole that must reflect her own personal experience.[131] Slaves belong to a human community, even if deprived of their physical freedom. They have homes, and they have human dignity (all of these propositions are obviously debatable). Stateless persons, on the other hand, by losing their polity have lost the most essential characteristic of their humanity in the Aristotelian sense. They have lost their "right to have rights" and are thus effectively expelled from humanity.

The crisis of stateless refugees in the 1930s was a prelude to the Holocaust. If statelessness meant expulsion from humanity, genocide was the culmination of the same logic: those who no longer belonged to a political community had no right to remain alive. Here, Arendt's interpretation of the Eichmann trial becomes relevant. Eichmann's heinous crime was neither murder writ large nor a crime "against the Jewish people," as the Israeli law read. The Holocaust was a new crime, a crime against humanity perpetrated "on the body of the Jewish people." It was a crime against humanity because the defendant sought to destroy the diversity that is essential to humanity: "it is an attack upon human diversity as such, that is, upon a characteristic of the 'human status' without which the very words 'mankind' or 'humanity' would be devoid of meaning."[132] This is a novel theory, but one that corresponds closely to the view that Arendt had already developed in 1951 in *Origins of Totalitarianism*.

The Jews constituted for Arendt not just one example of the failure of modernity, but the archetype. By beginning *The Origins of Totalitarianism* with anti-Semitism, she already signaled this intention. But she goes further, claiming that the "Jewish mission [is] to achieve the establishment of mankind."[133] What might this vision, messianic by her own admission, mean? If the essence of mankind is diversity, then it is the Jews who serve historically to "establish" this principle both by what they do and by what has been done to them. Moreover, the Jews, as the only "non-national European people" were "a kind of symbol of the common interest of the European nations."[134] Just as their lack of national territory made them the most vulnerable to the collapse of the nation-state in the face of totalitarianism, so they could model a new type of Europe, a united commonwealth of peoples in which national rights were divorced from territory.[135]

The use of the word "mission" suggests that Arendt is borrowing from the traditional terminology of the chosen people. Indeed, she argues that with secularization, chosenness was separated from messianic hope and became pure chauvinism (the most extreme example being Benjamin Disraeli who advocated the superiority of the Jewish race).[136] Instead of returning to some religious framework in which to situate the chosenness of the Jews, Arendt creates a new secular framework: the political question of human diversity. The role of the Jews is to teach the world this elemental fact of human nature. Thus, like Spinoza, she finds a political meaning in the concept of the chosen people, but, unlike Spinoza, she believes that this meaning can only achieve fruition in modernity or, more precisely, with the failure of modernity.[137]

In order for the Jews to fulfill this mission, they must become a political people. Like Spinoza and Mendelssohn—each for his own reasons—she too holds that the Jews in Diaspora have surrendered any political identity: "Jewish history offers the extraordinary spectacle of a people . . . which began its history with a well-defined concept of history and an almost conscious resolution to achieve a well-circumscribed plan on earth and then, without giving up this concept, avoided all political action for two thousand years."[138] Only the Sabbatian movement, which she understood politically, represented an exception to this passivity.[139]

For Arendt, the ostensible lack of a Jewish political tradition meant that in the modern period as well, the Jews failed to act politically. As they had in earlier centuries, they hitched their star to Gentile authorities, which meant they could survive as a group only as long as the state had some use for them. But now wealthy Jews attempted to assimilate into European society, thus creating the figure of the parvenu, who tries to escape the fate of his people by striking out on his own as an individual. As she had already discovered in her study of Rahel Varnhagen, the salon Jewess of the early nineteenth century, Arendt came to the conclusion that the fate of the parvenu was to become a pariah, just like the Jews themselves. Only the "conscious pariah" (all these terms are borrowed from Bernard Lazare) could find an escape from this fate by constructing a Jewish politics, a mobilization of the people against their enemies

Arendt concludes part 1 of *The Origins of Totalitarianism* on anti-Semitism with the Dreyfus Affair, which revealed once and for all the bankruptcy of the modern Jewish avoidance of politics: "The only visible result was that [the Affair] gave birth to the Zionist movement—the only political answer Jews have ever found to antisemitism and the only ideology in which they have ever taken seriously a hostility that would place them in the center of world events."[140] Like Lazare before her, Arendt came to see Zionism as the sole viable *political* response to anti-Semitism, but again like Lazare, she became a critic of Zionism for seeking salvation only in a nation-state. For if the modern European nation-state had failed to resolve the tension between majority and minority rights, a Jewish state conceived along the same lines would founder on similar shoals. Thus, in a series of articles from the 1940s, she castigated the leaders of the Zionist movement for seeking what others have called an "ethno-nationalist state," that is, a state based on a single national group. The Zionist movement, she argued, had surrendered to the maximalist demands of the Revisionists.

Moreover, by its alliance with British imperialism, it was making the same mistake as Herzl in depending on the major powers rather than on the Jews themselves. This form of Zionism, she implied, was a kind of parvenu nationalism. She also noted the irony that the Zionist solution to Jewish statelessness, the problem that gave it urgency in the first place, had resulted in statelessness for the Palestinians, proof that it was no better than European nationalism. Aligning herself with the Ichud group of Judah Magnes and Martin Buber that sought an Arab-Jewish confederation or binational state, she argued for "local self-government and mixed Jewish-Arab municipal and rural councils,"[141] a structure reminiscent of Lazare's anarchism and one which she identified elsewhere as representing the true revolutionary spirit.[142] She summarized her position in May 1948: "This goal [i.e., mixed councils] must never be sacrificed to the pseudo-sovereignty of a Jewish state."[143]

Despite Arendt's critique of pre-state Zionism and Ben-Gurion's government at the time of the Eichmann trial, she remained deeply sympathetic to Zionism in its utopian moments. She was neither a universalist nor a Diasporist, in the sense of someone who celebrates Diaspora as the ideal form of Jewish life. She believed that some of the elements of Zionist settlement in Palestine (the Yishuv) pointed in the right direction, although she held rather strangely that the kibbutz movement, which she otherwise applauded, should have been more political. And even though her critique of the Eichmann trial was often unjustifiably harsh, she did not doubt Israel's right to try Eichmann in the name of his victims, although they were not killed on its territory. On the contrary, Israel's right to do so rested on a highly original definition of territory:

> Israel could easily have claimed territorial jurisdiction if she had only explained that "territory" . . . is a political and legal concept and not merely a geographical term. It relates not so much, and not primarily, to a piece of land as to the space between individuals in a group whose members are bound to, and at the same time separated and protected from each other by all kinds of relationships, based on a

common language, religion, a common, history, customs, and laws. Such relation-
ships become spatially manifest insofar as they themselves constitute the space
wherein the different members of a group relate to and have intercourse with each
other. No State of Israel would ever have come into being if the Jewish people had
not created and maintained its own specific in-between space throughout the long
centuries of dispersion, that is, prior to the seizure of its old territory.[144]

The Jews have thus carried a "territory" with them wherever they went,
much like Heine's portable religion. They were no less a nation in Diaspora
than they are in their own land. Like Lazare, Arendt did not reject the importance of physical territory but held it to be secondary to this nonterritorial definition of the nation. She, too, came close to Simon Dubnow's autonomism, a Jewish politics based not on geography but on cultural affinity

It is not hard to find serious contradictions and even incoherence in
Arendt's position. How exactly she thought the Jews could mount a different politics in the face of Nazism remains unclear. At times, she sounds
like the Revisionists themselves, even though they were her worst enemies.
Thus, her criticism of the alliance between Zionism and British imperialism
was often precisely their position. And she called urgently for the formation
of a Jewish Army in the early years of World War II, a stance one associates
with more militant nationalists. On a more philosophical level, basing politics on "Jewishness"—the fact of being born Jewish—contradicts her attack
on Jewish parvenus for reducing their Jewishness to the same fact of their
birth. If nationhood consists in history, customs, even religion, then Arendt
scarcely allowed for any of these elements to characterize her own version
of Jewish identity. In the end, her politics were not as far from Herzl's as she
might have claimed: she, too, arrived at the need for a secular Jewish politics
as a response to an anti-Semitism that refused to allow any Jewish difference, even the minimal difference of having been born to Jewish parents

The idiosyncratic Zionism of Bernard Lazare and Hannah Arendt is emblematic of a Jewish politics based at once on a utopian ideology close to
anarchism and on a hardheaded response to modern anti-Semitism as a
threat unprecedented in Jewish history. The Jews were forced to recognize
that they were a nation, even if the definition of a nation did not require
territory. Despite their rejection of Herzl, they resembled him—as well as
other central European Jews who also became nationalists—in that their
path to a new Jewish politics started not with religion but with secularism.

The State of Israel:
David Ben-Gurion's Civic Identity for the Jews

The most uncompromising advocate of a territorial and statist solution to the problem of the Jewish nation was Israel's first prime minister, David Ben-Gurion. To be sure, Ben-Gurion came to the idea of Jewish sovereignty later than Jabotinsky, who was Ben-Gurion's greatest rival in the 1920s and 1930s. Jabotinsky argued that a national movement should not be diluted by other ideologies and that its sole "end goal" should be political sovereignty. Against what he called the *shaatnez* (the biblical prohibition on mixing flax and wool) of the socialist Zionists, who mixed their nationalism with Marxism, Jabotinsky articulated an ideology of "monism," a kind of secular equivalent of Jewish monotheism.[145] Just as biblical religion stemmed from the purity of monotheism, so Zionism must embrace a pure nationalism, devoid of socialist syncretism. Of course, as David Ben-Gurion and other socialist Zionist critics of Jabotinsky argued, the monism of the Revisionists was no purer than their own socialism: their claim to "class neutrality" actually concealed a capitalist ideology. Yet, even if open to such criticism, Jabotinsky's monism still represented a clear argument for the primacy of the nation and of politics over religion, class, and culture.

For most of the pre-state period, Ben-Gurion engaged and rejected Jabotinsky's argument about *shaatnez* Zionism. In 1932, he held that the social content of Zionism could be progressive or reactionary:

> A Zionism totally void of all social content, either good or bad, is a meaningless abstraction, lacking any living or concrete content. All talk of "monistic" Zionism, in contrast to "*shaatnez*" is a fraud. The fascist Zionist who advocates blood, mud and slavery, who wars on "Marxists" and "Leftists," the bourgeois Zionist who wants the rule of wealth and a class society, and the socialist Zionist who wants a free workers' society and a socialist land of Israel all have *shaatnez* Zionism. The difference is in the result of the admixture.[146]

A national politics, by definition, produces not unity but discord, since different class interests remain at stake. If Jabotinsky's argument was a secularized version of the biblical prohibition on mixing, Ben-Gurion's retort took the antinomian position: *shaatnez* was a necessary consequence of all politics, and therefore the Jewish tradition provided a model precisely in what it prohibited.

Ben-Gurion understood Zionism as a revolution, but not in the more traditional sense of overturning a political or economic regime. Due to the peculiar condition of the Jews as an apolitical, powerless people in exile, Zionism meant "a revolution in the mode of life of our people."[147] This revolution would take an unproductive people and turn it into a sovereign *am oved* ("working nation"). Whereas for Jabotinsky the symbol of Jewish politics was the rifle, for Ben-Gurion it was the plough.

Yet, in the struggle for independence after Jabotinsky's death in 1940, something significant changed in Ben-Gurion's outlook. Without saying so explicitly, he came to adopt many of Jabotinsky's fundamental positions. One of the first in the Labor movement to anticipate that Jewish sovereignty would only be won by military means, Ben-Gurion came to believe that Judaism, as a religion of this world, never rejected the use of physical force, even if it did not make it a supreme value.[148] Serving as both prime minister and defense minister in the first years of the state, he saw the army in virtually messianic terms, as the restoration of the Bible's martial virtues. It was the Revisionist underground, the Irgun Zvai Leumi, that engaged in retaliation in the 1930s, while the Labor movement's Haganah advocated restraint (*havlagah*). But in response to guerilla incursions in the early 1950s, the new Israeli army, under Ben-Gurion's leadership, made massive retaliation the cornerstone of its military doctrine.[149]

Most of all, Ben-Gurion abandoned the socialist rhetoric of the pre-state period and embraced instead a doctrine of statism, which he designated by the Hebrew term *mamlakhtiyut*.[150] Derived from the word "king" (*melekh*), the literal translation of the term would be "monarchism." Of course, Ben-Gurion had no intention of establishing a monarchy, and indeed, one of his greatest legacies was Israel's democracy. But by adopting this term, used also by Jabotinsky, Ben-Gurion was trying to ground a new theory of Jewish politics in a putative biblical tradition, a kind of secularized messianism. In this theory, "the state has become the principle and driving force in the achievement of Zionist aims."[151] These aims were primarily the ingathering of the exiles. In some places, though, Ben-Gurion even suggested that with the creation of Israel, Zionism itself was a thing of the past. No longer an *am oved*, the Jewish people in its own state was now an *am mamlakhti*, a sovereign or "statist" people. The state created a new identity, that of the Israeli, an identity grounded in the existence of a political entity.

Ben-Gurion did not only articulate a new theory; he also acted on it. The dissolution by force of the separate militias of the Irgun and Lehi groups during the 1948 war and the subsequent disbanding of the Palmach, the left-wing, quasi-independent strike force of the Haganah, demonstrated his desire to subordinate all force to the state. Even the incorporation of religious parties into his government, which would have lasting consequences for the identity of Israel, was an attempt to create a unified centrist governing bloc by freezing out parties on the far left and far right. Unable and unwilling to suppress the political diversity of the pre-state period, he settled instead for an ideology of the state as an institution above all parties.[152] In this way, and without admitting it, Ben-Gurion took on the mantle of Jabotinsky

Ben-Gurion was famously an unabashed admirer of Spinoza. He advocated an official rabbinic retraction of the seventeenth-century's philosopher's excommunication. Spinoza, for Ben-Gurion, represented the first modern secular Jew, the first as well in a long history of Jews who embraced natural science.[153] Science would be the key to the success of the Jewish state. Spinoza also stood for the Jewish return to politics, since he was the first to suggest a political reading of the Bible and to hold open the possibility of a renewed Jewish state. In his own incorporation of religious parties in his government and permission to continue the religious status quo with respect to laws of personal status and Shabbat observance, Ben-Gurion may have felt that he was only doing what Spinoza had already advocated: using religion as the handmaiden of the state. Could he have been unaware that some Orthodox Jews would construe these laws as the leading edge of a theocratic state, the opposite of what Spinoza intended? For Ben-Gurion, though, religion remained subordinated to the state, since it was the state itself, a secular entity grounded in consent of the people, that authorized these laws and could therefore equally revoke their authorization. The Jewish political revolution, secular by definition, had to produce a republic, envisioned by the first Jewish political theorist of the modern age.

Although Ben-Gurion did not write Israel's Declaration of Independence, he chaired the committee that gave it its final form. It is a document that bears his unique stamp with its combination of historical and secular political arguments: the legitimacy of the new state is grounded both in the age-old attachment of the Jews to the land of their national birth and in international resolutions from the Balfour Declaration to the UN General Assembly's partition vote of November 29, 1947. Self-confident statements of the natural right of self-determination coexist with anxious appeals for foreign recognition.[154]

However, the Declaration of Independence, although largely devoid of the force of law in Israeli jurisprudence, also contains the seeds of the internal contradictions in the state as the political identity of the Jewish people. On the one hand, the declaration quite naturally makes the pressing problems of the Jewish people, such as immigration and economic development, central to its argument for a Jewish state. On the other, it promises to develop the country "for the benefit of all its inhabitants" and guarantees equal rights and freedoms to all its citizens based "on the precepts of liberty, justice and peace taught by the Hebrew prophets." In what sense was the new Israeli identity also that of non-Jewish citizens of the state?

Although clearly motivated by modern liberal theories of the state, as the reference to the Hebrew prophets suggests, the declaration seeks to ground these in the Jewish tradition. Even the name of the document in Hebrew—*Megillat ha-Atzma'ut* (Scroll of Independence)—conjures up associations from the Jewish library (five of the minor books of the Bible are called *megillot*). But these gestures toward the tradition are remarkably hesitant; the closest the text comes to a religious affirmation is to invoke trust in the ambiguous "Rock of Israel." The latter was added to mollify Orthodox sensibilities, but it nevertheless betrays the unease of Israel's secular founders with any religious or traditional justification of the state.

Political sovereignty and majority status have fundamentally changed the discourse of Jewish politics. No longer a minority, the Jews now face the same issues in reverse that they confronted when they lived in Diaspora: how to reconcile majority and minority rights in the context of a nation state. But these are not only issues between Jews and non-Jews in the State of Israel. They are also issues between Jews, since once the exiles were gathered from the four corners of the earth, it became abundantly apparent that they were neither racially homogeneous, nationally cohesive, nor religiously united. Emma Lazarus turns out to have been more correct in her analysis than Moses Hess or Theodor Herzl. The class divisions intuited by Bernard Lazare and Hannah Arendt now appear to be much more pervasive, encompassing various cultural, ethnic, and religious conflicts.

From the point of view of Jewish secularism, the restoration of Jewish sovereignty produced a great irony. A secular, nationalist movement did not result in a secular state, but rather one deeply entangled with religion, in terms of the definition of citizenship, control of areas of law and foreign policy, and the struggle for political power. That Zionism would not only make space for religious forces but even empower them was remote from the visions of virtually all the founders of the movement, from Herzl and Ahad Ha'am to Jabotinsky and Ben-Gurion. Yet it was the founders' ideal of the nation, which in theory and practice included all Jews, that allowed the many stripes of Orthodox Jews to learn the secular craft of politics and make it their own. How ironic that Spinoza's idea that religion must be subordinate to the state might develop into religion as a competitor for power within the state. And equally ironic that it was the first modern Orthodox Jew, Moses Mendelssohn, who argued for the superiority of Judaism, since it asserted the separation of church and state, only to have his spiritual descendants in a Jewish state stand him on his head. If medieval theorists from Maimonides to Nissim Gerondi had imagined the possibility of a secular law for their communities, their modern heirs have been only partially successful in realizing this radical vision.

Much of this chapter has focused on Jewish nationalists from Moses Hess to Theodor Herzl, Vladimir Jabotinsky, and David Ben-Gurion. Their visions of a renewed Jewish nation with its own sovereign state were all predicated on a secular, political definition of the Jews. Not all those who sought a secular Jewish nation were necessarily statist nationalists, however. Bernard Lazare and Hannah Arendt represent two western European critics of political Zionism who nevertheless both shared with the Zionists the idea that the Jewish identity was national rather than religious.

Farther to the east, other theorists adopted the same secular national definition but also rejected the Zionist premise. Simon Dubnow, mentioned several times in this chapter, founded the movement of autonomism in the first decade of the twentieth century, a movement that sought Jewish cultural autonomy in eastern Europe. Around the same time, the Jewish Workers Bund demanded similar autonomy within the framework of a social democratic revolution in the Russian Empire. What these examples demonstrate is that the political dimension of a secular, national identity also frequently included a cultural dimension. The redefinition of Israel as a political nation often entailed the redefinition of Judaism from a religion to a culture. It is this cultural redefinition to which we now turn.

Chapter 4

Israel: History, Language, and Culture

In 1824, Heinrich Heine began writing a never-to-be-completed historical novel titled *The Rabbi of Bacherach*.[1] This was one of the first in what would become a genre of Jewish historical fiction, often based on actual figures such as Uriel da Costa or Baruch Spinoza. Heine was evidently influenced by the medieval romances of Sir Walter Scott, who also, at times, featured Jewish characters. Although deeply flawed from a literary point of view, Heine's *Rabbi* is notable for what its author was trying to accomplish. The work starts out in the Rhineland town of Bacherach (the correct spelling is actually Bacharach) from which the archetypically named Rabbi Abraham and his wife Sarah flee on the eve of Passover after the body of a Christian child is deposited under the table by two mysterious guests. Since this Sarah cannot conceive, these two guests are malign versions of the angels from Genesis who announce that the biblical Sarah is to give birth to Isaac. The rest of the town's Jews are then slaughtered in the wake of this ritual murder libel. Abraham and Sarah flee to Frankfurt where they enter the ghetto and encounter there a baptized Spanish Jew, Don Isaac Abarbanel, a real figure from Jewish history who did not, however, convert. Heine's fictional Spaniard is clearly his own alter ego, since he too had converted to Christianity a year after he began the book. In his identification with this Spanish Jew, he was taking part in and contributing to the German Jewish fascination with the Spanish Jews as the true aristocracy of the Jewish people.

Don Isaac agrees with the rabbi's accusation that, despite his conversion, he (like Heine) is really more pagan than Christian: "Yes, I am a heathen. And as obnoxious to me as the arid, joyless Hebrews are the gloomy self-tormenting Nazarenes. May our Lady of Sidon, holy Astarte [i.e., the Canaanite goddess], forgive me for kneeling and praying before the sorrowed Mother of the Crucified." But the Spanish knight has still retained one tie to his ancestral people:

> I have no special liking for the company of God's people, and verily, it is not to pray but to eat that I visit Jew Street. . . . My nose has kept the faith. When chance brought me into this street one day about noon and I smelled the well-

known odors from the Jews' kitchens—then the same longing seized me which our forefathers felt in thinking aback to the fleshpots of Egypt; tasty childhood memories awoke in me.[2]

Don Isaac goes on to describe in mouthwatering detail the cuisine of the Frankfurt ghetto. Heine himself, even when he was mostly alienated from Judaism and the Jews, repeatedly invoked Jewish cooking as the essence of Jewishness (his poem comparing the taste of the Sabbath *cholent* stew to Elysium is as hilarious as it is affecting).

This paean to the Jewish kitchen reveals Heine's purpose. Although he renewed work on *The Rabbi of Bacherach* after the Damascus Blood Libel of 1840 and therefore made the medieval origins of this accusation central to his book, what he was really trying to do was to evoke the daily lives of ordinary Jews in the past. Their lives certainly included terror and suffering at the hands of the Christians, but also food, carnal love, and other everyday joys and sorrows. While food is certainly bound up with the religious practices of Judaism, Heine emphasizes instead cuisine as a symbol for the *secular* culture of the Jews.

Heine's turn to history reflected the view that not just the Bible needed to be subjected to historical criticism. Just as he and others had transformed the Bible into a cultural instead of a religious document, so they sought the traces of a secular culture in all of Jewish history. The study of history is, of course, itself a secular discipline since it rejects any supernatural causation, and it becomes doubly secular if it insists, as Heine did, on focusing its attention on the nonreligious dimensions of the past. Moreover, constructing a historical sphere of life beyond religion—call it "culture"—was a distinctly modern move, allied as it was with contemporary movements to create a secular Jewish culture. In answer to those who claimed that Judaism was a medieval religion that had nothing to offer modernity, proponents of a secular Jewish culture argued that those artifacts and texts created by Jews in the past or in the present were part of a *national* culture, as legitimate as the national cultures of the French, Czechs, or Poles. The emergence of this secular culture happened at the same time that modern Jews increasingly embraced the national cultures of their surroundings or, alternatively, a presumed cosmopolitan culture. Some argued that the contributions of Jews to these national cultures or to the construction of a cosmopolitan culture ought to be considered part of Jewish culture, even if the content of that culture had nothing to do with Jews or Judaism. Heinrich Heine became a symbol of a Jew who had contributed to European culture with a particular irony that some saw as typically Jewish. This reading of Heine was adopted by some Zionists, like Herzl and Max Nordau, who saw in Heine a cosmopolitan who nevertheless retained a sense of Jewish national identity.[3] This tension between cultural particularism and universalism weighed heavily on many modern Jews, so that one might even say that a central feature of modern Jewish culture is the debate over this very tension.

The question of language, which we already encountered in Hayim Nahman Bialik and Gershom Scholem, became one of the central questions for a modern, secular culture. In an age when nationalism was closely associated with language, what was the national language of the Jews? Was it Yiddish, spoken by the vast majority of the Jews of eastern Europe but not by Jews farther west or, for that matter, in North Africa and the Middle East? Those who argued for Yiddish could point to the way other peasant dialects, like Magyar and Czech, served as the founts for new national cultures. But Yiddish was seen by many intellectuals as a *jargon*, a derivative, vernacular dialect with no literary value. If not Yiddish, was it possible to revive Hebrew as a spoken language? To do so was to accomplish something unheard of in European nationalism. It was the equivalent of taking Latin, a high, literary language, and making it once again a vernacular. Or was it possible to construct Jewish culture in a non-Jewish language, whether it be Russian, German, or English? Although there was less theoretical argument for this option, it was certainly one adopted by many Jewish writers as traditional Jewish languages gave way to the languages of the Jews' habitations.

Finally, given the complex nexus between cosmopolitanism and nationalism in modern Jewish culture, it is no surprise that the inventor of the utopian, universal language, Esperanto, was a Polish Jewish philologist, Ludwig L. Zamenhof (1859–1917). Zamenhof was also the author of a work on Yiddish linguistics and a member of the proto-Zionist Hovevei Zion.[4] Thus, in the battle over Jewish languages, Zamenhof fought on all sides and even invented one of his own. He therefore represents, perhaps better than most, how secular Jewish culture might encompass Jewish and non-Jewish languages, nationalism and universalism.

In the previous chapters, I have argued that modern, secular ideas about God, Torah, and the political identity of Israel all had their analogues in premodern Jewish thought. But the ongoing debt that secular thinkers owed to premodern sources is more complicated with respect to culture. The idea that Israel might be defined in cultural rather than religious terms was peculiarly modern because the terms themselves were modern. Culture and religion as separate categories had no real meaning in traditional Jewish life, just as they had no real meaning in premodern Europe generally. The modern Hebrew term for culture (*tarbut*) does derive from a talmudic source: the greatest rabbinic heretic, Elisha ben Abuya, was said to have "gone after evil *tarbut*" (b. Hagigah 15a). But the rabbis made no distinction between the cultural practices of the Greeks and Romans and their religion. The very word for "religion" in modern Hebrew (*dat*), which appeared originally in the biblical book of Esther, is a Persian loan word meaning a royal decree. Biblical Hebrew has no indigenous word for religion, and the way later rabbinic Hebrew uses *dat* is in the sense of custom or practice.

As Max Weinreich, the scholar of Yiddish, wrote, the popular culture of the Ashkenazi Jews was permeated with locutions drawn directly from rabbinic literature.[5] Was this culture religious or secular, or are the terms anachronistic? The argument for an autonomous sphere of "culture" as opposed to "religion" required new definitions of these categories, definitions that were in part borrowed from European culture, which itself came to use the word "religion" in the sense of beliefs held by an organized institution only in the seventeenth and eighteenth centuries.[6]

At the same time, though, it is possible to demonstrate that a culture encompassing, but not limited to, religion certainly did exist throughout Jewish history.[7] A good example is the role of custom (*minhag*), especially in Ashkenazi culture of the Middle Ages and early modern times. Assuming virtually the force of law, local custom could become as important as what the rabbis held to have been revealed at Sinai.[8] Another example is the daily practice of Jewish women, which might have its origins in revealed law but often took on a life of its own. For instance, the daily liturgy prescribed by the rabbis includes a man's blessing thanking God for not making him a woman and a woman's blessing thanking God for making her "according to His will." But two Italian Renaissance prayer books commissioned specifically for women contain a radical revision: the prayer thanks God "for making me a woman and not a man."[9] The context is religious, to be sure, but the virtually antinomian sentiment suggests a women's culture independent of the religion of the rabbis.

Thus, the new definition of Judaism as a culture had a basis in earlier tradition and it was a basis that the proponents of this new definition elaborated and developed in their historical writings. As with the other chapters in this book, one might legitimately ask whether the search for a Jewish culture in the past was an optical illusion of those in the present or whether it was a real object that required modernity in order to reveal it. Either way, secular Jewish thinkers found reflections of themselves in the past, even as they blazed new trails.

To write a history of this new secular culture, which flourished in far-flung regions—eastern and western Europe, North and South America, the Ottoman Empire, and the State of Israel—would take several volumes.[10] Instead of doing so, I propose to examine a few theorists who set forth the major issues and took representative positions. We will start with the Odessa school represented by the "secular rabbi" Ahad Ha'am, the Hebrew national poet Hayim Nahman Bialik, and the social historian and activist Simon Dubnow. We will then turn to two "counterhistorians," Micha Yosef Berdichevsky and Gershom Scholem, who argued that historical Judaism— and implicitly modern Jewish culture—is marked by a dialectic between orthodoxy and heresy, religion and secularism. Then we will examine perhaps the most radical of the nationalist thinkers, Joseph Hayim Brenner, who rejected the dialectical argument connecting the religious past and the secular present in favor of a Hebrew culture severed from history. Brenner's radicalism led him to embrace Jews who converted to Christianity, a position also adopted by his contemporary, Chaim Zhitlowsky, who argued for a secular culture in Yiddish instead of Hebrew. While secular Hebrew culture came to flourish in Palestine and, later, the State of Israel, Zhitlowsky found the most ready audience for his message among the eastern European immigrants to America. But with the waning of Yiddish in America, several thinkers, specifically Horace Kallen and Mordecai Kaplan, proposed a new Jewish culture in English, and it is with them that we will conclude this examination of history, language, and culture as new categories to define the community called Israel.

Most of these thinkers wrote in the early years of the twentieth century, since it was at that pivotal moment that the questions were most hotly debated and when matters were most in flux. Today, with the disappearance of the once-flourishing cultures in the diasporic languages of Yiddish, Ladino, and Judeo-Arabic and with the emergence of powerful secular cultures in

Hebrew and English, and (to a lesser degree) Russian, French, and Spanish, the debates of the turn of the previous century appear almost quaint and antiquated, a development to which I will return in the epilogue. But it was out of that crucible that the choices were made that led to today's reality.

Ahad Ha'am: The Secular Rabbi of Zionism

Odessa in the latter part of the nineteenth century was the hothouse for the creation of a secular Jewish culture for the Jewish nation in the Russian Pale of Settlement.[11] The maskil Moses Leib Lilienblum, whom we discussed in chapter 1, fled there when he sought an enlightened community. S. Y. Abramowitsch (1835–1917), the "grandfather" of modern Yiddish literature, known by his pseudonym as Mendele Mokher Sforim, found a congenial home there from which to write his satirical stories of traditional Jewish life. It was in Odessa as well that Simon Dubnow, the great historian of the eastern European Jews, conducted his groundbreaking work collecting the artifacts of the culture of the folk. The free air of the new port city on the Black Sea also attracted the Hebrew poet Hayim Nahman Bialik and the Hebrew prose writer and polemicist Micha Yosef Berdichevsky, both refugees from the famous Volozhin yeshiva. And it was also there that Ahad Ha'am held court as the secular rabbi of the new Jewish culture.

Ahad Ha'am was perhaps the most important theoretician of secular Jewish culture.[12] Although he was a fervent advocate of Hebrew in the language wars of the fin de siècle, his ideas had a profound impact on all the belligerent parties, as well as on those in North America, seemingly far removed from the theater of combat. In our chapter on the Bible in secular Jewish thought, we observed how Ahad Ha'am identified the "national spirit" of the Jews, which he substituted for God, with biblical ethics. The rabbis had fossilized this national spirit in the Talmud, a sin perpetuated by the nineteenth-century German Reformers. Only a revived national culture in Hebrew could return the Jews to the "inner morality" of the Bible.

It is to this national culture in Ahad Ha'am's thought that we now turn. Ironically for one writing in the Russian Empire, it was the cultural plight of Judaism rather than the political plight of the Jews that Ahad Ha'am found most distressing. Yet, even in a time when the Jews were suffering severe economic and legal hardships that led to mass emigration, the cultural question had also become pressing. Increasing numbers of young Jews were joining Russian revolutionary movements and/or converting to Christianity. The specter of assimilation, hitherto confined to western and central Europe, had now come to haunt the Jews of the east. In Ahad Ha'am's eyes, the question of cultural identity was therefore the foremost one facing the Jews, and against Herzl's political Zionism, he argued that the national movement must undertake to solve this problem along with the problem of political oppression.[13]

Ahad Ha'am was an avowed secularist with respect to the religious tradition. In his 1891 attack on the assimilationists and reformers of western Europe, he stated: "I can pass judgment of my own on the beliefs and opinions bequeathed to me by my forefathers without fear that the connection that binds me to my nation will be severed; I can embrace the 'scientific heresy that carries the name of Darwin' without endangering my Judaism."[14] The very lack of political freedom in eastern Europe paradoxically allowed for much greater freedom of opinion than in the West. Yet his secularism was moderated by two issues: he substituted a national essence for a religious one, and unlike some of his opponents, he sought continuities with the religious past. For example, although he labeled Hasidic literature "childish," he still preferred it over the literature of the Haskalah, the Jewish Enlightenment.[15] The texts produced by Hasidism and other premodern Jewish movements, no matter their flaws, were part of a national literature, something he found lacking in their nineteenth-century successor. Indeed, even though he argued that the Jews had become enslaved to The Book, a much worse slavery emerged with modernity, a "slavery within freedom."[16] This slavery was a result of the sterile attempt to ape European culture rather than to cultivate a true Hebraic spirit. With religion now divorced from the day-to-day life of the people, it had lost touch with the national spirit.

That premodern Jewish literature was religious was not its essence; religion was merely an instrument for expressing that essence.[17] As Ahad Ha'am put it in a letter to the historian Israel Abrahams, "religion itself is only one of the forms of [Jewish] culture."[18] Or, in a letter to Judah Magnes, the American Reform rabbi who had written to him of his aspirations for revolutionizing the synagogue: "our religion is national—that is to say, it is a product of our national spirit—but the reverse is not true. . . . [I]t is possible to be a Jew in the national sense without accepting many things in which religion requires belief."[19] Therefore, he recommended to Magnes to turn the synagogue into house of study with "Jewish learning as its first concern and prayer as a secondary matter. Cut the prayers as short as you like, but make your synagogue a haven for Jewish knowledge."[20] The bet *midrash* (house of study) and not the bet *knesset* (synagogue) was the historical "heart of the Jewish people."[21] He might have noted that traditional Ashkenazi culture calls the synagogue a *shul* ("school"), since the house of prayer was also commonly a house of study. It is not surprising, then, that Ahad Ha'am was one of the earliest and most devoted advocates of creating a secular Jewish university in Palestine.

In a secular age, the essence of Judaism, previously cloaked in religious garments, could find its expression only in a national culture. To create such a national culture could be accomplished only in Hebrew since "a people's literature is the literature written in its national language."[22] For that reason, he argued surprisingly that there could be no national literature in the United States or Switzerland, since those countries had no national language of their own. If, on the other hand, one wrote about the Jews in a European language, as was already increasingly common in Ahad Ha'am's time, one created a "literary ghetto," presumably since few Jews could read such literature. Thus, the paradoxical way out of the cultural ghetto was to write in Hebrew, a language only available to an educated elite, but one that had the status of a national language.

The alternative, though, was Yiddish (Ahad Ha'am, like most of his contemporaries, did not relate at all to other Jewish languages, like Ladino or Judeo-Arabic, since the majority of Jews at the fin de siècle still spoke Yiddish). Here, as we will see when we turn to Chaim Zhitlowsky, was a language that might also claim to be national. In waging war against Yiddish, Ahad Ha'am noted something paradoxical: "So long as it was really the spoken language of all East-European Jews . . . it never occurred to anybody that Yiddish was our national language."[23] It was only when Yiddish was waning (inaccurate when he wrote it, but ultimately prophetic) that its proponents advanced it as comparable or even superior to Hebrew. For Ahad Ha'am, although Yiddish was the vernacular of the Jews of eastern Europe, it did not express their deepest longings and emotions. Even those women for whom a literature was written in Yiddish, since they could not read Hebrew, recognized that "the substitute language was merely a convenience, not an object of any special affection."[24]

In this argument for a literary language poorly understood by most Jews, even if they could read it, Ahad Ha'am was the child of the Hebrew Haskalah that he otherwise criticized. And he was arguing for a linguistic nationalism that had no parallel in Europe. Ahad Ha'am's vision of a secular Jewish culture based in Hebrew was therefore highly utopian and manifestly elitist. It is also peculiar that in these debates over a national language, proponents of Hebrew like Ahad Ha'am rarely referred at all to non-Ashkenazi Jews; surely one of the strongest arguments for Hebrew, which later Zionists made when they "discovered" the Mizrahi Jews, was that only the ancient language of the Jews had the capacity to unite a linguistically fragmented people.

Ahad Ha'am's brief for Hebrew had another paradoxical dimension. While Yiddish was a fusion language—that is, composed of Hebraic and European elements—Hebrew as a Semitic language was utterly foreign to European Jews. Yet, he claimed, only in Hebrew could a secular Jewish culture have a healthy relationship to European culture. Only the language with the least European resonance was, on the one hand, the most open to worthy ideas from the dominant culture but, on the other, the least likely to be assimilated into that culture.

This claim flowed from a historical argument that Ahad Ha'am made in an important, early essay titled "Imitation and Assimilation" (1893).[25] Throughout history, he argued, the Jews were highly adept at imitating the cultures of their surroundings. Yet, instead of assimilating into those cultures, the new ideas they imitated produced a kind of competition with the foreign cultures so that the imitation then became part of the national Jewish culture. Openness to the outside was a necessary component in national survival and creativity, since without it, the nation would have fossilized. Lack of such imitation could paradoxically produce assimilation. Ahad Ha'am mused: what would have happened had Plato been translated into Hebrew? The philosopher of Athens would have then become a part of Hebrew culture. As a result, the wave of hellenization in the second century BCE and the Maccabean Revolt against it might not have taken place. Imitation of the Greeks would have meant less assimilation and also less conflict. Hebrew culture in the present age must therefore do what it had failed to do in the Second Temple period: translate European culture into a Jewish idiom. Only Hebrew had the capacity to imitate without assimilating.

In another essay, Ahad Ha'am gives a surprising example of what he has in mind: Salomon Maimon.[26] Just as Maimon learned European languages and philosophy as an adult, so the Jews need not start over like children in absorbing modern culture. On the contrary, as an ancient people, they could produce a fruitful synthesis between their culture and that of the modern world on the foundation of their past. Once again, it is implicitly possible to accomplish this task in Hebrew because it is only in Hebrew that the Jews are not like schoolchildren. Of course, Maimon is a strange example, because he broke his ties with the Jewish world, but perhaps Ahad Ha'am viewed him as a Hebrew secularist before his time. As we have seen in chapter 1, Maimon's debt to the Hebrew intellectual tradition was one that he translated into his German philosophy (and vice versa), clearly a model of what Ahad Ha'am intended. Had a national culture existed in the eighteenth century, perhaps Maimon would have found his home there and not in exile.

Another example Ahad Ha'am took from history is Maimon's namesake, Moses Maimonides. Participating in the cult of Maimonides as a modern philosopher *avant la lettre*, Ahad Ha'am celebrated the eight hundredth anniversary of Maimonides' death with an essay extolling the "emancipation of reason from its subordination to an external authority [as] the great and lasting achievement . . . [of] Maimonides."[27] Here, Maimonides became the harbinger of secular reason as opposed to blind religiosity. Against those who see Judaism as secure because it is above reason, "Maimonides came and said: 'Judaism is secure because *it* is reason.' "[28] In keeping with his own philosophy, Ahad Ha'am found in Maimonides his precursor in privileging "national sentiment" over God and in reducing religion to a tool for education. Maimonides became preeminently a moral philosopher, thus foreshadowing Ahad Ha'am's own philosophy of Judaism.

The debate over assimilation in which Ahad Ha'am participated revolved around the question of whether the Jews could persist as a distinct people in the face of modern culture. Extreme Zionists argued that if life in Diaspora led to abandonment of Jewish culture, then the only place that a healthy culture might flourish had to be in a Jewish national territory. Ahad Ha'am's response to this binary was to suggest a third way: a spiritual center in Palestine whose renewed national culture would also renew the Diaspora. In part, this compromise reflected his skepticism that the majority of the Jews would immigrate to the land of Israel; a Diaspora would perforce continue to exist. But it also suggested his position that land was not necessary for culture. He understood the importance of an economic and social infrastructure for providing the basis for his cultural center. But once a minimal infrastructure was created, the cultural center could flourish and influence the Diaspora.

In the historical moment at which Ahad Ha'am made these arguments—when the vast majority of the Jews lived in eastern Europe and traditional education still created a constituency for Hebrew writings—this position was not entirely utopian. In the interwar period, when Zionism in Poland promoted secular education in Hebrew, Polish Jews eagerly consumed the culture produced in the Yishuv, the Zionist settlement in Palestine. Following the Holocaust, however, this readership largely disappeared, murdered in the Diaspora that Ahad Ha'am thought would remain the reservoir of secular Hebrew culture. It is ironic that the high water mark of Ahad Ha'amism was before the Jews attained their state and not after.

Hayim Nahman Bialik: The Poet as Modernist Muse

Perhaps the main Hasid of the secular rebbe Ahad Ha'am was Hayim Nahman Bialik, poet laureate of the national renaissance of Hebrew culture. As he wrote later, "Every word that Ahad Ha'am wrote seemed addressed to me, to my innermost thoughts."[29] When he fled the Volozhin yeshiva in 1891 for the modern Jewish city of Odessa, Bialik entered the charmed circle of secular intellectuals that centered around Ahad Ha'am. In his search for a bridge between modernity and tradition, Bialik would find in Ahad Ha'am's philosophy a persuasive program. Yet Bialik's was a much more experimental, modernist sensibility than his mentor's, and his relationship to the religious tradition was at once more hostile and more enmeshed. As we observed in chapter 1, Bialik's poetic struggles over language found expression in a kind of existentialism, an evacuation of biblical theology of its positive content. But Bialik articulated his extreme—even atheistic—stance in the language of the religious tradition that he commanded perhaps better than any modern Hebrew writer. Where Ahad Ha'am pioneered a new Hebrew prose style with only fleeting references to traditional locutions, Bialik mined every stratum of the language to create a personal vocabulary and syntax that few have successfully imitated.

Bialik's relationship to Ahad Ha'am was therefore predictably complicated. The older writer commanded his reverence, but his own view of the
new culture was at times quite different. Ahad Ha'am's elitism seemed to
Bialik misplaced. Instead of a linguistic revival limited to a small circle of
scholars and writers, Bialik envisioned something much more capacious.
Thus, in an essay from 1905, "The Birth Pangs of Language" (*Hevlei
Lashon*),[30] Bialik sharply criticized Ahad Ha'am's argument that the cultural renaissance would be primarily written. For common emotions, Ahad
Ha'am suggested, one could use *mame loshen*, Yiddish, but when one wanted
to speak of "Judaism" (by which Ahad Ha'am obviously meant more than
the religious tradition), one should turn to Hebrew, the only language that
contained the historical resonances of the tradition. This sharp dichotomy
between the spoken language of the emotions and the written language
of reason was foreign to Bialik's sensibility. National poet of the Hebrew
renaissance he may have been, but he never scorned Yiddish and, indeed,
wrote some important works in his mother tongue.[31]

Bialik's main criticism of Ahad Ha'am, however, rested on a different theory of language, one that we may recognize from "Revelation and Concealment in Language." For Bialik, language is a living thing, and it grows by
absorbing and transforming words. Only spoken language has this power:

> The mere existence of linguistic assets alone, as plentiful as they may be, still will
> not suffice. Rather [these assets] need a turning and overturning, the perpetual,
> cyclical motion of life. . . . Great is the power of living speech. . . . To obliterate
> completely the barrier between our soul and our tongue, to put an end to all the
> "birth pangs of language" all at once—all this will become possible only through
> a total rejuvenation of the language and a renaissance of speech and writing.[32]

In other words, only the interaction between the spoken and the written can
create a living language since only a spoken language is truly creative. This
creativity lies in breaking linguistic conventions, even subverting the rules
of grammar, and thereby producing new words and new forms. Indeed, Bialik's own oeuvre is filled with neologisms that he coined.

To limit a language to the "four cubits of writing" is to condemn it to
"permanent burial."[33] This is a cunning appropriation of religious language
for a secular purpose. The phrase "four cubits" is traditionally applied to
the *halakhah*, or Jewish law. To immure language in this structure is to condemn it to the same death as the one suffered by Jewish culture at the hands

of religion. Only the subversive power of a spoken language, like the antinomian power of secularism, can liberate this culture from its tomb. Here, Bialik takes a positive view of the process that had so terrified Gershom Scholem in his letter to Franz Rosenzweig discussed in chapter one.

Bialik does not fear the secularization of a religious language. The speaker who creates freely "rises above language and becomes a lord and king over it, enslaving it voluntarily."[34] Moreover, the process of linguistic creation is necessarily subversive: one "commits a transgression that becomes a commandment." Bialik may well be alluding here to the heretical seventeenth-century Sabbatian doctrine of "a commandment that is fulfilled by transgression" (*mitzvah ha-ba'ah be-averah*). Shattering the law and shattering language are part of the same revolutionary process that gives rise to a new culture. We are now very far from Ahad Ha'am's evolutionary philosophy and closer in some ways to the antinomianism of Friedrich Nietzsche.

Bialik contends that a "holy spirit" is necessary for this revolutionary process to take place, but he means something far from this traditional way of referring to God. The spirit is one internal to the creative person. If one may be permitted a pun on Bialik's own name: it is "the god within" (*bi-el*: "God is within me"). Ten years before the pessimism of "Revelation and Concealment," Bialik speaks confidently here of the divine force behind the poet's creativity. But while he may have been concerned with the individual sources of poetry in "Birth Pangs of Language," Bialik was equally preoccupied with how a nation collectively renews its language. Here, too, a "holy spirit" is at work and, indeed, a spoken language can only be renewed collectively, by the interchange between speakers.

Despite the revolutionary utterances of this important essay, Bialik also reveals a certain conservatism. As opposed to Ahad Ha'am's argument for cultural imitation, Bialik holds that language must grow internally: translation from one language to another is "1/60th part of death" (here, too, he uses another rabbinic phrase for a secular purpose). Although he was deeply influenced by his reading of Russian poetry, his position is that a spoken language has its own resources for creativity. He also admits that his own method relies on the tradition he is overturning, since, as he says, sometimes the new combination of old words has greater creative power than the invention of new ones. Thus, we find in Bialik an extraordinary dialectic between the old and the new, the treasure house of the past and the antinomian urge to burn it down.

Between 1908 and 1911, Bialik and his collaborator, Y. H. Ravnitsky, undertook an extraordinary project of remodeling that treasure house into a national library. *Sefer ha-Aggadah* (*The Book of Legends*) culled legendary material from rabbinic sources and organized it topically. In an essay that served as the introduction to the volume, Bialik describes the aggadah in secular terms as the embodiment of the collective, literary spirit of the nation.[35] Fashioned by many hands over many centuries, this massive body of literature required an act of synthesis in the age of national renaissance. In other words, organizing the material chronologically and by topic not only gave order to it but actually produced something new.

In this respect, Bialik and Ravnitsky's project resembled a secular version of Maimonides' great code of Jewish law, the *Mishneh Torah*, since, like their twelfth-century predecessor, they made significant judgments about what to include and what to omit and thus created something greater than the sum of its parts. Just as Maimonides believed that his generation was too distant from the Talmud to be able to distill its reasoning without mediation, so *Sefer ha-Aggadah* stemmed from a sense of modern alienation from the sources of tradition, which now needed to be recast in accessible form. That Bialik may have seen himself as a twentieth-century Maimonides gains further credibility from one of his last major projects: a commentary on the first order of the Mishnah, which was how the great philosopher started his career of legal commentary. Unlike Maimonides, though, Bialik and Ravnitsky did not rewrite their material, a point Bialik makes explicitly in his essay, probably aimed against Louis Ginzberg, who famously rewrote the legends in his own voice.[36] Thus, *Sefer ha-Aggadah* appears on the one hand to be a thoroughly traditional text, perhaps like the thirteenth-century *Yalkut Shimoni*, a compilation of aggadot arranged according to the order of the Bible. But its intent was anything but traditional. Instead, it was designed to create a national literature based on historical texts, not because of their divine source but, on the contrary, as evidence of the creativity of the nation.

In the decade after the essay "Birth Pangs of the Language" and *Sefer Ha-Aggadah* were published, Bialik began to reevaluate some of his earlier positions. If in *Sefer Ha-Aggadah*, he had seen aggadah as the literary spirit of the nation that could be detached from the halakhah (Jewish law), now he came to believe that the two might not be so easily separated. In 1917, he wrote "Halakhah and Aggadah," a reformulation of the relationship between the two genres in terms that had contemporary cultural resonance as well.[37] He begins with an antithesis that sounds like his earlier position: the halakhah has an angry face, while the aggadah has a laughing face. Yet the two are equally valuable: "These and these are the words [*divrei*] of creation."[38] Here, once again, Bialik plays with a rabbinic phrase: "these and these are the words of the living God."[39] The Talmud brings this saying to state that the contradictory teachings of the Schools of Hillel and Shammai are both grounded in divine revelation. However, Bialik attributes the contradictory stances of halakhah and aggadah not to God but instead to human creation.

Even though halakhah and aggadah are ostensibly polar opposites, they are linked. Bialik gives several examples, the first surprising. The Christians build cathedrals, which, in their concrete structure, are like the halakhah. But the spirit that animates the cathedral, that makes it a home for the spirit, is the same as the aggadah. Where the Christians build their "halakhah" with stones, the Jews build theirs with words. In both cases, though, a creative spirit lies behind what otherwise appears static. In the Jewish context, all of the minute legal distinctions inherent in the Shabbat are animated by aggadah, since, for Bialik, the Shabbat is a "day that is wholly aggadah" (a takeoff from the liturgical expression "a day that is wholly Shabbat"). In other words, the strictness of the law grows directly out of the creative spirit of the aggadah.

Far from enshrining only dogmatic commandments, both the halakhah and aggadah express the disputations and contradictions in Jewish culture. Bialik gives an example that is explicitly relevant to his own time: the question of language. The Mishnah debates whether on the Sabbath one can save from a fire a Torah scroll translated into a foreign tongue. The contradictory legal positions taken on this question find expression as well in the aggadah. On the one hand: "God spoke to Israel in a language it could understand—Egyptian." On the other: "Speak to the children of Israel in my language—Hebrew." Both the halakhah and aggadah reflect the language wars that have persisted from ancient to modern times. Bialik strikingly does not take his own position on this conflict but instead uses it to show the disputatious character of both law and legend. He leaves the impression that it is the very lack of a decisive conclusion to these controversies that allows for creativity. Jewish culture is a culture of contradictions, not of dogmatic law or theology.

The reason for this move in the direction of halakhah becomes clear toward the end of the essay. Today, says Bialik, we live in an age that is "all aggadah."[40] The halakhah, in its deeper meaning, has been lost. Literature is now consumed only by the aesthetic question of beauty and love: "love of the land, love of the language, but what is the price of this abstract love?"[41] Where is the obligation (*hovva*) that ought to accompany this love (*hibba*)? The word for love that Bialik uses here is the name chosen by the early Zionists: *Hibbat Zion* ("love of Zion"). The focus of the essay now has shifted from the historical distinction between the genres of halakhah and aggadah to the contemporary cultural question of the role of literature. If the new Hebrew literature is to create something concrete in the world, it must do more than preoccupy itself with abstract aestheticism; it must create a new halakhah. This new law is anything but religious; it is instead the new national culture. And, if one can infer from Bialik's description of both the traditional halakhah and aggadah, the new secular culture in all its forms would have to be characterized by the same spirit of disputation and controversy. It is this, as well as Bialik's exploitation of traditional resources for modern purposes, that links the religious past with the secular present.

Simon Dubnow: The Collector as Historian

Bialik and Ravnitsky's work of collection (called *kinus* in Hebrew) seems to have been in the Odessa air. Already a decade and more before them, the Russian Jewish historian Simon Dubnow (1860–1941) initiated a massive project of collecting materials from far-flung corners of the Pale of Settlement by enlisting volunteer "collectors" to send him local artifacts and texts. Dubnow's project of collecting texts and other materials from the farthest reaches of Russian Jewish society was not unique. The Yiddish writer and social revolutionary, S. Ansky, for example, led an expedition in 1912 to recover the folk traditions of the Russian Jews. These efforts were part and parcel of a sense, on the one hand, that the world of tradition was vanishing and, on the other, that a national culture required assembling the wisdom of the folk, a motive, like that of the Brothers Grimm in Germany, common to most European nationalisms. Among these Jewish intellectuals, the folk was sometimes paradoxically portrayed as a source of secularism since its culture was perceived to be antithetical to that of the rabbis.

In addition to these sources of social history, Dubnow also focused his attention on the documents of Jewish self-government, such as the minute books of the *Vaadot* (councils) of Poland and Lithuania. This concern with political history grew out of Dubnow's commitment to "autonomism," the political alternative to Zionism that sought Jewish autonomy in eastern Europe and that was influenced by the Slavophilic idea of Vladimir Soloviev that a nation's soul need not be connected to territory.[42] Dubnow therefore wanted to show that Jews had always exercised forms of political autonomy throughout the Diaspora, and not only in the land of Israel. Dubnow's "world history of the Jews" traced these centers of autonomy as they shifted from one place to another in the different periods of Jewish history. This idea of a world history was also a subtle response to the status of the Jews in Imperial Russia, a national minority on the Western borderlands. Like other historians of minorities in the Russian Empire—which Lenin called the "great prison house of nations"—Dubnow's was a voice from the margins, yet one that insisted that his nation, possessing as it did a "world history," was anything but marginal.[43]

In the introduction to his *World History of the Jewish People* (1937–38), Dubnow issued a call for a new kind of history of the sort that Heine might have advocated: "The subject of investigation is not an abstraction but a living organism, which has developed out of an original biological germ, the tribe, into a complex cultural historical whole, the nation."[44] Following the organic or biological vocabulary of German and Russian nationalism of the late nineteenth and early twentieth centuries, Dubnow held that the Jews are like an organism that starts as an "amorphous national cell" and then differentiates by establishing itself in different environments. The nation follows the laws of nature in its development until it eventually reaches maturity—in Dubnow's own period—as a complex, cultural entity.

Given his approach, it is no surprise that Dubnow subordinated religion to these social and political tendencies: "The religion of Judaism was fashioned in accordance with the image of the social conditions of the nation's existence, and not the reverse."[45] Although by no means a Marxist, Dubnow nevertheless wanted to see religion as a product of social history and not its cause. But this new, secular approach to Jewish history was itself the product of social conditions, namely, the secularization of Jewish life in the modern period. As Jews came to define themselves more as a nation than only a religious community, historical writing also became more secular:

The secularization of the Jewish national idea was bound to affect the secularization of historical writing, liberating it from the shackles of theology and, subsequently, of spiritualism or scholasticism. . . . This conception [i.e., of a sociological history] provides a way out for our historiography from the labyrinth of theological and metaphysical theories and places it upon a firm bio-sociological foundation."[46]

Thus, the secularization of the writing of Jewish history created the possibility for a much broader and more inclusive view of the past, which was, in turn, linked to a more secular future.

History and Counterhistory

Dubnow and Bialik sought in the voice of the folk and the national literary tradition antidotes to the theological bent of nineteenth-century historical science. A different antidote with similar intent might be called "counterhistory." [47] By counterhistory I mean the argument that the vital forces of Jewish history lie in the margins—in the subterranean, ignored, and even despised traditions, further even from the center than the vox populi. A counterhistorian might find the true history of the Jews among the heretics rather than the Orthodox. In addition, what characterizes counterhistory is its resistance to reducing history to a single, dogmatic essence. The vital forces may be found in the margins, but their vitality comes from the dynamic conflict with establishment or official traditions. Pluralism rather than singularity is its hallmark. Counterhistory has a strongly secular flavor, since it insists that the history of mainstream religious authorities does not tell the whole story. While heretical rejections of authority were typically religious themselves in the premodern world, counterhistorians frequently hint—or even explicitly say—that these movements either prefigure or even dialectically produce modern secularism.

We have already encountered Micha Yosef Berdichevsky's counterhistory of the Bible in which the traditions of Sinai competed with the countertradition of Gerizim. A culture celebrating nature and strength struggled with—and ultimately lost out to—a religion of ethics and law. Jewish history is the record of this battle of "Judaism" against "the Jews." There is therefore no single "essence" of Judaism but rather continual conflict between different forces:

The Hebrews do not have a single literature of a single mind, given by a single leader[,] but we have a multitude of diversified parts of literature. . . . The Hebrew people [are] not a single unique nation having but a single mind and spirit, but [they include] conflicting tribal forces which have different temperaments.[48]

Berdichevsky railed against history for suffocating the life force of the nation, and it was here that he warred bitterly against Ahad Ha'am, the more moderate representative of the older generation of Hebrew nationalists. For all his Nietzschean anarchism, however, Berdichevsky also recognized that this revolt against history and the religious tradition carried with it a paradox: "When we defeat the past, we ourselves are defeated. And, conversely, when the past defeats [us], we and our children's children are defeated. A potion of life and a potion of death in one thing."[49] History is what constitutes us and gives us our existence, but it is also history that robs us of our vitality.

The way out of this dilemma for Berdichevsky was counterhistory, the quest for vitalistic forces in history that resisted the hegemony of stultifying law. The traditions of Gerizim extended beyond the Bible and into later rabbinic literature, which never fully suppressed them. The sword and the book that came down from heaven joined together continued to compete throughout all the centuries of Jewish history: "The children of Israel tended in general 'to do evil,' that is to say, to live like all the other nations. The war between the secular and the sacred, between material life and spiritual life[,] took on great force through all the days of [Israel's] spiritual and political culture. . . . But the efforts to restore vitality to life were in vain."[50]

Berdichevsky searched for signs of his countertradition among the heretics and rebels who "refused to take part with us, refused to be counted with us, and, yet, how much more are they connected with us."[51] At times, he turned certain rabbis, like those of the School of Shammai, into his heroes, since they opposed the dominant School of Hillel. During the Great Revolt against Rome (66–70 CE), he championed the nationalist Zealots against the "pacifist" Pharisees. Despite the supremacy of the rabbis throughout the Middle Ages, movements of vitalistic resistance repeatedly emerged to challenge their authority: "Pharisees opposed Sadducees, Karaites opposed rabbis, and the Kabbalah and esoteric doctrines opposed the explicit. In other words, nothing genuine exists except when one extreme party does the thing completely and without tolerant compromise."[52] That none of these movements of spiritual opposition could even remotely be identified with the militaristic traditions of the sword shows the ambiguity of Berdichevsky's terms. But in stressing the common critical function served by all these traditions, he pointed out that the rabbis had no easy monopoly.

Berdichevsky was equally attracted to modern heretics such as Spinoza. In a notebook entry from 1890, he described his excitement at discovering the Hebrew translation of Spinoza's *Ethics* while spending the year in Odessa.[53] In a review of this translation, he expressed his displeasure at many of the modern interpretations of Spinoza.[54] He attacked those who tried to integrate Spinoza back into the Jewish tradition by arguing (as the author of this book has done) that his sources were in medieval Jewish thought. He was equally critical of those modern thinkers who wanted to claim direct spiritual descent from Spinoza. Both of these approaches to Spinoza—which could be held by the same people—tried to normalize him either in prior or subsequent Jewish history, while the real Spinoza was a much more radical heretic than they wanted to admit. Although Berdichevsky does not say so explicitly, he apparently wanted to embrace precisely the Spinoza who had departed radically from Jewish tradition and therefore still remained an outcast. Only as such could he serve as a hero for Berdichevsky's radical revolution.

Berdichevsky's attraction to the heretics and rebels of Jewish history was part and parcel of the modern recuperation of these figures by a wide range of writers and artists. But rather than fully embracing these heretics as he did, modern Jewish culture often celebrated them only after reinterpreting the meaning of their heresies. Uriel da Costa and Baruch Spinoza became heroic figures in the nineteenth century, but as Berdichevsky observed, their truly radical heresies were domesticated into precursors of respectable nineteenth-century Judaism. Heretics from within the religious tradition, such as Jesus, Elisha ben Abuya (the arch-heretic of the Talmud), and Shabbtai Zvi (the mystical Messiah of the seventeenth century), also became popular subjects in nineteenth and twentieth-century Jewish writing and art. Here, too, the religious heresies of these figures were often reinterpreted to point toward modernity.[55]

Perhaps the most important historian of such heresies was Gershom Scholem, who explicitly connected his rehabilitation of heretics with the new interpretative freedom promised by Zionism: "the new evaluations and emphases which Zionism has established have blown a fresh breeze in a house which had seemingly been all too well-ordered by the nineteenth century."[56] This was the same "anarchic breeze" that he believed apocalyptic messianism had blown through the "well-ordered house" of the halakhah, infusing the static law with renewed vitality.[57] By uncovering the hidden sources of vitality among the heretics, the historian fulfilled the same function as the apocalyptic messianists.

Scholem's greatest work was his biography of Shabbtai Zvi, published first in Hebrew in 1958 and in an expanded English edition in 1971.[58] Scholem saw Sabbatianism as the dialectical watershed that prepared the ground for modernity. He first made this argument at an early stage in his career in a 1928 article on the Sabbatian theology of Abraham Cardozo. Cardozo was a converso who had returned to Judaism. His response to Shabbtai Zvi's apostasy was to see the erstwhile Messiah as a Marrano like himself. Since the doctrine of reincarnation of the soul seemed to make man no longer responsible for evil actions in earlier incarnations, Cardozo interpreted the Kabbalah as pointing to a kind of moral anarchism. With Cardozo's Sabbatianism, says Scholem, the anarchism implicit in this doctrine burst outward into the world and exploded Judaism from the inside: "Thus it was that before the powers of world history uprooted Judaism in the nineteenth century, its reality was threatened from within. Already at that time [the time of Sabbatianism] the 'reality of the Hebrews,' the sphere of Judaism, threatened to become an illusion."[59]

This argument found fuller expression in a powerful article written in Hebrew in 1936 titled "Mitzvah ha-Ba'ah be-Averah" ("The commandment that is fulfilled through its transgression" or, as it was titled in English translation, "Redemption through Sin").[60] Scholem distinguished here between moderate and radical Sabbatians. The first believed that only the Messiah needed to convert to Islam. Like the Marranos, they maintained their faith in him inwardly, while acting outwardly like fully Orthodox Jews. In this way, they anticipated the modern splitting of identity into private and public compartments. The radicals, on the other hand, believed in the "holiness of sin" for themselves as well, embracing antinomian acts and, ultimately, apostasy from Judaism. However, in the case of the Frankists in Poland (an eighteenth-century offshoot of Sabbatianism), apostasy meant not a sincere acceptance of the new religion but a dialectical nihilism expressed through the mask of Christianity. According to Scholem, Frankist nihilism ultimately turned outward to a desire for political liberation, and certain Frankist tracts made the connection between heretical mysticism and the political ideals of the Enlightenment and the French Revolution.[61]

Scholem's argument is thoroughly dialectical—the most irrational and religious forces in Jewish history produced a messianic movement whose collapse led, in turn, to modern secularism, religious reform, and political revolution: "The desire for total liberation which played so tragic a role in the development of Sabbatian nihilism was by no means a purely self-destructive force; on the contrary, beneath the surface of lawlessness, antinomianism and catastrophic negation, powerful constructive impulses were at work."[62] Sabbatianism undermined the hegemony of rabbinic law. While individual Sabbatians in the eighteenth century found their way to the European Enlightenment, since the movement was worldwide, its shock waves weakened the rabbinic establishment in many different lands. As radically different as the Enlightenment may seem in contrast to mystical messianism, there was, then, a hidden connection between them in which Sabbatianism unwittingly prepared the ground for secular modernity.

In Scholem's philosophy we find a counterhistory similar to Berdichevsky's. Conservative forces such as law, philosophy, and rationalism contend constantly with the countervailing forces of myth, mysticism, and irrationalism. Judaism consists of a plurality, even an anarchism of ideas, rather than a single essence. Indeed, Scholem was perhaps the single most vehement critic of the nineteenth-century Science of Judaism, the founding school of Jewish historiography, on the grounds that it reduced Judaism to a single rational, theological principle while suppressing the mythic and the irrational.[63] It is the creative conflict of opposing ideas in the realm of history, rather than their harmonization in the realm of theology, that gives Judaism its vitality.

Yet, in his own politics, Scholem shied away from the full consequences of the apocalyptic and the heretical. As fascinated as he was by these phenomena in Jewish history, he feared their practical consequences for Zionism.[64] Just as he warned Franz Rosenzweig of the dangers inherent in reviving Hebrew as a secular language—since the apocalyptic energies inherent in the language could not be controlled—so he denounced the right-wing militant nationalists of his day as "latter-day Sabbatians." Zionism, for Scholem, meant the pragmatic return of the Jews to history and such latter-day apocalypticists threatened to destroy the movement by reaching for the *eschaton*. The dialectic between the religious past and the secular future was always in danger of imploding.

Joseph Hayim Brenner: Against the Dialectic

Challenges to this dialectic came from many directions, from the ultra-Orthodox to the ultra-secular. Perhaps none of the latter was as uncompromising as Joseph Hayim Brenner, the writer and critic who came to Palestine as part of the Second Aliya and was murdered by Arabs in the riots of 1921. We have already considered Brenner's harsh rejection of the Bible, which staked out the farthest border of Jewish secularism. Now we turn to Brenner's militantly secular vision of a modern Hebrew culture divorced from the Jewish past.

Brenner wrote at a time when the young Hebrew culture in Palestine was still very much in formation, in the process of establishing its identity. A child of the national Hebrew renaissance represented by such figures as Ahad Ha'am and Bialik, the culture that Brenner wanted to create was to be rooted in the new-old land. No longer interested in just a literary exercise, Brenner and his comrades hoped to decisively break with the Diaspora and found something new. Yet this process of creation was wracked with self-doubt and fears of failure. Never had a national cultural movement been so riven between revolutionary zeal and despair, with Brenner representing more than most both poles of this syndrome.

Brenner clearly regarded Bialik with enormous respect, yet, for all that he admired the Hebrew national poet, he could not accept his relationship to the religious tradition.[65] Where Bialik believed that one could turn the halakhah and the aggadah into the sources for secular epic and lyric poetry, Brenner dissents with an ironic reference to a ritual object: "Even an omnipotent artist can't weave a prayer shawl from purple thread out of the peel of a garlic."[66] Brenner finds nothing to redeem in the halakhah. Where Bialik spoke of the "angry face" of the law versus the "laughing face" of the aggadah, Brenner bitterly responds that the angry face is that of the rabbi in J. L. Gordon's famous nineteenth-century poem, "On the Point of a *Yod*," which tells the tale of a rabbi who denies a woman a divorce because of a minute defect in the *get* (divorce writ) that her husband had written her. And the "laughing face" of the aggadah is that of the woman "Bat-Shua with her children hanging on her skirts" or of Bialik's own mother, kneading the dough, from whom he inherited his poetry.[67]

This turn toward women is highly significant, since the literature of the Haskalah had used the fate of women as evidence for the brutality of traditional Jewish life. If the aggadah is symbolized by these tormented women, then it hardly has a "laughing face." Here, the aggadah becomes an expression not of poetry but of real life, a motif of great importance in Brenner's philosophy. Linked together in this way, the halakhah and the aggadah—the twin genres of traditional Judaism—have no saving virtues. Brenner, like Bialik, was educated in the *bet midrash*. But where Bialik retained a certain ambivalent nostalgia for this age-old institution, Brenner claims that his years studying the intricacies of Jewish law left little impact. Only the wars of Joshua, the history of the Judges, and the tales of the destruction of the Temple provided spiritual nourishment, themes that clearly point toward nationalism instead of religion.[68] The law itself, he argues, may have been created out of good motives, but after these have passed into history, all that remains is evil, "weighing like a stone on the lives of men and fighting against every new law, the need for renewed life."[69]

Brenner's savage critique of halakhah, like Berdichevsky's, was grounded in a kind of Nietzschean anarchism, which saw all law as a yoke on the human spirit. But his anarchism was not only aimed at the law. It was grounded in a profound individualism in which the human being and his fate must be wrested free from the weight of collective tradition. Thus, as Menahem Brinker notes, Brenner was even more radical than Berdichevsky.[70] Where Berdichevsky expressed his revolt against the religious tradition by seeking a countertradition, Brenner had no use for such historical ruminations: we must decisively divorce ourselves from the past in order to live in the present. As he puts it at the beginning of one of his longest and most important pieces of criticism, "Evaluation of Ourselves in Three Volumes" (1914), rabbinic literature is lacking in the self-consciousness needed to live in the present, since "everything [in that literature] is the words of the dead God."[71]

There is, of course, a great irony in Brenner's use of this phrase. He is playing here upon the rabbinic saying that we encountered also in Bialik: "these and these are the words of the living God." But where Bialik used this affirmation of controversy in a positive sense, Brenner gives it the kiss of death. The additional irony is that in seeking a total rupture with tradition, Brenner invokes a traditional phrase, a move clearly reminiscent of Bialik. Indeed, throughout Brenner's oeuvre, the reader encounters many rabbinic locutions, including phrases in Aramaic of the sort that a talmudic scholar might employ. The yeshiva student has run away from the yeshiva, but he still carries it within him.

Where Berdichevsky shared with Ahad Ha'am the pressing need to address the problem of assimilation—and proposed a revolutionary Hebrew culture to do so—Brenner's problem was not assimilation. One might say that he rejected the very antinomy of "assimilation" versus "nationalism" that Ahad Ha'am, among others, had posed. The cultural question of his age did not interest him, since it was rooted in the Diaspora, which deserved nothing but contempt and negation. Indeed, Brenner wrote some of the most scathing criticisms of the Jewish world in which he grew up, criticisms that verge, at times, on self-loathing. Taking his cue from the Yiddish writer Mendele Mokher Sforim, whose Yiddish and Hebrew fiction he celebrates in "Evaluation of Ourselves in Three Volumes," he mocks the Jews because they cry to God: "a people of faith is what this cursed people of tears is called." But, in truth, it is not faith that characterizes the Jews of the Pale: "Laziness and submission and depression in front of the great punisher who sits in the heavens, but not faith."[72] Judaism, this religion of complaint, says Brenner, is "a wound [*maka*—the word can also mean 'plague'] that is always bleeding."[73]

Judaism is tied to Brenner's other main target, one he shared with the earlier Haskalah, that is, the unproductive nature of the Jewish economy, which has left the Jews miserable and impoverished. Poverty has yielded not some higher morality but the opposite: the Jews are "stooped, bedraggled, depressed figures, placing all their faith in the psalms of David, the son of Jesse, king and poet of Israel. Which is more than the other: ugliness or immorality? Whether we like it or not, we are forced to say: there is too much of both of them at the same time!"[74] An earlier consensus held that the Jews built a spiritual nation after they lost their material one, that they represent a protest against materialism, and that they will survive no matter what. But Brenner will have none of it. The Jews survive, but at what price? Their survival is merely biological, like ants, as "gypsies, peddlers, traveling salesmen and bank clerks"; it is not a "sociological survival" that guarantees continuity from one generation to the next. On the contrary, these Jews leave nothing to inherit and nothing to pass on. If the rabbinic literature is their only inheritance, it would have been better if it had never been.[75]

Brenner goes so far as to express understanding for anti-Semites who accuse the Jews of using blood for ritual purposes. Against Ahad Ha'am, who wrote in denunciation of the modern revival of the "blood libel," Brenner argues that the accusation is not the cause of anti-Semitism but its result. Hatred of the Jews is a response to their foreignness and to their negative qualities, particularly their economic behavior. It is therefore based in reality.[76] The only problem with combating the blood libel, which Brenner obviously did not believe to possess any truth, is that it will blind people to the real faults of the Jews, which are the cause of hatred in the first place. If the tables were turned and others were like the Jews, he asks, wouldn't we have good cause to hate them as well?[77]

Only now, in the modern period, when the Jews no longer believe that they are the chosen people, has it become possible to listen unflinchingly to the accusations of the anti-Semites and affirm those that are correct. Here, in Brenner's brutal self-criticism, the implied political alliance that Herzl sought between Zionists and anti-Semites found its cultural and social analogue. Not for nothing have some critics discerned an almost anti-Semitic tone in the literary and political ideology of *shelilat ha-gola* ("negation of the Exile") with which Brenner's name is so intimately associated.

Brenner argues that if the Jews wish to survive, they must "become a chosen people, that is like all the other nations, each of which is chosen by itself."[78] Without explicitly invoking Spinoza, he seems to have had in mind something like what the Dutch philosopher meant. Only by embracing "normality" could the Jews be "chosen," that is, determining or choosing their own identity. And such normality requires a Jewish territory: "Now we live without an environment (*sevivah*). Totally without an environment. We need to start anew, to lay the first stone. . . . This is the question. In order that our character be changed as much as possible, we need our own environment; in order to create such an environment ourselves, our character must be radically changed."[79] A revolution required territory but a territory could not be won without a prior revolution. Those are the horns of the dilemma on which Brenner found himself impaled and that explain the despair and pessimism of his fiction, as expressed in the title of his most famous novel, *Breakdown and Bereavement*.

Unlike his compatriots, such as Ahad Ha'am, Bialik, and Berdichevsky, Brenner put forward no program for the future Hebrew culture. He was too wracked by the seemingly insurmountable problems of his generation. Literature, at best, could only serve the necessary role of self-criticism:

> The literature of self-criticism since Mendele says: Our function now is to recognize and admit our lack of pedigree since the beginning of history to the present day, all the faults in our character, and then to rise up and start all over again. . . . Logic will come and pose a puzzle: how can we become ourselves and not ourselves? But let logic argue what it may. Our urge for life, which stands above logic, says otherwise. Our urge for life says: All this is possible. Our urge for life whispers hopefully in our ear: workers' settlements, workers' settlements. Workers' settlements—this is our revolution. The only one.[80]

Only the practical "religion of labor" preached by Brenner's friend, Aaron David Gordon, a secular religion drawn in equal parts from Tolstoyan populism and Hasidic pantheism, could create a new culture based on a new Hebrew worker.[81] These Hebrews would be as distant from the religion of their fathers and mothers as from the Diaspora lands where that religion was practiced. For now (i.e., in 1914), the promise of this new secular religion remained at best a faint whisper.

It was in language that Brenner believed the seeds of this new religion might germinate. Here, too, his critique was scathing: "We, the Jews, are a nation without a language, and what makes the tragedy worse, almost without the need for a language. Our relationship to language is mechanical and not organic."[82] Unlike many of those who took up cudgels in the language wars between Hebrew and Yiddish, Brenner did not utterly reject the position of the other side. He believed, like Ahad Ha'am, that Hebrew lay at the vital core of Yiddish, but he admired Mendele for treating Yiddish not as a "jargon" but as a living language.[83] Many of his critical essays were devoted to works in Yiddish; he clearly appreciated the literary renaissance taking place in that language at a time that he was struggling to express his innermost feelings in the Hebrew that was not his mother tongue. It was, however, in Hebrew that a true secular Jewish culture could emerge. As he wrote in celebration of Bialik's poetry: "Just as language is not a mere garment for poetry, but instead its foundation, its essence, so it is not a national ornament or a national heritage for generations, but rather the foundation of nationalism for all the generations, the essence of nationalism."[84]

The radical nature of Brenner's critique of the Jewish religion found per-haps its most extreme expression in a controversy that broke out in 1911 over an article Brenner wrote anonymously about the ongoing wave of Jew-ish conversions to Christianity in Russia.[85] The importance of this con-troversy lies in defining where one believed the borders of the new Jewish culture should be drawn. Ahad Ha'am, for example, wrote against Brenner's article (without knowing at the time that Brenner was its author): "He who denies the God of Israel, the historical force that gave the nation life and in-fluenced its character throughout thousands of years can be a good person (*adam kasher*), but he cannot be a national Jew, even if he lives in the land of Israel and speaks Hebrew."[86] A Jewish Christian was an impossibility for Ahad Ha'am, and such a person had no place in the national renaissance.

But was it really impossible for a "national Jew"—and not a religious one—to affirm belief in Jesus? This was the issue that Brenner took up in his characteristically acerbic style. He expresses bafflement over the hul-labaloo in the Jewish press over the many young converts to Christianity. Much of this literature treated theological questions, as if to defend Judaism against Christian dogma. Brenner argues that the vast majority of Jews have no interest in theology and that those who convert to Christianity do so purely for material reasons. But these young Jews are no more satisfied with their spiritual life, since they recognize "the lack of a complete Hebrew lan-guage, the lack of a Hebrew homeland and the lack of a Hebrew culture."[87] By implication, if such a Hebrew culture existed and they lived in a Hebrew homeland, they might have no need to convert.

Religion with all its vanities and dissonances, Brenner argues, is noth-ing but a part of life that human beings created as a result of economic and national human conditions. Religion comes and goes, takes on new forms, is born and dies. Christianity, as we know it today, "the Roman, the pagan, the inquisitional, that suppressed exalted Greek philosophy . . . hangs from the tree of the miserable Jew, Joshua of Nazareth—but is there any similarity between them?"[88] Note that Brenner deliberately refers to Jesus, not by the name "Yeshu" traditional to Jewish culture, but by the far more neutral "Joshua." The disparity between historical Christianity and its founder is no different than the disparity between historical Judaism and its biblical origins.

In the "Brenner Affair," Christianity became a symbol for whether Jew-ish culture would be bounded by religion alone. For Brenner, secular Jews had no dog in the fight over who was the Messiah, since they did not believe in messiahs sent by Gods from elsewhere. Thus, for a Jew to affirm that Jesus was a Jew was a paradoxical way of using the religion of the Other to assert a secular identity. And in challenging those like Ahad Ha'am who denounced these conversions, Brenner was staking out a radically new claim about Jewish identity: it was an individual decision one made about what religion if any to follow, and as such, it had no bearing on one's national identity. The latter, for Brenner, was primarily linguistic, and he was prepared to welcome to it anyone who wished to join, regardless of his or her religious preference.

Chaim Zhitlowsky: Yiddish as a Secular Identity

Brenner was not alone in staking out such a radical position on Christianity. Several years before he wrote his notorious article, a similar "crucifix question" (*tzeylem frage*) enraged the world of Yiddish letters, demonstrating that the same cultural questions crossed the linguistic barricades.[89] The debate took place in 1908 in the pages of the short-lived Yiddish periodical *Dos naye Leben*, edited by Chaim Zhitlowsky (1865–1943), one of the leading ideologues of the secular Yiddishist movement. Zhitlowsky had provoked the conflict by publishing stories by Lamed Shapiro and Sholem Asch that used Christian imagery in ways never seen before in Jewish fiction. He also appended his own review—a kind of extended "blurb"—of the stories in the same issue of the journal.

Zhitlowsky used the two stories as a vehicle for his own view of how Jews and Christians might reconcile under the umbrella of a humanist culture. This was, in fact, his central project: to construct a universal, socialist culture within which a secular Yiddish culture could also flourish.[90] Since Enlightenment universalism was the secular product of Western Christian culture, Jews must overcome their instinctive hatred of Christianity if they wish to join the modern world. The paradoxical path to Jewish secularization led through the Christian religion, not by conversion but by renouncing the Jewish religion's teaching of contempt. Yet, by reclaiming Jesus as one of their own, the Jews might argue that their culture was a key source for Western civilization. Jewish national pride could thus coexist with Enlightenment universalism.

Zhitlowsky's positive view of Christianity went back to his first written work in Russian, "Thoughts on the Historical Destiny of Judaism" (1887).[91] There, he rejected the traditional teaching of the chosen people in favor of the social and moral ideals of the Bible, which, he claimed implausibly, became the doctrine of the Second Temple Essenes. It was the Christians who inherited these ideals, while the Pharisees, responding to the destruction of the Temple, turned toward "religion" in place of ethical idealism. The essence of the Bible was not religion, therefore, but instead values that might be co-opted for a secular program of social revolution. Prefiguring the later debate over conversion, Simon Dubnow attacked Zhitlowsky's attempt at a rapprochement between Second Temple Judaism and Christianity as an invitation to Jews to abandon Judaism.

Like Brenner, Zhitlowsky was willing to accept Jews who converted to Christianity as part of the "spiritual Jewish national home"—as long as they spoke Yiddish.[92] This idiosyncratic position points to several crucial signposts of his philosophy: rejection of the Jewish religion in favor of a secular definition of Jewish identity, the search for a synthesis between universalism and nationalism, and above all, the central role of the Yiddish language. His goal was to create a secular space between the extremes of assimilation and Zionism, since he believed that the Jewish religion could not ensure national survival.

Zhitlowsky's own biography is replete with similar idiosyncrasy. Like his boyhood friend S. Ansky (1863–1920), who was his main opponent in the "crucifix debate," Zhitlowsky was raised in an Orthodox milieu in White Russia, but he journeyed through the Haskalah to revolutionary socialism. However, unlike others who abandoned any Jewish identity when they embraced revolutionary politics, Zhitlowsky, again like Ansky, returned to his people and advocated a number of specifically Jewish positions. To follow his political biography is often bewildering since, at one time or another, he embraced Russian populism, socialism, Bundism, leftwing Zionism, autonomism, and—in the last decade of his life—even Soviet Communism. As a believer in the peasantry as the source of revolution, his brief membership in the Bund came to an end with the emphasis of the Jewish Worker's Union on the urban proletariat. On the other hand, he was briefly enthusiastic about Zionism for its effort to create a Jewish peasant class in Palestine but, like Bernard Lazare, criticized Theodor Herzl for relying too much on capitalists.[93]

If there was any common thread to his political peregrinations, then, it was his belief in the peasantry as the motor of socialism, a stance he adopted in his youth under the influence of the Narodniki, the Slavophilic movement that tried to "go to the people." Zhitlowsky subsequently became one of the founders of the Social Revolutionary Party, which was the successor to the earlier populist movement. He believed initially that the Jews must become peasants in Russia and find common cause with Russian peasants, a doomed project, but one that attracted some short-lived support.

Although Zhitlowsky was a tireless advocate for socialism in both its universal and Jewish forms, his importance lies more in promoting secular Yiddish culture. When he came to New York in 1904 and gave his first speech, he electrified the crowd with his rich language and rapidly became the most popular speaker in front of Yiddish audiences.[94] For Zhitlowsky, Yiddish was the quintessential national language of the Jews. The other languages used by eastern European Jews, especially Russian and Hebrew, did not address the concerns of the folk and, moreover, wittingly or not, promoted assimilation.[95] He envisioned a full national culture in Yiddish, which, as opposed to Hebrew, had primarily secular connotations:

> We hope that the Yiddish language, which is to us as dear and holy as German is to the Germans, Russian is to the Russians and Hebrew to the old-fashioned Jews, will become richer in words and expressions. . . . Only when Yiddish literature becomes rich in books and in all branches of science will the new generation not have to look for knowledge among the foreign peoples. . . . Everything [the Jews] will achieve in art and science will be brought out in Yiddish, and Yiddish culture and Yiddish education will grow continuously and will become a formidable force that will bind together as one not only the educated people with the folk, but also all Jews from all countries.[96]

Yiddish would unify the nation, the role the Zionists foresaw for Hebrew (it is an ironic fulfillment of Zhitlowsky's prophecy that Moroccan Jews studying in Lithuanian yeshivot in Israel today learn to speak Yiddish). Zhitlowsky also envisioned the creation of Jewish universities that would be conducted in Yiddish, again a parallel to Zionist aspirations. In addition, because Yiddish, unlike Hebrew, was a partially European language, it could serve as the essential bridge between Jewish nationalism and European cosmopolitanism.

Zhitlowsky makes it clear that Yiddish literature is not just anything written in the Yiddish language. Yiddish literature is *any* literature written by Jews, including both religious literature, like the Bible, and modern scientific literature. This claim was made possible by the multivalent meaning of the word "Yiddish" as both the fusion language spoken by eastern European Jews *and* the adjective "Jewish." Thus, at the 1908 Yiddishist conference in Czernowitz, Zhitlowsky gave a fiery address in which he advocated translating Jewish religious texts into Yiddish in order create a secularized, national literature available to the masses.[97] Like Bialik's *Sefer Ha-Aggadah*, this call was very much in line with other nineteenth-century projects of turning historical traditions into national treasures.

A good example of what Zhitlowsky had in mind for how a secular Yiddish culture might appropriate the religious tradition is his reading of the biblical book of Job.[98] He understood the book as antireligious, a critique of the Bible's conventional ideas of divine justice, an interpretation similar to the one I suggested in chapter 2 and to that of Bernard Lazare discussed in chapter 3. Since there is no biblical doctrine of life after death, one must acquiesce in death as an act of divine justice. Job revolts against this view, seeing himself as a lonely individual facing a meaningless death. Job thus foreshadows modern man, since the book champions individualism and also, in places, suggests that human powers rival God's.[99] It is specifically in the realm of morality that human beings demonstrate their autonomy, since there are no ethics grounded in God. Job offers a new, unconditional moral code: "love your neighbor as yourself" (although the phrase is not actually found in Job). For Job, God exists and is manifest in the grandeur of creation, but this has nothing to do with morality. Zhitlowsky explicitly compares this view to Nietzsche's *Beyond Good and Evil*. Job is thus revealed as a precursor to modern, radical secularists, who share with him the sense that only humans are responsible for social justice.

Zhitlowsky proposes that, like his reading of Job, traditional religious symbols and rituals be subjected to "scientific criticism" that will turn them into secular symbols and rituals.[100] This process of secularization, like Bialik's appropriation of the religious tradition, is a product of the dialectical development of modern Jewish history. The first stage in the modern period Zhitlowsky labels that of the *apikoros*, the heretic who rebels from within but who leads many other Jews to the European Enlightenment. The Jewish form of Enlightenment accomplished something decisive by relegating religion to the private sphere, but it opened the door to assimilation. The second stage was that of the *baal teshuva*, the romantic return to religion. This stage is similar to Slavophilism and Teutomania; Zhitlowsky dubs it "Judeomania." He has some sympathy with this movement, since he understands that the Jewish religion played a key role in national survival. But in a secular age, it can no longer do so, and Judeomania must give way to its successor, Yiddish culture, which will put new wine in old bottles. Since Yiddish culture is secular, it will keep religion private, but by reinterpreting religion in secular terms, it will avoid the pitfalls of Judeomania.

Zhitlowsky calls the third stage in his historical scheme "the poetic-nationalist renewal of the Jewish religion." By "poetic-nationalist," he means secular. The Passover, for example, stripped of all its divine miracles, now becomes the story of national self-liberation. The holiday of Sukkot, consonant with Zhitlowsky's agrarian socialism, needs to return to its biblical roots as an agricultural festival. But the holiday also shows that Judaism is a culture with a big tent (the *sukka*) that has space for all Jews: the Orthodox can wave the *lulav*, a Christian Jew can hang an icon of Jesus, a Sabbatian Muslim can read the Koran, an atheist can read Schopenhauer, and a pantheist (or Spinozist) can unite himself with the universal substance. In this ecumenical embrace, Zhitlowsky goes even further than he had in the "crucifix debate," including every kind of Jew (it is fascinating that the Dönmeh sect of Sabbatian Muslims in Turkey was still sufficiently active to merit inclusion).

However, one might wonder what exactly unites these disparate Jews who believe in all sorts of things, most of them antithetical to the religious tradition? Here, Zhitlowsky at times veered toward a quasi-racial definition of Jewish identity based on his reading of contemporary science. He was an enthusiastic popularizer of modern science in Yiddish and wrote lengthy essays explaining Darwin and Einstein, among others, to his readers. In a long, theoretical treatise, "What Is a Nation?" he argues that the contemporary biological theory of race cannot adequately explain nations.[101] After all, the "Aryan" race contains different nations, each with its own characteristics. The theory of the nation must take into account the impact of nature upon culture. Just as the more one plays music, the more one becomes attuned to music, so the more a nation is forced to respond to particular natural stimuli, the more their innate character will consist of this characteristic. Without mentioning the name of Lamarck, Zhitlowsky appears to endorse the inheritance of acquired characteristics: "the more mysterious the process may be, the more its traces are passed by inheritance from one generation to the next."[102] This process creates much more productive combinations than the random effects of nature, thus putting Zhitlowsky in seeming opposition to Darwin but in some relation to Freud.

In an essay from the late 1920s, "Jews and Jewishness," Zhitlowsky applies these ideas to the Jews.[103] In his desire to create a secular identity, he flirts with a racial definition in which certain innate characteristics, acquired throughout history, are passed down in the blood. The Jewish quality of mercy, for example, is not derived from the Jewish religion but is instead part of this innate character for which he used the term *Yiddishkayt*. This "Jewishness" is different from Judaism, even though it contains the religion signified by the latter term. This idea of a "Jewish sensibility" allows him to attribute Jewish characteristics to movements like Marxism and psychoanalysis: even when Jews like Marx no longer considered themselves Jewish, they could not help importing an innate Jewish ethos to their universalist philosophies.

Matthew Hoffman has pointed out how Zhitlowsky's secular concept of *Yiddishkayt* is quite similar to the popular concept, derived from Hasidism, of *dos pintele Yid*, the "quintessential Jew." Jewish folk tradition thus already contained the concept of a Jewish essence outside of religion. Indeed, the nineteenth-century ultra-Orthodox Hungarian rabbi Akiva Schlesinger argued that beyond the traditional realm of the halakhah lay the category of "Jewishness" (*yahadus*—here the Hebrew equivalent of *Yiddishkayt*) which he contrasted with "gentileness" (*goyus*): these were no longer mere religious categories, but instead something like essential national or ethnic characteristics.[104] Thus, in his ostensibly secular category of *Yiddishkayt*, Zhitlowsky created a strange marriage between secular-scientific ideas of race and notions of a Jewish essence already circulating in the world of Orthodoxy.

The irony of Zhitlowsky's position lies in the term *Yiddishkayt* that he employs as the ostensibly eternal essence of Jewishness. This innate and permanent trait ought to persist even after one leaves the traditional world. Yet it was precisely the Yiddish language, which Zhitlowsky placed at the center of his philosophy as the carrier of *Yiddishkayt*, that vanished so quickly in the twentieth century. Despite his episodic use of racial arguments, Zhitlowsky's nationalism was grounded in contingent cultural forces.[105] Once the conditions for a culture's existence disappeared, the culture itself could not survive. Zhitlowsky himself can be forgiven for not foreseeing such a development. He died in 1943, just as the Holocaust was consuming the vast majority of Yiddish speakers and, with it, much of the culture on which he had based his ideology.

American Crucible

Zhitlowsky settled for good in the United States in 1908 and remained there until his death in 1943. As Tony Michels has shown, he was one of the catalysts, along with Abraham Cahan (the storied editor of the Yiddish daily *Forverts*) and other lesser known writers and activists, for the socialist Yiddish culture that dominated Jewish life for the first decades of the twentieth century.[106] By wedding Yiddish with radical politics, these intellectuals believed that they were riding the wave of history that would lead at once to a socialist utopia and a solution to Jewish marginalization.

⌐ Since the Jewish immigrants from the Russian Empire were typically more willing than those who remained behind to abandon the religious tradition and embrace new values as they entered the American working class, America became the main site for the new Yiddishist politics and culture at the fin de siècle. Where radical politics had to be carried on in secret and even cultural activity was subjected to censorship in the Russian Empire, America provided a free arena and a ready audience for both. It was, in fact, for this reason that Zhitlowsky, followed later by the great Yiddish writer Sholem Aleichem, saw New York as the secular Promised Land. Only in the interwar period did rival centers of secular Jewish culture spring up in the Soviet Union, Poland, and Palestine (Stalin ultimately destroyed the first and Hitler the second; only the last remained as a competitor to its American cousin).⌐

The fate of this culture in America was not, however, what its founders envisioned. Political repression in the 1920s and again in the 1950s, as well as the attraction of the Democratic Party under Franklin D. Roosevelt during the Great Depression, pushed Jews—and others too—away from revolutionary politics and toward ameliorative liberalism. Since the Yiddishist culture of the immigrant period was so closely tied to political radicalism, the waning of the latter clearly weakened the former. But Americanization accomplished the rest. If secular Yiddish culture and politics had initially served as vehicles toward an American identity, they were increasingly seen by the next generations as roadblocks. In retrospect, the ideology that Zhit-lowsky preached lasted only two generations before it dissipated and became fully American. Of course, it had lasting impact on both American politics and culture, as Jews continued to espouse a progressive politics out of sync with their class status and as many of the themes and locutions developed initially in Yiddish were translated into English. And the dominant secularism incubated in Yiddish continued in new forms among American Jews, of whom nearly 50 percent in the year 2000 still identified as "secular," a number about twice the average in the American population as a whole.

The translation into English of the ideas of Zhitlowsky and his comrades produced a peculiarly American form of Jewish secularism. The constitutional mandate separating church and state found many of its greatest adherents among secular Jews, who had much to gain from relegating religion to the private sphere. Many such Jews advocated the "melting pot" theory of America.[107] The crucible of America would melt all of the immigrant cultures and create a new alloy, greater—and different—than the sum of its parts. This new American culture would not be religious or, for that matter, ethnic; it would be united by a common citizenship rather than by origin or belief.

As we saw in the previous chapter, it was the English Jewish writer, Israel Zangwill who popularized the phrase "melting pot" in his play of that name. But just as Zangwill's views of Jews as a race were highly ambiguous, so, too, the way he described the melting pot yielded contradictory results. On the one hand, the play seems to advocate intermarriage as the road to Americanization. On the other hand, Zangwill surreptitiously makes this argument, not so much by stripping his Jewish characters of their Jewish characteristics as by making America more Jewish. Thus, for example, the feisty Irish house servant, who initially denounces Jewish religious practices in virtually anti-Semitic terms, ends up speaking Yiddish and celebrating Purim. Despite its title, *The Melting Pot* actually treats the Jews as the model toward which this new America would aspire; its assimilationist message contains an undercurrent of Jewish ethnic pride. Jews, it transpires, are not just any immigrant group but the quintessential Americans.

Zangwill's play spawned immediate, as well as longer-term, responses from Jews and others. Within a year of the play's first production, Judah L. Magnes, the eloquent New York rabbi and follower of Ahad Ha'am, preached that "America is not the melting pot. It is not the Moloch demanding the sacrifice of national individuality. The symphony of America must be written by the various nationalities which keep their individual and characteristic note, and which sound this note in harmony with their sister nationalities."[108]

A more sustained response came from the Jewish social thinker Horace Kallen, who published a series of articles in 1915 in *The Nation* titled "Democracy versus the Melting Pot."[109] Kallen argued that the melting pot could only be achieved by the violation of democratic principles, that is, by coercing the immigrants to accept Americanization and by forbidding the expression of their original cultures. Kallen advocated instead what he called "cultural pluralism." Also invoking the metaphor of a symphony, Kallen envisioned the United States as a "democracy of nationalities," united politically, with English as its common language, but in which each nationality would cultivate its own dialect of English under the influence of its native culture. Kallen's essay clearly reflected the cultural reality of the immigrant period, when it was hard to imagine immigrants freely giving up or even inevitably losing their ethnic identities. Yet, as opposed to the Yiddishists, he believed that the cultures of the immigrant groups would find expression in English.

Kallen's primary example of an ethnic group with a strong cultural heritage was the Jews. Both the persistence of anti-Semitism and the dynamic character of Jewish culture in America seemed to suggest to him that Jews would remain an identifiable group: "Of all group-conscious peoples they are the most group-conscious. . . . [O]nce . . . the Jewish immigrant takes his place in American society a free man . . . and an American, he tends to become rather the more a Jew."[110] Kallen's theory of immigration, based largely on his observation of the Jews, argued that after an initial period of attempting to assimilate, the immigrant group discovers its "permanent group distinctions" and is "thrown back upon . . . [its] ancestry." At this stage, "ethnic and national differences change in status from disadvantages to distinctions."[111] It is American democracy that allows this flourishing of ethnic cultures. Toleration of cultural and ethnic differences flows directly from the federalist principles on which America was founded. For Kallen, cultural pluralism was much truer to American ideals than the totalizing ideology of Americanization.

⌈Cultural pluralism, in Kallen's account, was based on the involuntary influence of ethnicity. As he wrote in a much quoted passage: "Men may change their clothes, their politics, their wives, their religions, their philosophies, to a greater or lesser extent; they cannot change their grandfathers."[112] Blood, and not culture, is the foundation of identity. To force the immigrants to Americanize would be counterproductive since their very sense of self would be destroyed: a new culture would be grafted onto them without a new identity. ⁊

The intrinsic difficulty with Kallen's position, at least in the 1915 essays, is that it attributes autonomous power to ethnic or racial origin, as one of his critics, Isaac Berkson pointed out.[113] For Kallen, culture, as opposed to ethnicity, is an epiphenomenon that can be changed. But if an ethnic culture changes so much that it no longer resembles its origins, what would be the meaning of an identity based solely on one's ancestry? Kallen himself was later to recognize the problems in his original position, and he took pains to distance himself from a racial definition of identity.[114]

Arguably the most influential and prolific theoretician of a new Jewish culture in America was Mordecai Kaplan. Kaplan published his magnum opus, *Judaism as a Civilization*, in 1934, just over a half century after the mass Jewish immigration to America from eastern Europe first began. With immigration now effectively ended by the quota law of 1924 and the coming of age of a generation of English-speaking Jews, the time had arrived to formulate a vision of Jewish culture appropriate to the new American reality. For many of Kaplan's readers, the Jewish religion was part of a larger ethnic culture rather than a separate belief system. To be Jewish meant to speak "Jewish," to associate with Jews, and to practice behaviors that one thought of as common to Jews. For the immigrant generations, one could shed the religious commandments without shedding one's ethnic or cultural identity.

It was this cast of mind that Kaplan theorized in *Judaism as a Civilization*. To be sure, he insisted that he was not a secularist and explicitly distinguished his "religious culturalism" from "secular culturalism."[115] Yet his claim that Judaism is a civilization and not just a religion, combined with his naturalistic theology and rejection of the idea of the chosen people, brings his thought in close proximity to secularism. Deeply influenced by cultural Zionism, Kaplan might be seen as an American avatar of Ahad Ha'am in his claim that the Jews are essentially defined by peoplehood.[116]

Kaplan characterizes civilization as "that nexus of a history, literature, language, social organization, folk sanctions, standards of conduct, social and spiritual ideals, esthetic values which in their totality form a civilization."[117] Religion, which in Kaplan's vocabulary is limited to doctrinal issues or matters of belief, is therefore secondary to the "folkways" of a civilization. He even considers the 613 commandments to fall under the category of folkways rather than religion. Only by conceiving of Judaism as a civilization could the modern crisis of Judaism be solved by reinforcing a sense of otherness, which, in Kaplan's vocabulary means a sense of difference more essential than religion.

America, he says, may provide the most fertile soil for retaining Jewish otherness. Following Kallen, he suggests that America will never become the kind of monolithic nation-state envisioned by French revolutionary republicanism, since American Catholicism incites a militant Protestant reaction. This rivalry between a Protestant majority and a Catholic minority will both keep America a Christian nation and prevent the full assimilation of the Jews. In other words, the cause of Jewish separatism is furthered by Catholic separatism: the Catholic Church is the unwitting handmaiden of the Jews! Where others might decry the forces of anti-Catholicism, which were also typically anti-Semitic, Kaplan sees a virtue: "perhaps America is destined to depart from the strict logic of democratic nationalism and to achieve a new cultural constellation in which historical civilizations, or churches, may be permitted to conserve the finest products of their experience and contribute them to the sum total of American culture and civilization."[118] Kaplan's analysis reflects the realities of the interwar period in which anti-Catholicism was at least as strong as anti-Semitism. Although anti-Catholicism is now largely a thing of the past, Kaplan's vision was prophetic in several ways: he imagined what we would today call multiculturalism, and he envisioned the possibility that a Christian revivalism in America might ironically come to benefit the Jews.

The idea that American civilization could be shaped by the contributions of separate civilizations, such as that of the Jews, led Kaplan to argue for hyphenated identities in contemporary America. There should be no prohibition on adopting non-Jewish folkways, provided that this is a conscious and explicit process. He even welcomed intermarriage, provided the homes are Jewish and the children are given a Jewish upbringing: "It is only an openly avowed policy of this kind [i.e., an acceptance of mixed marriage] that can make the position of the Jews tenable in America. For nothing is so contrary to the ideal of cultural and spiritual cooperation as the unqualified refusal of one element of the population to intermarry with any other."[119] It is hard to reconcile this openness toward non-Jews with Kaplan's simultaneous argument for Jewish otherness.

In the end, though, Kaplan reinstates religion at the center of his philosophy. The divorce between modern civilization and religion is, at best, a temporary phenomenon; in the future, religion will again become central to civilization. To be sure, what Kaplan means by religion is idiosyncratic: it must be redefined to exclude the idea of a transcendent God. Kaplan's notion of God as the spirit of nature looks very much like Spinoza's, even though he hardly mentions the seventeenth-century heretic. For Kaplan, religion represents the "will to live." Redefined in this secular way, Judaism turns out to be the most "religious" of all religions and therefore the one best suited to animate American civilization in the future.

Despite this unexpected swerve toward religion, Kaplan's concept of a civilization, like Ahad Ha'am's cultural Zionism, was an attempt to reach beyond the religious tradition toward a more capacious vision of Jewish identity. Although the movement that Kaplan founded never achieved significant numbers, his understanding of Jewish culture in America is perhaps the closest to an umbrella theory for the striking varieties in that culture, from the Orthodox to the secular. Despite its claims of universality, Kaplan's Judaism has an American specificity. As opposed to Ahad Ha'am's view, this civilization expresses itself not in Hebrew or, for that matter, in Yiddish, but in English. Its very interaction with its surroundings is thematized by its language, which is not a fusion language like Yiddish, Ladino, or Judeo-Arabic but the language of the majority that the Jews must adopt, even if they bend it to their own uses. In this sense, English, like German for the Jews of pre-Nazi Germany, is akin to Greek in late antiquity: a language that the Jews spoke and wrote and in which they expressed their own culture.

American Jewish English is not a dialect, but it does reflect indirectly the legacy of the Yiddish spoken by the ancestors of most of its speakers, just as modern Hebrew has absorbed the Yiddish, Judeo-Arabic, and other languages spoken by immigrant Jews while transmuting these languages into something new. Similarly, the way a host of American Jewish writers, poets, and comedians have used English has both echoed and transformed the voices that make American Jews distinct in their larger culture. This English may therefore be said to be a Jewish language. In a real sense, the language wars of the early twentieth century were resolved not so much by the victory of Hebrew over the diasporic Jewish languages as by the replacement of the old Jewish languages with new ones. Hebrew itself has evolved so radically over the last century that some linguists prefer to call it "Israeli," suggesting its intimate connection to the state in which it resides.

The invention of new political, cultural, and ethnic definitions of the old community of Israel has been one of the greatest contributions of secular thinkers to modern Jewish identities. While some of these identities included elements from the Jewish religion, they often did so by transmuting their meaning into a national or cultural idiom. History, language, and the broader umbrella of culture now subsumed religion. The series of writers we examined—Ahad Ha'am, Bialik, Dubnow, Berdichevsky, Scholem, and Zhitlowsky—each found different ways of reinterpreting the past to point toward a secular present. This reinterpretation was accompanied by passionate campaigns for Hebrew or Yiddish as the language of secular Jewish culture. At the most extreme, Joseph Hayim Brenner exploded the dialectic, arguing for a complete divorce between the Jewish religion and contemporary Jews: the new Hebrew culture would reflect the pressing contemporary concerns of its members, not the concerns of the past. Israeli culture still owes much to Brenner and his secularist colleagues. In America, such radical secularism waned by the early postwar period, but as transformed by Horace Kallen, Mordecai Kaplan, and other creators of American Jewish culture, it continues to resonate into the twenty-first century.

Conclusion: God, Torah, and Israel

This book is based on a contrarian argument: that many of the most avowed critics of religion, those we call secularists, could never escape the tradition they overturn. At times, this debt to the past was conscious and explicit, as was certainly the case for Hayim Nahman Bialik or Gershom Scholem. At other times, it requires archaeological excavation to unearth, as with Theodor Herzl or Hannah Arendt. Others fall in between. Salomon Maimon, for example, adopted Maimonides as his namesake but often tried to hide the traces of his traditional education by ridiculing the world of his origins. Unraveling these subterfuges yields a complex pattern in which Maimon read medieval Jewish philosophy through Enlightenment eyes but also read the Enlightenment through Jewish eyes. Similarly, Sigmund Freud reread the Bible through his own version of the Enlightenment, but he too was not immune from reading the Enlightenment through Jewish eyes. Even that most radical of secularists, Joseph Hayim Brenner, could not avoid the rabbinic locutions he had drunk with his mother's milk. Jewish secularists—the subjects of this book, as opposed to mere secularists—are defined by this dialectic between modern rationalism and the Jewish tradition.

I have argued that Judaism, with its lack of a dogmatic theology, was perhaps more open to secular possibilities than, say, Christianity. It was not only the absence of theology, however, that prepared the ground for secularism but also important elements in the premodern tradition itself. I began this book by quoting Isaac Deutscher, who located the modern Jewish secularist in a tradition of heresies. The secularist who searches for a countertradition in which to situate him or herself might well find intellectual ancestors in Elisha ben Abuya, the rabbinic heretic, or Shabbtai Zvi, the seventeenth-century antinomian. Yet these historical heretics are not the only source for their modern heirs. Perhaps more significant are the canonical figures of the establishment tradition, like Moses Maimonides, who might also be turned into icons of secularism. Maimonides' powerful argument for God's utter transcendence could be stood on its head to deny the existence of such a remote deity. Thus, even strong theistic positions could feed their dialectical negation.

A major figure in this story has been Baruch/Benedictus Spinoza. That the seventeenth-century heretic is equally known by the Hebrew and Latin versions of his name tells us a great deal about his liminal status. His feet were planted in the soil of the medieval Jewish tradition while his arms reached for a world not yet born. Spinoza, as I have argued, would not have recognized the way later thinkers turned him into a forebear, the founder of Jewish secularism. But his ideas about God as nature, the Torah as a historical artifact, and Israel as a political nation resonated loudly in the various permutations of Jewish secular thought we have surveyed in these pages. Spinoza did indeed pioneer the alchemical transformations of these three cardinal religious categories into their secular equivalents.

The question of God, never a central Jewish concern in premodern times, loomed much larger in the modern period. Since the law assumed divine revelation, however, challenges to the law inevitably led to challenges to the God whom tradition believed to have been its source. Atheism, a mere theoretical possibility to the medieval mind, now became a real philosophical option. Inspired in part by Spinoza, several traditions of secular thought took up this challenge. There were those, such as the cultural critic and early Zionist, Max Nordau, or Sigmund Freud, who dismissed the existence of God *tout court* as a barbaric superstition ill suited to the modern mind. Freud, for one, reduced God to a psychological projection, the father transported to the heavens. But he nevertheless argued that it was Judaism, which had reduced God to a father and spoke of him as one, that prepared the ground for the psychoanalytic revelation of his absence.

Others preferred to retain theistic language for their own purposes. Those I have called "Spinoza's children"—Salomon Maimon, Heinrich Heine, Albert Einstein, and Leo Strauss—took the path of pantheism by infusing nature with divinity. Others, notably Bialik and Scholem, found powerful sources for the modern sense of God's absence in the medieval Kabbalistic tradition. This view may be considered a modern version of Gnosticism in which the *deus absconditus* remains inaccessible to human knowledge. For Bialik, God's absence turned the divine into death. Scholem, on the other hand, nourished the hope that traces of the hidden God might be found in the detritus of history. Finally, another strain of secular thought abandoned Jewish theism for paganism, a return to the ancient gods of Canaan. With this paganism, we come full circle back to pantheism, for these gods were preeminently the gods of nature.

No wrestling with God could ignore the book in which that wrestling first took place, the Hebrew Bible. Even within the Bible itself, contradictory voices challenge the fundamentalist idea that the text itself conveys a homogeneous message. The Bible is, in truth, a book of books. The rabbis added to this welter of voices with their own legal and legendary readings. But it was in the Middle Ages that Abraham Ibn Ezra and Moses Maimonides, to name the two important philosophers and exegetes whom we studied, prefigured modern historical criticism of the Bible with their very different but similarly radical biblical interpretations. The former pioneered an immanent exegesis that limited the knowledge contained in Scripture, while the latter, in his "reasons for the commandments," offered a historical reading of the sacrifices that looks uncannily modern.

Spinoza explicitly acknowledged his debt to Ibn Ezra, if not to Maimonides. But his decentering of the Bible from The Book to just *a* book laid the groundwork for all modern criticism. While Spinoza believed the Bible was thoroughly antiquated, he nevertheless opened the door for new ways of making it relevant. Whether as a source for Heine's politics of social justice, Freud's psychological Jew or Ben-Gurion's Jewish state, the Bible could be mobilized to do service outside the house of religion. The secular Jewish Bible was no longer Torah in the traditional sense, but it now served as the fount for a variety of modern political and cultural ends. Only the most hardened secularists, whether Nordau or Joseph Hayim Brenner, threw the book into the dustbin of history. But the very vehemence of their attack spoke volumes about the continued power of the ancient text.

Reconfiguring God and Torah led ineluctably to rethinking Israel. As a community that was historically at once an *ethnos*, a nation, and a state, in addition to the bearer of a religion, traditional definitions of Israel provided a firm historical basis for secular versions of the nation, whether racial or political. In addition, a group of medieval theorists—Maimonides, Moses Nahmanides, Solomon ibn Adret, and Nissim Gerondi—carved out a startling realm of secular law within the four cubits of the halakhah. Modern thinkers may have been ignorant of this tradition, but its very existence demonstrates that secular politics are not exclusively a modern invention.

Spinoza was, once again, a key figure in proposing that the true identity of Israel was not religious but political. He thought such politics thoroughly antiquated. But his modern successors thought otherwise. Moses Hess, an avowed disciple of Spinoza, linked Jewish nationalism to a quasi-racial definition of the Jews. So, too, did Vladimir Jabotinsky. Other Zionist thinkers—Herzl and Ben-Gurion—rejected such thinking, arguing instead for either anti-Semitism or the formation of a Jewish state as the factors that constituted the nation. Critics of political Zionism such as Bernard Lazare and Hannah Arendt, both of whom started as Zionists, offered their own versions of a secular political identity for the Jews, based on the poor sitting on Job's dung heap.

The fin de siècle was as much a time of cultural as it was political revolution. In addition to the various political definitions of Israel, the final chapter of this book examined the search for a secular Jewish culture, marked by debates over history and language. By finding the roots of this culture in history, secular thinkers grounded their contemporary innovations in a historical tradition. Whether that culture would find expression in Hebrew, Yiddish, or non-Jewish languages was a war waged on many fronts, but all the combatants agreed that language was an essential element in any secular culture as a substitute for religion. This war also had certain precursors in earlier periods of Jewish history, but never before had it been fought with such vehemence.

The search for a secular Jewish culture played out on different stages: Europe, Palestine, the United States, as well as North Africa and the Middle East. While the secular revolt against religion was a central chapter in the modernization of the Jews everywhere, it was not a uniform revolt. Its capital was in eastern Europe where the peculiar conditions of Jewish life under czarist oppression gave rise to a dichotomous division between Orthodox authorities and their opponents. While there were attempts at reform in the east, the hegemony of Orthodoxy spawned revolutionary secular alternatives. This internecine warfare gave rise in part to the Zionist movement, and it was in Israel that the religious-secular binary was to have its longest life, in large measure due to the surprising success of the Orthodox in controlling certain aspects of Israeli law. On the other hand, the eastern European Jewish immigrants who came to North and South America with secularism and socialism in their suitcases lost much of their militancy as integration and acculturation took hold. Especially in the United States, with its strong civic culture of religious pluralism, secularism began to dissolve as Jews entered the American mainstream.

For Jews elsewhere, the conflict was less vituperative than in eastern Europe. Although many central and western European Jews also embraced secularism, religious alternatives in the guise of Reform, as well as the emergence of a partially "neutral" non-Jewish society, moderated the bitter battle that was waged to the east. An interesting exception was France, where the Republican ideal of *laïcité* (an almost untranslatable term that means more than mere secularism) was closely linked to Jewish rights, especially after the Dreyfus Affair. For many French Jews, secularism associated with the French state became a powerful form of Jewish identity.

Finally, the Jews of North Africa and the Middle East underwent a different process of modernization, much of it mediated by both Western colonialism and European Jewish paternalism. Secular rebellion against tradition certainly took place in the Orient, but it was a relatively small elite that became modern. For the rest of these Jews, only evacuation from their ancestral homes—coerced and voluntary—in the 1950s and 1960s created the confrontation with modernity and secularism. For those who immigrated to the State of Israel, the face of secularism was Ashkenazi, and thus a new internal Jewish conflict broke out in which religious-secular and ethnic divides were mapped onto one another.

The trajectory of secularism thus changed according to the political and cultural climate in which the Jews found themselves. And processes of migration, whether from the countryside to the cities or from one continent to another, deflected this trajectory even further. Over the twentieth century, Jewish secularism mutated in response to the differing environments of Jewish life. What can we say about the legacy of these varied forms of the secular in the early twenty-first century, and what future directions might they take?

Epilogue: Legacy

⌈The rise of Jewish secularism was largely a story of the turn of the twentieth century. This secular "moment" in Jewish history had its precursors, as
this book has argued, and it is by no means entirely over. But for all of the
Jewish communities in which secular political, cultural, and philosophical
movements flourished, the great ideological struggles of a century ago have
been transformed and, in many cases, vanquished. Yet their legacy in the
form of cultural memory remains alive and not only within memory. On the
contrary, the concept of *legacy* suggests a memory that continues to haunt
its inheritors and to affect their beliefs and actions in conscious and unconscious ways.[1] That Jews throughout the world today are disproportionately
more secular than their Gentile neighbors in all the ways articulated in this
book is one piece of evidence of the ongoing nature of this legacy.⌉

Yet it would be a mistake to draw a direct line between the secularism
of the last fin de siècle and its more recent versions. It has been frequently
argued that we live in a "postsecular" age, meaning an age in which religion
and its negation are no longer polar opposites.[2] Religion is part and parcel
of the secular world in all of its aspects. Religion is permeated with the secular, just as the secular is permeated with religion. Nationalist movements
exhibit the characteristics of religions, while religious revivals often find
their expressions in political practice. The Enlightenment's claim to have
slain the gods appears increasingly hollow.

In the Jewish world, as well, the old dichotomies appear less set in stone.
Let us examine the two largest Jewish communities, first in the State of Israel and then in North America, to see how the themes propounded by the
thinkers treated in this book resonate in more recent years and where they
might go in the future. The founders of secular Hebrew culture would no
doubt have been surprised to discover that religion was flourishing in the
state created by the Zionist movement. Political sovereignty for the early
Zionists was intimately bound up with a secular alternative to the Jewish
religion. Such a cultural alternative, fueled by the phenomenal success of

modern Hebrew, has surely struck deep roots in the State of Israel. But even if the seminal Zionist thinkers—Herzl, Nordau, Ahad Ha'am, Berdichevsky, and Brenner—envisioned a Jewish state largely without religion, the ambiguous concept of a *Jewish* state has made it difficult ideologically, and not only practically, to effect a divorce between them. So, ironically, the state founded by the most radical secularists has turned out to enshrine religion in its laws of marriage, divorce, and inheritance as well as its public holidays. The definition of who is a Jew, which dictates who can be a citizen, also falls back on religious categories.

Thus, the secular revolution prophesied by modern Hebrew culture did not entirely reach its promised land. In the 1950s, the ultra-Orthodox rabbi Abraham Karelitz, also known as the Hazon Ish, met David Ben-Gurion and insisted that only the religious tradition can be considered a "full wagon." The phrase refers to a talmudic passage which rules that when a full wagon and an empty wagon meet on a narrow bridge, it is the full that must be given the right of way. At the time, confident that history was on his side, Ben-Gurion made certain concessions to the Orthodox in the belief that they were fossils about to disappear from the world. However, in the years since the Six-Day War, two powerful religious movements challenged the hegemony of secular Hebrew culture: the anti-Zionist ultra-Orthodox and the messianic religious Zionists. The first, benefiting from a high birthrate and from recruitment among Mizrahi Jews, and the second, riding the wave of religious fervor spawned by the conquest of the biblical Judea and Samaria, both argued that secular Zionism was culturally bankrupt, an empty wagon. Each for its own separate reasons believes that the tables have turned, and it is rather the secularists who are a passing aberration, a century-long deviation from the *longue durée* of Jewish history.

Not merely throwbacks to a premodern past, these religious movements are both creatures of and responses to modernity. If secularism was originally a reaction against religion, Orthodox Zionism, non-Zionism, and anti-Zionism are, as their names suggest, reactions to the dominant secular Israeli culture. Intent on negating the religious cultures of the Diaspora with a new and unitary Hebrew culture, the Zionist movement gave rise instead to unanticipated pluralism and diversity, not only of ethnicities but of religious expressions as well.

As a result of the persistence of orthodoxy and its political power, the secular culture that is otherwise dominant has an oppositional character:

it derives at least some of its meaning from rejecting theocratic politics. In this respect, one can draw a line from the eastern European Haskalah and nationalist writers of the nineteenth and early twentieth centuries to their spiritual descendents in the early twenty-first. Of course, the former were in the minority, while the latter are themselves the establishment. But one can still discern many of the mentalities and motifs of the founders of modern Hebrew culture in contemporary Israel.

Let us consider the response to this situation by several contemporary Israeli writers, each of whom has inherited in a different way the legacy of secular Zionism. Amos Oz, for example, has taken up the cudgels in defense of the secular tradition. In his book of encounters in post-1967 Israel, Oz devotes one chapter to the ultra-Orthodox anti-Zionists in the quarter of Jerusalem where he grew up: "In these neighborhoods where I was born and raised, the battle has been decided: Zionism has been repulsed, as if it had never been."[3] It was this world that Brenner, Berdichevsky, and Bialik had sought to banish forever: "In an eruption of rebellion and loathing, they portrayed this world as a swamp, a heap of dead words and extinguished souls. They reviled it and at the same time immortalized it in their books."[4] But, at least in this corner of Jerusalem and elsewhere in the land of Israel, the secular revolution has failed, and it failed, in part, because "you [that is, contemporary secular Jews] cannot afford to loathe this reality, because between then and now it was choked and burned, exterminated by Hitler," says Oz. The Holocaust forbids the kind of wholesale assault undertaken by the founding fathers of modern Hebrew culture, yet this resurgent Orthodoxy stands as a mortal threat to that culture. Oz cannot resist falling into language reminiscent of Brenner, language dangerously close to anti-Semitism: "Only Hitler and the Messiah are alive and well here, burning like twin pillars of fire above this swarming tuberous growth, which is practical, quick and clever . . . adding up its pennies."[5]

Oz undertakes to construct a renewed rationale for secular Zionist culture, arguing head-on against the notion that secularism is an empty wagon.[6] The culture of Israel, he says, has a kind of anarchistic core: "we don't want discipline." This resistance to authority and the desire for democratic pluralism are not just contemporary but derive from historical Judaism: "Democracy and tolerance are but expressions of a deeper matter: humanism, the essence of which is that the individual human being is always an end and never a means. This ideal is not a foreign body, nor an import; it flows from the core of Jewish civilization." If humanism and democracy are inherently Jewish, then their close cousin, secularism, must also be rooted in Jewish civilization. Oz's project is to wrest Judaism—the wealth of the historical Jewish tradition—from the rabbis and from religion.

The secular Israeli poet most in dialogue and disputation with the religious tradition was Yehuda Amichai (1924–2000).[7] Raised, like Bialik, in the Orthodox tradition, Amichai constantly contrasts traditional tropes with the contradictory reality of his own—and his people's—life. In the wake of the Holocaust and the wars of Israel, he cannot see the God of Israel as benevolent. Thus, in one of his most famous poems, *El Maleh Rahamim*, based on the prayer recited at funerals, he begins ironically:

> God Full of Mercy
> If God weren't so full of mercy
> There would be mercy in the world, and not just in Him.[8]

In another poem, the God of tradition with whom the poet struggles is a figment of man's own fabrication:

> I declare with perfect faith
> that prayer preceded God.
> Prayer created God.
> God created human beings,
> human beings create prayers
> that create the God that creates human beings.[9]

A central theme of Amichai's is that small, everyday realities are much "holier" than bombastic theology or ideology. He writes in a prose poem of pausing to rest by the walls of Jerusalem while bringing home a basket of groceries.[10] A group of tourists come and use him as a point of reference to look at an archway. The poet's response: "Redemption will come only when they are told, 'you see that arch from the Roman period? It doesn't matter, but near it, a little to the left and then down a bit, there's a man who has just bought fruit and vegetables for his family.'" The messianic age of the secular Jew is found not in the walls of Jerusalem or its Temple but in the simple act of putting food on the table. In this turn to the everyday and the individual, Amichai has realized the promise for Hebrew culture set forth by Brenner. Like Brenner, Amichai cannot divorce himself from the religious tradition that gives his secularity its language, but living in that culture of colloquial Hebrew that Brenner and Bialik created, he is able, perhaps much more than they, to write a poetry of the quotidian.

That one important work of the younger generation of Hebrew writers was by an Israeli Palestinian writer, Anton Shammas, is perhaps the best testimony to the secular revolution of Hebrew literature presaged by Brenner. Shammas chose to write his *Arabesques*, a major novel of the Palestinian experience, in Hebrew. To be sure, Brenner's own attitude toward the Arabs of the land was ambivalent, and he was ultimately murdered by some of them. But one wonders if he would not have celebrated three-quarters of a century later the fact that a non-Jew could write a compelling work in a "Jewish" language as a sign that secular Hebrew culture had finally cast off the parochialism of the religious tradition.

Shammas's intervention in what had seemed an intra-Jewish dialogue heralded a new movement, loosely called "post-Zionism," which seeks to turn Israel from a Jewish state into a state of all its citizens. The claim of the post-Zionists (and there is no uniform ideology that they all subscribe to) is that the secularism inherent in the original Zionist movement can only be realized when Israel gives up the last semblance of a religious identity and adopts a neutral category of citizenship. The post-Zionists also call into question the homogeneity of the category "Jewish." If the contemporary Jewish state has to contend with a significant minority of non-Jews—Palestinian Arabs, Russians, and foreign workers—it also has to confront the extraordinary diversity of its Jewish population. Israel might be a Jewish state according to some formal criteria, either religious or secular, but it is manifestly not the unitary ethnic state the founders of Zionism envisioned.

The most provocative theoretician of post-Zionism in terms of secular engagement with the religious tradition is the philosopher Adi Ophir. Ophir undertakes a thoroughgoing critique of theological texts and demonstrates how this religious discourse continues to reverberate in secular Israeli culture. He argues implicitly that the religious-secular dichotomy assumed by nearly everyone to be the fundamental divide going back to the origins of Zionism is, in fact, an illusion. Secular Zionism, even in its most liberal forms, has unconsciously taken over cardinal categories from Judaism and dressed them in secular, nationalist garb. Here, one might say, is a critique similar to Berdichevsky's attack on Ahad Ha'am a century earlier.

The most central categories, according to Ophir, are those of the Jew and the goy.[11] Or, rather, the two categories are really one since the Jew defines himself against the goy, who, in turn, has no independent existence outside of the dyad. This fundamental division goes back to the very beginnings of the Jewish religion, and although it assumed different forms throughout Jewish history, it remained essentially the same. The Zionists secularized and nationalized this binary, which led them to create an exclusionary state. We recall that Spinoza had argued similarly that the Jews preserved themselves after they lost their state by self-segregation, which in turn provoked the hatred of the non-Jews; because the Jews had survived in this fashion, they might in the future go on to regain political sovereignty. But Spinoza was clearly no more sympathetic to Jewish self-segregation than is Ophir. Indeed, Ophir's project may be seen as a working out of Spinoza's three-hundred-year-old argument.

One powerful example that Ophir gives for his thesis is the Passover Haggadah.[12] He shows that the Haggadah is the one text that unites both religious and secular in modern Israel, since an overwhelming majority of Israelis attend a Passover seder and read the text. He argues that the Haggadah's fundamental message is one of segregation: God "passes over" the houses of the Israelites to smite only the houses of the Egyptians. Liberated from oppression, the Jews are free to reverse the power equation and oppress others. If this was a revenge fantasy for several millennia, it has now become true in the State of Israel: the Israelis read the Haggadah no longer as the oppressed but as oppressors of both the Palestinians in the territories occupied in 1967 and those who are nominally Israeli citizens. Going a step beyond the theology of the Haggadah, Ophir argues that whereas in the religious tradition, it was God whose mighty arm intervened to save his people, in a time of secular nationalism, this role is played by the Israeli army—the worldly equivalent of divine wrath. Faith in arms now replaces faith in God, but the function of the one is the same as the other: to ensure that God's people will remain isolated from the everpresent threat of the goy.

Ophir's post-Zionism may be seen as an effort to realize the fundamental premise of Zionism itself: to "normalize" relations between Jews and non-Jews. Herzl's utopian novel, *Altneuland*, promised just such a normalization: the Arab in the Jews' state is a full-fledged citizen who praises the Zionists in perfect (if Berlin-accented) German. The Zionists, Ophir suggests, did not realize this revolutionary promise, which requires, in his view, not just a secularization of religious categories but their deconstruction from within. Ophir's secularism is therefore not like that of Herzl, whose ignorance of the Jewish tradition was matched only by his unwitting appropriation of its inner categories. Ophir, by contrast, constructs his position by a criticism of the tradition itself. Yet, one might say that just as the Jew requires the existence of the goy, so Ophir's secularism requires the existence of Judaism, either in its religious or secular Zionist forms. Exactly what positive content it has on its own remains unclear.

Ophir's avowedly secular engagement with the religious tradition demonstrates that the specter of that tradition continues to haunt those who contest its fundamental truths. Like Ophir, young secular Israelis have been turning in increasing numbers to the study of traditional texts. Secular *batei midrash* (houses of study)—Elul and Alma to name two—have sprung up since the 1990s. Similarly, the Orthodox practice of studying all night on the holiday of Shavuot (known in Hebrew as *tikkun layl Shavuot*) has become a popular custom among some secular Israelis as well. Coinciding roughly with the rise of post-Zionism, these nonacademic institutions and activities reflect a desire to wrest the tradition away from the Orthodox and make it the patrimony of all Jews. If the secular-religious divide was the product of Zionism and all its precursors, these new secular students of the rabbis are challenging the very binary. Whether or not this relatively small phenomenon signals a movement of real significance, it does demonstrate that secularism in Israel is not always driven by Brenner's renunciation of anything smacking of the religious tradition. It is rather the indirect legacy of Ahad Ha'am who also wanted to take back the tradition from the rabbis.

Turning now to the American Jewish community, we find a different history of secularism since the turn of the twentieth century. Whereas the dialectic of secularism and religion in Israel owes a great deal to the persistence of rabbinic authority, the lack of rabbinic power in America has created a different dynamic. Since Alexis de Tocqueville's *Democracy in America*, it has been a commonplace to observe that America's separation of church and state has created the most religious society of any modern country. Civil society teems with religious diversity, including the constant creation of new religions. Jewish Americans have benefited greatly from this peculiar form of secularism. With the state as guarantor of religious freedom and tolerance, the Jews too have innovated and adapted their religion in the New World.[13] As opposed to its eastern European and Israeli variants, Orthodoxy has to compete with a marketplace of religious alternatives, not only with secular ones.

The majority of this community derives from the great migration of 1881–1924. It therefore mirrors chronologically the State of Israel's founding generations, who also fled eastern Europe during the same time period. The generation (or generations) of immigrants often cast off religion and embraced progressive politics and a secular Jewish culture, as we saw in chapter 4. The next generation, in its passage from the cities to the suburbs, frequently turned back to religion, finding its Jewish identity in the synagogue. Thus, in 1955, Will Herberg could describe the Jews as the third leg in the American religious tripod: Protestant, Catholic, Jew.[14] A full embrace of America seemed to require turning Judaism into primarily a religion.

Yet just as religion was never absent in the first generation, neither was secular culture in the second. The political and cultural legacy of the immigrants persisted, even as it was translated from Yiddish to English. A wonderful passage from Philip Roth's *The Plot Against America* captures the sense in which the generations born in America came to be associated with a secular, ethnically inflected English:

> Their being Jews didn't issue from the rabbinate or the synagogue or from their few formal religious practices. . . . Their being Jews didn't even issue from on high. . . . These were Jews who needed no large terms of reference, no profession of faith or doctrinal creed, in order to be Jews, and they certainly needed no other language—they had one, their native tongue, whose vernacular expressiveness they wielded effortlessly and, whether at the card table or while making a sales pitch, with the easygoing command of the indigenous population. . . . Their being Jews issued from their being themselves, as did their being Americans.[15]

For these Jews, so accepting of their Jewish identities in an entirely secular sense, American English had become a thoroughly Jewish language, Jewish in the sense that it was how they expressed who they were.

Moreover, the postwar appropriation of religion was not only religious. The tradition served as a source for secular expressions as well. Thus, as Hana Wirth-Nesher has noticed, the kaddish, the traditional prayer for the dead, appears frequently in the secular culture produced by American Jews.[16] The most renowned of these appropriations is probably Allen Ginsburg's beat-generation poem "Kaddish" (1960), written three years after the death of his mother. Ginsburg was famously a Buddhist and he seemingly equates the "Hebrew Anthem" with "the Buddhist Book of Answers." But it is to the kaddish that he turns when thoughts of death—his mother's, his own, the planet's—come to mind. Ginsburg evokes his mother's experience as an immigrant, and the poem thus becomes an elegy for the transformative movement in American Jewish history from immigrant to native culture.

Other works conjure differently with the kaddish. Charles Reznikoff's poem of the same name from 1942 is a call for identification with the weak and for social justice, while Leonard Bernstein's *Kaddish* Symphony was dedicated to the memory of the recently assassinated John F. Kennedy. Only Leon Wieseltier's *Kaddish* truly comes to grips with the historical and textual resonances of the prayer.[17] Occasioned by the death of Wieseltier's father, who was a Holocaust survivor, the book is at once a work of historical scholarship and a personal spiritual meditation. As such, one might argue that it walks the fine line between religion and secularism, a line that has often become fuzzy in the recent history of American Jewish culture.

Why is the kaddish is so frequently invoked in works of American Jewish artists and writers? Could it be the long shadow of the Holocaust, which has become a kind of secular religion of the American Jews? But with the exception of Wieseltier's book, the various works cited here, as well others, such as Tony Kushner's play *Angels in America*, do not explicitly invoke the Shoah. Perhaps instead, since a secular culture may not provide the tools with which to confront death—the death of individuals and the death of a lost European culture—even the most secular Jews turn to this quintessential expression of religious tradition to mine its historical associations for nonreligious ends.

With the rise of ethnicity and multiculturalism in the late 1960s, the third generation of Jews returned, often nostalgically, to an earlier self-definition as a people. This shift was also influenced by the post-1967 identification with Israel, which prompted many to see themselves as part of a nation rather than only a religion. Here, one might find the residue of Ahad Ha'am's idea of Zion as a cultural center radiating its light upon the Diaspora, although it was Israel as a state rather than Hebrew culture that had the greatest resonance for American Jews. None of the theoreticians of secular Zionism quite anticipated this effect of a Jewish state: not Herzl, who mistakenly thought it would end anti-Semitism, and not Ben-Gurion, who also mistakenly thought it would bring about the ingathering of all the exiles.

As the cultural critic Andrea Most suggests, this third generation might be labeled "modern" because "they believe that a wholeness once existed that has since been shattered . . . and [they have] a lingering faith in the possibility of repairing the fragmentation of modernity."[18] This drive to recover a lost culture might take religious forms, such as Jewish Renewal, or equally secular forms, through fiction, theater, and film. In the San Francisco Bay Area, for example, a highly unaffiliated Jewish community attends its annual film festival in greater numbers than the total average weekly attendance in synagogues. Of course, the audience for this film festival overlaps to some degree with those who do attend synagogue, but that is exactly the point: secular and religious expressions of Jewish culture are no longer so easily separable.

The explosion of interest in academic Jewish studies—virtually every American university and college now has at least one professor in the field—is another example of the overlap between the religious and the secular. It has been estimated that some 40 percent of Jewish university students take at least one course in Jewish studies. As an academic discipline, Jewish studies, the heir to the historical scholarship pioneered by Baruch Spinoza, uses thoroughly secular methods, even when it takes up religious texts or is taught by an observant teacher. A secular approach to such texts may, at times, produce conclusions radically antithetical to those of the mainstream religious tradition. For example, some who study the Talmud, the quintessential religious text, find in it a source for something as antitraditional as gay rights. Like secular Hebrew culture in Israel, where academic Jewish studies has less of a mass impact, the field can provide a way of partaking in Jewish culture without necessarily subscribing to the religion of Judaism.

The academic and lay interest in Spinoza, discussed in chapter 1, is itself an expression of Jewish studies. Rebecca Goldstein's popular book on Spinoza opens with the author, raised Orthodox and later trained in academic philosophy, describing how her Orthodox day school teacher warned the students about the dangers of reading the seventeenth-century heretic.[19] Spinoza thus retains the same fascination and the same absolute threat to religion that he had for Salomon Maimon in the eighteenth century and Leo Strauss in the 1920s. Goldstein's own path to philosophy seemingly begins with this threat of heresy. As someone who teaches Spinoza regularly, I can confirm Goldstein's account: undergraduate students of every sort of background find him exceptionally riveting. Spinoza's mesmerizing power clearly stems from the fact that the battle between religion and secularism is still joined.

The present generation, roughly the fourth in American Jewish history, is now in the process of redefining this battle. Lacking their parents' anxieties over anti-Semitism and assimilation, these Jews are often alienated from the focus on intermarriage, continuity, and synagogue membership, as well as from the travails of the State of Israel. This generation, which has been labeled "postmodern," often regards identity as constructed and malleable: there is no such thing as an "essential" Jewishness—racial, religious, political, ethical, or otherwise. Everyone, and not just converts, is a "Jew by choice," and the meaning of "Jewish" is fluid and often situational. The old categories of "religious" and "secular" are therefore no longer fixed. One might experiment with religious ritual one day and take up social activism the next.

It is significant that some of the acclaimed authors of this generation, such as Shalom Auslander and Nathan Englander, are Jews who grew up Orthodox but now write about that world from the outside.[20] Their ironic, at times comic, distance from religion is somewhat reminiscent of the Haskalah and turn-of-the-century Hebrew and Yiddish literatures, which often used satire to pillory the world of the rabbis. Auslander in particular is at war with the God of his father. But where those nineteenth-century writers had nowhere to flee—and therefore searched for utopian addresses in Zion or elsewhere—the fallen Orthodox Jews of today have a whole secular world at their fingertips. Late-twentieth-century American secularism may present its own challenges, but they are fundamentally different from those of a century and more ago. By writing about religion from a stance that is both inside and outside, these writers only complicate the line between them.

And, finally, for contemporary American Jews, Jewish identity is but one identity among many. The postmodern turn in contemporary Jewish culture is quintessentially "anti-essentialist" and therefore open to plurality of new possibilities. Fluidity is itself a sign of secularism, since its opponent—religion— demands binary divisions: us versus them, with no grey area in between. Intermarriage is the most visible sign of this fluidity, but it is a fluidity that challenges religion on many levels, including the Orthodox.

We recognize in this challenge the same issues raised a century ago by advocates of secular Jewish culture like Zhitlowsky and Brenner. Zhitlowsky's "big sukka" could accommodate believers and heretics alike, while Brenner's vision of a new Hebrew culture was equally open to all who wished to join it. Both, however, came from a culture in which the vast majority of Jews knew instinctively what it meant to be Jewish. Their revolutionary alternatives assumed a stable identity against which they revolted. A century later, no such stability could be assumed, especially in a society like America where self-fashioning and self-invention are quintessential marks of the culture. Neither religious nor secular in the way these terms used to be used, Jewish culture in America is in the process of defining both of them anew. The only definite thing one can say about the future of these categories is that they will not look anything like they did a century ago, when ideological secularism became a mass movement. The secularism of American Jews today is not ideological in that sense, and perhaps that is why it is writers of fiction and memoirists rather than ideologues who are giving it expression.

The majority of Jews in the world today are, in some sense, secular. They either doubt the existence of God or consider the question superfluous. They believe in the separation of religion from the state. Even Orthodox Jews outside of the State of Israel would probably agree with Moses Mendelssohn that church and state should be separated: religious in private, they are secular in public. And most Jews now define their identities in historical and/or cultural terms. But in a nonideological age, "secular" has largely ceased to be a fighting word and, for that reason, it may not be the first word most Jews choose to identify themselves. In one sense, this means that the ideologues of Jewish secularism won their battle, but in another sense, they did not, since the secular culture that they had in mind was one intentionally chosen.

If the hallmarks of secularism are lack of dogma and resistance to uniformity, as Amos Oz argues, then the totality of Jewish culture in Israel and North America, including its Orthodox elements, is profoundly secular. No hegemonic authority, either religious or nationalist, can dictate its agenda.

No trajectory toward the future can be charted with confidence. Secularism can make no promise of continuity or survival, but it does guarantee the freedom to experiment, without which neither continuity nor survival is possible.

• • •

I began this book with a personal story, and I would like to end it that way. In the preface, I told the story of my father's antinomian Yom Kippur. The socialist and Zionist ideologies that he had imbibed in the Hashomer Hatzair youth movement fed a secular rebellion against the religion of his parents. It was that secularism, combined with profound Jewish commitments, that he bequeathed to me and that served as one motivation to explore the ideas discussed in this book. But that secularism lost its ideological edge in the passing of the twentieth century and came to mean something quite different for him and, in other ways, for myself as his son. In his later years, he returned to the synagogue, albeit only a few times a year. On coming home from Kol Nidre, the evening of Yom Kippur, something of the rebellion of his youth reawakened: with an impish twinkle in his eye, he would call for tea and cake, as if to say that no amount of religious devotion could erase a lifetime of skepticism.

As for myself, a different way of marking the holiest day of the Jewish year marks my own "postsecularism." With a minyan (prayer quorum) of friends, my family and I repair to Muir Woods, where, I like to think, the Almighty himself (if he exists) must pray among the giant, ancient redwoods. A religious or secular ritual? Neither and, yet, both—a paradoxical hybrid only possible in the wake of a century and more of the tradition of Jewish secular thought that has been the subject of this book.

Notes

Preface

1. For a similar story about the Polish Jewish revolutionary, Isaac Deutscher, see Tamara Deutscher, "Introduction," Isaac Deutscher, *The Non-Jewish Jew and Other Essays* (Boston, 1968), 21.

2. Rakovsky's memoir was published in an abbreviated Hebrew translation in 1951 and in the Yiddish original in 1954. For the English, with an excellent introduction by Paula E. Hyman, see Puah Rakovsky, *My Life as a Radical Jewish Woman*, trans. Barbara Harshav with Paula E. Hyman (Bloomington, IN, 2002). See also the preface by Yitskhok Niborski in the French translation, *Mémoires d'une révolutionnaire juive*, trans. Isabelle Rozenbaumas (Paris, 2006). For the brilliant use of Tevye's daughters to mark out the different paths of eastern European Jews, see Yuri Slezkine, *The Jewish Century* (Princeton, NJ, 2002), chap. 4.

3. Shmuel Feiner, "Haskalah, Secularization and the Discovery of the Jewish 'New World' in the Eighteenth Century," *Simon Dubnow Institute Year Book* 6 (2007): 1–13; and idem, *Shorshei ha-Hilun: Matiranut ve-Safkanut be-Yahadut ha-Me'ah ha-18* [The *Sources of Secularization: Permissiveness and Skepticism in Eighteenth-Century Judaism*] (Jerusalem, 2010). With this thesis of the pre-Haskalah secularization of central European Jewish society, Feiner has updated the older work of Azriel Shochat, *Im Hilufei ha-Tekufot* (Jerusalem, 1960).

4. See his encounter with the Jewish historian Heinrich Graetz at Karlsbad in 1876 described in Pierre Birnbaum, *Geography of Hope: Exile, the Enlightenment, Disassimilation*, trans. Charlotte Mandell (Stanford, CA, 2008), 36–43.

5. Together with Frederick Engels he also repeated with some modifications the arguments from this 1843 essay in *Die heilige Familie* (*The Holy Family*, Frankfurt, 1845), chap. 6.

6. See Julius Carlebach, *Karl Marx and the Radical Critique of Judaism* (London, 1978).

7. In *Geography of Hope*, Birnbaum provides a brilliant exposition of the relationship of modern Jewish intellectuals to their Jewish identity. Some of the thinkers he treats overlap with those I deal with here, but our approaches diverge.

Introduction: Origins

1. Isaac Deutscher, "The Non-Jewish Jew," in *The Non-Jewish Jew and Other Essays* (Boston, 1968), 26.

2. Mark Lilla, *The Stillborn God: Religion, Politics and the Modern West* (New York, 2007). For a good discussion of the secularization theory as well as a critique, see José Casanova, *Public Religions in the Modern World* (Chicago, 1994), 11–39.

3. For a recent work that operates with this paradigm, see Charles Taylor, *A Secular Age* (Cambridge, MA, 2007).

4. See Peter Berger, *The Heretical Imperative: Contemporary Possibilities of Religious Affirmation* (Garden City, NY, 1979).

5. See, among other recent works, Peter Berger, ed., *The Desecularization of the World: Resurgent Religion and World Politics* (New York, 1999); David Martin, *On Secularization: Towards a Revised General Theory* (Burlington, VT, 2005); Talal Asad, *Formations of the Secular: Christianity, Islam, Modernity* (Stanford, CA, 2003); David Scott and Charles Hirschkind, eds., *Powers of the Secular Modern: Talal Asad and His Interlocutors* (Stanford, CA, 2006); and Vincent P. Pecora, *Secularization and Cultural Criticism: Religion, Nation and Modernity* (Chicago, 2006).

6. See Casanova, *Public Religions*, 12–14

7. Quoted in *Oxford English Dictionary*, s.v. "Secular," 3.a.

8. Amos Funkenstein, *Theology and the Scientific Imagination* (Princeton, NJ, 1986). Hans Blumenberg formulated this relationship somewhat differently by arguing not so much for a dialectical progression as for modern ideas occupying the places vacated by medieval theology. See *The Legitimacy of the Modern Age*, trans. Robert M. Wallace (Cambridge, MA, 1983).

9. Karl Löwith, *Meaning in History* (Chicago, 1949).

10. Carl Schmitt, *Political Theology*, trans. George Schwab (Cambridge, MA, 1985). For a more recent treatment of political theology, albeit unaccountably without any mention of Schmitt, see Lilla, *Stillborn God*.

11. Peter Berger, *The Sacred Canopy: Elements of a Sociological Theory of Religion* (Garden City, NY, 1967).

12. Marcel Gauchet, *Le désenchantement du monde: Une histoire politique de la religion* (Paris, 1985); English version, *The Disenchantment of the World: A Political History of Religion*, trans. Oscar Burge (Princeton, NJ, 1997).

13. See, among other recent works, Casanova, *Public Religions*; Rajeev Bhargava, ed., *Secularism and Its Critics* (Delhi, 1998); and Janet R. Jakobsen and Ann Pellegrini, eds., *Secularisms* (Durham, NC, 2008).

14. For example, Leviticus 21:4 referring to the ritual pollution acquired from contact with a corpse or 21:9 to the pollution acquired by the daughter of a priest through illicit sex. The root *hll* also means "wounded" or "fallen" (as in battle), which corresponds to the law that a damaged or wounded animal cannot be consecrated.

15. 1 Samuel 21:5.

16. See Azzan Yadin and Ghil`ad Zuckerman, "*Blorít*—Pagans' Mohawk or Sabras' Forelock? Ideologically Manipulative Secularization of Hebrew Terms in Socialist Zionist Israeli," in Tope Omoniyi, ed., *The Sociology of Language and Religion: Change, Conflict and Accommodation* (London, 2010), chap. 6. *Hiloni* was not the only word that denoted a secular person: *hofshi* (free or freethinking) had a similar connotation, but by the late twentieth century, the former had largely replaced the latter.

17. Leviticus Rabba 25.5. The word derives from the Aramaic for a stranger.

18. M. Avot 2.14

19. B. Sanhedrin 99b–100a.

20. Berger, *Heretical Imperative*.

21. B. Baba Metzia 59b.

22. For the partial substitution of the *bat kol* for the prophet, see b. Yoma 9b

23. Jeffrey Rubenstein, *Talmudic Stories* (Baltimore, 1999), 34–63.

24. B. Baba Batra 12b. On our text and the end of prophecy, see Joseph Blenkinsopp, "'We Pay No Heed to Heavenly Voices': The End of Prophecy and the Formation of the Canon," in *Treasures Old and New: Essays in the Theology of the Pentateuch* (Grand Rapids, MI, 2004), 192–207.

25. B. Eruvin 13b.

26. See David Sorkin, *Moses Mendelssohn and the Religious Enlightenment* (Berkeley and Los Angeles, 1996). Sorkin shows how the Andalusian traditions of exegesis were the ones particularly influential for Mendelssohn, but the point can be generalized.

27. Naomi Seidman suggested this metaphor drawn from literary theory.

28. These anecdotes are from the autobiographical introduction written by Deutscher's wife Tamara in Deutscher, *Non-Jewish Jew*, 17 and 19

29. Talal Asad, *Formations of the Secular: Christianity, Islam, Modernity* (Stanford, CA, 2003), introduction.

30. For a parsing of the different types of secular political theories, see Charles Taylor, "Modes of Secularism," in Bhargava, *Secularism and Its Critics*, 31–53.

31. See Jonathan Frankel, *Prophecy and Politics* (Cambridge, UK, 1981); Eli Lederhendler, *The Road to Moderen Jewish Politics: Political Tradition and Political Reconstruction in the Jewish Community of Tsarist Russia* (Oxford, 1989) and Ezra Mendelssohn, *On Modern Jewish Politics* (Oxford, 1993).

32. Maurice Halbwachs, *La mémoire collective* (Paris, 1997).

33. I therefore disagree with Yosef Hayim Yerushalmi's argument in *Zakhor: Jewish History and Jewish Memory* (Seattle, 1982) that collective memory is primarily a characteristic of premodern times and that modern identity is characterized instead by critical history. Memory is a characteristic of modern, secular Jewish culture as well.

34. For the identity of Israel and the Torah, see Zohar 3:73a. For the identity of God and Israel, see ibid. 3:93b. For the very prevalent view on the Torah as God's name, see Zohar 2:60a, 87a, 90b, 124a, 161b; 3:13b, 19a, 21a, 35b–36a, 73a, 89b, 98b, 159a, 265b, 298b. See further Isaiah Tishby in *Kiryat Sefer* 50 (1975): 480–92, 668–74; and Bracha Sack, *Kiryat Sefer* 57 (1982): 179–84. I thank Daniel Matt for providing me with these references.

35. Mordecai Kaplan, *Judaism as a Civilization* (New York, 1934), 328.

36. Leo Trepp, *A History of the Jewish Experience* (Springfield, NJ, 2000), 537.

37. Blumenberg, *Legitimacy of the Modern Age*, 48–49. See further David Ingram, "Blumenberg and the Philosophical Grounds of Historiography, *History and Theory* 29 (1990): 1–16.

38. For the idea of countertradition, see my *Gershom Scholem: Kabbalah and Counter-History* (Cambridge, MA, 1979).

Chapter 1. God: Pantheists, Kabbalists, and Pagans

1. See Robert S. Kawashima, "The Priestly Tent of Meeting and the Problem of Divine Transcendence: An 'Archaeology' of the Sacred," *Journal of Religion* 86 (2006): 226–57.

2. On the literature of this period, see Elias Bickerman, *Four Strange Books of the Bible: Daniel, Jonah, Kohelet, Esther* (New York, 1968).

3. The letter was written 1 February 1877 and was published by Arthur Prinz in "New Perspectives on Marx as a Jew," *Year Book of the Leo Baeck Institute* 15 (1970): 121. The letter was discovered by Boris Nikolayesky and first published in *Yivo Historishe Shriften* 2 (1937). See further Pierre Birnbaum, *Géographie de l'espoir* (Paris, 2004), 41–42. Graetz's translation of and commentary on Ecclesiastes was published as *Kohélet oder der Salomonische Prediger: Übersetz und kritisch Erläutert* (Leipzig, 1871). Graetz's interpretation of Ecclesiastes is actually strikingly different—and more conservative—than the one he advanced to Marx. The secular point of view of the book was really a political satire directed against Herod the Great, the first century BCE ruler during whose reign Graetz believed it was written. The author does not embrace the pessimistic tendencies that were the result of Herodian misrule but fights against them. His actual philosophy was therefore much closer to that of the Bible than to the views he satirically attributes to the camouflaged Herod.

4. See Robert Gordis, *The Book of Job: Commentary, New Translation and Special Studies* (New York, 1978).

5. Menahem Kellner, *Dogma in Medieval Jewish Thought: From Maimonides to Abravanel* (Oxford, 1986).

6. See Daniel Jeremy Silver, *Maimonidean Criticism and the Maimonidean Controversy, 1180–1240* (Leiden, 1965).

7. For an account of the way Moses Mendelssohn—hardly a secularist—built his own philosophy around the teachings of the medieval Spanish Jewish Enlightenment, and especially Maimonides and Ibn Ezra, see David Sorkin, *Moses Mendelssohn and the Religious Enlightenment* (Berkeley and Los Angeles, 1996).

8. The most recent treatments of Maimonides are Herbert A. Davidson, *Moses Maimonides: The Man and His Works* (New York, 2005); Joel Kraemer, *Maimonides: The Life and World of One of Civilization's Greatest Minds* (New York, 2008); and Sarah Stroumsa, *Maimonides in his World: Portrait of a Mediterranean Thinker* (Princeton, 2009).

9. Moses Maimonides, *The Guide of the Perplexed*, trans. Shlomo Pines (Chicago, 1963), 1:55 (hereafter cited as *Guide*).

10. The argument is to be found in *Guide*, 1:55–60.

11. For his naturalistic explanation of events in nature or by humans that the Bible seemingly attributes to God's direct intervention, see ibid., 2:48. On Maimonides' position on the impossibility of violating the laws of logic or mathematics, see ibid., 3:15. On the idea of a "realm of the possible," see ibid., 3:26.

12. Ibid., 3:26.

13. See especially ibid., 3:32.

14. Ibid., 1:66.

15. See Moses Narboni, *Perush al-Moreh Nevukhim*, s.v. 1:66. Profiat Duran, the author of the *Efodi*, another commentary on the *Guide*, offers virtually the identical interpretation. Both Narboni and Duran claim to have actually seen a stone from Sinai, which they broke into pieces, only to discover that each piece still contained an image of the bush. Narboni is almost certainly the source for Duran. Narboni says that one of the notables of Barcelona actually brought back such a stone from Sinai, which he gave to a relative who was one of Narboni's students. See further Maurice R. Hayoun, *Moshe Narboni* (Tübingen, 1986), 90–91. I thank Abe Socher for this reference in Narboni.

16. Catherine Chalier, *Spinoza, lecteur de Maimonide* (Paris, 2006).

17. See Yosef Kaplan, *Mi-Notzrim Hadashim le-Yehudim Hadashim* (Jerusalem, 2003); Yosef Kaplan, *From Christianity to Judaism: The Story of Isaac Orobio de Castro*, trans. Raphael Loewe (Oxford, 1989); Miriam Bodian, *Hebrews of the Portuguese Nation: Conversos and Community in Early Modern Amsterdam* (Bloomington, IN, 1997); and Yosef Hayim Yerushalmi, *From Spanish Court to Italian Ghetto: Isaac Cardoso, a Study in Seventeenth-Century Marranism and Jewish Apologetics* (New York, 1971).

18. Yirmiyahu Yovel, *Spinoza and Other Heretics* (Princeton, NJ, 1989), 70–71. On Prado, see further Kaplan, *From Christianity to Judaism*, passim.

19. Rebecca Goldstein, *Betraying Spinoza* (New York, 2006). See also Yovel, *Spinoza and Other Heretics*; and Steven Nadler, *Spinoza: A Life* (Cambridge, 1999), both of which predate Goldstein in this analysis.

20. Thomas Nagel, *The View from Nowhere* (New York, 1986).

21. Willi Goetschel, *Spinoza's Modernity: Mendelssohn, Lessing, and Heine* (Madison, WI, 2004), 3–32.

22. See particularly Spinoza's *Ethics*, I, Props. XIV and XV. The literature on this question is vast. For an excellent synopsis, see Alan Donagan, "Spinoza's Theology," in Don Garrett, ed., *The Cambridge Companion to Spinoza* (Cambridge, 1996), 343–82. A highly engaging analysis of Spinoza's philosophy is Matthew Stewart, *The Courtier and the Heretic: Leibniz, Spinoza and the Fate of God in the Modern World* (New York, 2006). On the *Ethics* generally, see Steven Nadler, *Spinoza's Ethics: An Introduction* (Cambridge, 2006). On the medieval origins and meaning of the concept of substance, see Harry Austryn Wolfson, *The Philosophy of Spinoza* (Cambridge, MA, [1934] 1962), chaps. 3–5.

23. Spinoza, *Ethics*, I, Prop. XV, note.

24. Ibid., Prop. XVII, note.

25. Here I follow Wolfson, *The Philosophy of Spinoza*, although he probably assumes that Spinoza was more conversant with medieval Jewish philosophy than the evidence supports. See also Shlomo Pines, "Spinoza, Maimonides and Kant," *Scripta Hierosoymitana* 20 (1968): 3–54; and idem, "Spinoza's Tractatus Theologico-Politicus and the Jewish Philosophical Tradition," in Isadore Twersky and Bernard Septimus, eds., *Jewish Thought in the Seventeenth Century* (Cambridge, MA, 1987), 499–521. Rebecca Goldstein thinks that the Kabbalah furnished the questions to which Spinoza composed his philosophical answers, but there is little to indicate that Spinoza was conversant with the Kabbalah or that it served as his major source.

26. Spinoza, *Ethics*, V, Prop. XVII.

27. Ibid., Prop. XIX.

28. Baruch Spinoza, *Theological-Political Treatise*, 2nd ed., trans. Samuel Shirley (Indianapolis, 2001), 36.

29. Ibid., 53–54.

30. For a discussion of the scholastic origins of the debate over God's powers, see Funkenstein, *Theology and the Scientific Imagination*, chap. 3.

31. Spinoza, *Theological-Political Treatise*, 76.

32. For a full translation of the *herem* against Spinoza, see Steven Nadler, *Spinoza's Heresy: Immortality and the Jewish Mind* (Oxford, 2001), 2.

33. Spinoza, *Ethics*, V, Prop. XXIII.

34. For a review of the literature, see Nadler, *Spinoza's Heresy*, 203 n. 35.

35. Gersonides takes up this question in his *Milhamot ha-Shem*, book 1.

36. Yovel, *Spinoza and Other Heretics*, chap. 2.

37. Wolfson, *Philosophy of Spinoza*, 1:vii.

38. See Jonathan Israel, *Radical Enlightenment: Philosophy and the Making of Modernity 1650–1750* (Oxford, 2001), 159. Israel argues provocatively for Spinoza's profound influence on the European Enlightenment. See also his *Enlightenment Contested: Philosophy, Modernity and the Emancipation of Man 1670–1752* (Oxford, 2006).

39. On the pantheism controversy, see Fredrick C. Beiser, *The Fate of Reason: German Philosophy from Kant to Fichte* (Cambridge Mass., MA, 1987), chaps. 2–4.

40. See Mordechai Breuer, *German-Jewish History in Modern Times*, ed. Michael A. Meyer, trans. William Templer (New York, 1996) 1:244–50.

41. See Steven Lowenstein, *The Berlin Jewish Community: Enlightenment, Family and Crisis, 1770–1830* (New York, 1994), 25–32.

42. Azriel Shochat, *Im Hilufei ha-Tekufot* (Jerusalem, 1960); and Shmuel Feiner, *Shorshei ha-Hilun: Matiranut ve-Safkanut be-Yahadut ha-Me'ah ha-18* [The Sources of Secularization: Permissiveness and Skepticism in Eighteenth-Century Judaism] (Jerusalem, 2010)

43. See Salomon Maimon, *Lebensgeschichte*, ed. Zwi Batscha (Frankfurt, 1995), p. 156, for his conversion to Spinozism and p. 163 for his views as a "free thinker."

44. Ruth Gay, *The Jews of Germany* (New Haven, CT, 1992), 37.

45. Abraham P. Socher, *The Radical Enlightenment of Salomon Maimon: Judaism, Heresy, and Philosophy* (Stanford, CA, 2006). For additional background on the *Lebensgeschichte*, see Liliane Weissberg, "1792–93: Salomon Maimon writes his *Lebensgeschichte* (Autobiography), a reflection on his life in the (Polish) East and the (German) West," in Sander L. Gilman and Jack Zipes, eds., *Yale Companion to Jewish Writing and Thought in German Culture, 1096–1996* (New Haven, CT, 1997), 108–15.

46. See in particular the contemporary material collected by Sabbatia Wolff under the title *Maimoniana oder Rhapsodien sur Charakteristik Salomon Maimons* (Berlin, 2003).

47. See Maimon, *Lebensgeschichte*, I, 152.

48. Salomon Maimon, *Givat Ha-Moreh* (Jerusalem, 1966), 161.

49. For an excellent discussion of Maimon's philosophy, see Samuel Hugo Bergman, *The Philosophy of Salomon Maimon*, trans. Noah J. Jacobs (Jerusalem, 1967). See also Socher, *Radical Enlightenment*, chaps. 2 and 3.

50. See Maimon's entry for "Atheist" in his *Philosophisches Wörterbuch* (Berlin, 1791), 25–27.

51. See S. H. Bergman, "The Principle of Beginning in the Philosophy of Hermann Cohen" [in Hebrew], *Keneset* 8 (1944): 143–53.

52. See Hermann Cohen, *The Religion of Reason Out of the Sources of Judaism*, trans. Simon Kaplan (New York, 1972). This work became the source for the religious existentialism of Franz Rosenzweig and, to a lesser degree, Martin Buber.

53. For a history of Spinoza's Jewish reception in the nineteenth and twentieth centuries, see Daniel Schwartz's forthcoming book to be published by Princeton University Press.

54. Moses Hess, *The Holy History of Mankind and Other Writings* (Cambridge, 2004)

55. Emma Lazarus, "Was the Earl of Beconsfield a Representative Jew?" *Century* 23, no. 6 (April 1882): 939–42. See Esther Schor, *Emma Lazarus* (New York, 2006), 128–133.

56. M. L. Lilienblum, *Ketavim Autobiographiyim* (Jerusalem, 1970), 2:45–51.

57. Ibid., 1:143.

58. Ibid., 1:108.

59. See George Mosse, *German Jews beyond Judaism* (Bloomington, IN, 1985); idem, *Germans and Jews: The Right, the Left and the Search for a "Third Force" in Pre-Nazi Germany* (New York, 1970); and David Sorkin, *The Transformation of German Jewry, 1780–1840* (New York, 1987).

60. On Heine's Jewish writings, see S. S. Prawer, *Heine's Jewish Comedy: A Study of his Portraits of Jews and Judaism* (Oxford, 1983); and Harmut Kircher, *Heinrich Heine und das Judentum* (Bonn, 1973).

61. Heinrich Heine, *The Poetry and Prose of Heinrich Heine*, ed. Frederic Ewen (New York, 1948), 806–7.

62. Heinrich Heine, "Deutschland—Ein Wintermärchen," 1.12 in *Heinrich Heine Werke* (Basel, 1956), 2:97.

63. Heine, *Poetry and Prose*, 682–83.

64. Ibid., 502. The passage is from a posthumously published letter.

65. Heinrich Heine, *Zur Religion und Philosophie in Deutschland*, ed. Wolfgang Harich (Frankfurt, 1965), 148.

66. Heine, *Poetry and Prose*, 349–50.

67. Ibid., 669.

68. Ibid., 140–44. I have modified the translation slightly.

69. Sigmund Freud, *The Future of an Illusion*, trans. James Strachey (New York, 1961), 63.

70. *The North Sea III*, in Heinrich Heine, *Historisch-kritische Gesamtausgabe der Werke*, ed. Manfred Windfuhr et al. (Hamburg, 1973–), 6:736. Jeffrey Sammons notes that Heine removed the phrase from the printed edition of this essay. See Jeffrey L. Sammons, *Heinrich Heine: A Modern Biography* (Princeton, NJ, 1979), 305.

71. The literature is vast. Worth mentioning in particular are Peter Gay, *A Godless Jew* (New Haven, CT, 1987); Yosef Hayim Yerushalmi, *Freud's Moses: Judaism Terminable and Interminable* (New Haven, CT, 1991); Sander L. Gilman, *Freud, Race, and Gender* (Princeton, NJ, 1993); Moshe Gresser, *Dual Allegiance: Freud as a Modern Jew* (Albany, NY, 1994); Richard J. Bernstein, *Freud and the Legacy of Moses* (Cambridge, 1998); and Eliza Slavet, *Racial Fever: Freud and the Jewish Question* (New York, 2009).

72. Letter from Freud to Pfister, 9 October 1918, in *Psycho-Analysis and Faith: The Letters of Sigmund Freud and Oskar Pfister*, trans. Eric Mosbacher (London, 1963), 63.

73. The letter was written 6 May 1926. See Gay, *A Godless Jew*, 137.

74. Freud, *Future of an Illusion*, 8 and 19.

75. Ibid., 21.

76. Ibid., 24.

77. For a recent biography, see Walter Isaacson, *Einstein: His Life and Universe* (New York, 2007).

78. See ibid., 79–84.

79. See the full text in Max Jammer, *Einstein and Religion: Physics and Theology* (Princeton, NJ, 1999), appendix.

80. *New York Times*, 25 April 1929, quoted in Ronald W. Clark, *Einstein: The Life and Times* (New York, 1971), 413.

81. *New York Times Magazine*, 9 November 1930, reprinted in Albert Einstein, *Ideas and Opinions* (New York, 1954), 38.

82. See Ernst Bloch, *Atheism in Christianity*, trans. J. T. Swann (New York, 1972).

83. E. Salaman, "A Talk with Einstein," *Listener* 54 (1955): 370–71, quoted in Jammer, *Einstein and Religion*, 123.

84. Quoted, including German original, in Abraham Pais, *Subtle Is the Lord: The Science and Life of Albert Einstein* (New York, 1982), 114.

85. Jammer, *Einstein and Religion*, 222 (n. 124 for original German).

86. Moshe Pearlman, *Ben Gurion Looks Back* (London, 1965), 216–17.

87. Jammer, *Einstein and Religion*, 185–86. From Albert Einstein, *Mein Weltbild* (Amsterdam, 1934).

88. Moritz Lazarus, *The Ethics of Judaism* (Philadelphia, 1900). For a similar voice earlier in the nineteenth century, see Samuel Hirsch, *Systematischer Katechismus der israelitischen Religion: Aus Beschluss des Vorstandes der israelitischen Gemeinde zu Luxemburg* (Luxembourg, 1856).

89. Einstein, *Ideas and Opinions*, 194. The quotation is from an article on anti-Semitism that appeared in *Collier's Magazine*, 26 November 1938, and thus in the immediate aftermath of Kristallnacht.

90. Leo Strauss, *Spinoza's Critique of Religion* (New York, 1965), 15.

91. Benjamin Lazier, *God Interrupted: Heresy and the European Imagination between the Wars* (Princeton, NJ, 2009), part 2.

92. See Daniel Chanan Matt, "'Ayin': The Concept of Nothingness in Jewish Mysticism," in Robert K. C. Forman, ed., *The Problem of Pure Consciousness* (New York, 1990), 121–59; and Gershom Scholem, "Schöpfung aus Nichts und die Selbtsverschräkung des Gottes," *Über einige Grundbegriffe des Judentums* (Frankfurt, 1970), 53–89.

93. See Isaiah Tishby, *Torat ha-Ra ve-ha-Klippa be-Kabbalat ha-Ari* (Jerusalem, 1942).

94. Hayim Nahman Bialik, "Gilui ve-Kishui ba-Lashon" in *Kol Kitve H. N. Bialik* (Tel Aviv, 1938), 202–4. For an English translation by Jacob Sloan, see Robert Alter, ed., *Modern Hebrew Literature* (New York, 1975), 130–37.

95. Ariel Hirschfeld, "When the World Is Shocked: On Bialik's Relationship to his Sources" [in Hebrew], in Zvi Luz and Ziva Shamir, eds., *Al "Gilui ve-Kishui ba-Lashon"* (Ramat Gan, Israel, 2001), 145–50.

96. See Ziva Shamir, "Libels Grew in the Land: The Essay 'Revelation and Concealment in Language' and Its Place in Bialik's Works" [in Hebrew] in ibid., 151–70.

97. Bialik, "Gilui ve-Kishui," 202.

98. Nahman of Braslav, *Likkutei Moharan* (Jerusalem, 1969), part 1, homily 64.

99. Azzan Yadin, "A Web of Chaos: Bialik and Nietzsche on Language, Truth and the Death of God," *Prooftexts* 21 (2001): 179–203.

100. See especially Steven Aschheim, *The Nietzsche Legacy in Germany, 1890-1990* (Berkeley and Los Angeles, 1992).

101. For an English translation, see Gershom Scholem, *On the Possibility of Jewish Mysticism in Our Time*, trans. Jonathan Chipman (Philadelphia, 1997), 27–29. For a commentary connecting the letter to Bialik's essay, see Galili Shahar, "The Sacred and the Unfamiliar: Gershom Scholem and the Anxieties of the New Hebrew." *Germanic Review* 83 (2008): 299–320.

102. See Michael Brenner, *The Renaissance of Jewish Culture in Weimar Germany* (New Haven, CT, 1996); and Asher D. Biemann, *Inventing New Beginnings: The Idea of Renaissance in Modern Judaism* (Stanford, 2009).

103. Gershom Scholem, *Tagebücher*, vol. 1 (Frankfurt, 1995). See also idem, *From Berlin to Jerusalem*, trans. Harry Zohn (New York, 1980); and Lazier, *God Interrupted*, chap. 10.

104. Gershom Scholem, "Offener Brief an den Verfasser der Schrift, 'Jüdischer Glaube dieser Zeit,'" *Bayerische Israelitische Gemeindschaft*, 15 August 1932, 241–44.

105. Scholem, "Offener Brief," 243. In "Revelation and Tradition as Religious Categories in Judaism," an essay first published in *Eranos Jahrbuch* 31 (1962): 19–48, Scholem uses the identical terms to characterize the Kabbalah, which suggests that his own theological position, at a minimum, developed in interaction with his study of the Kabbalistic sources and, at a maximum, even preceded his Kabbalistic studies. For the English version with the relevant passage, see Gershom Scholem, *The Messianic Idea in Judaism and Other Essays in Jewish Spirituality* (New York, 1971), 296.

106. Gershom Scholem, "Reflections on Jewish Theology," in Werner Dannhauser, ed., *On Jews and Judaism in Crisis* (New York, 1976), 268–69. See also idem, "Revelation and Traditions as Religious Categories" and "Reflections on the Possibility of Jewish Mysticism in our Time," [in Hebrew] *Amot* 2, no. 2 (1963–64): 11–19.

107. See my *Gershom Scholem: Kabbalah and Counter-History* (Cambridge, MA, 1971), 74–76 (English translation), 215–16 (original German text).

108. For a discussion of Scholem's and Benjamin's readings of Kafka, see Robert Alter, *Necessary Angels: Tradition and Modernity in Kafka, Benjamin, and Scholem* (Cambridge, MA, 1991).

109. Franz Kafka, *The Complete Stories* (New York, 1983), 3–4.

110. For what is still the best treatment of the *hekhalot* literature, the earliest stratum of Jewish mysticism, see Gershom Scholem, *Major Trends in Jewish Mysticism* (New York, 1961), Second Lecture.

111. Richard Rubenstein, *After Auschwitz* (Indianapolis, 1966).

112. Shaul Tchernikhovsky, *Shirim* (Jerusalem and Tel Aviv, 1945), 72–74. The translation is by Azzan Yadin with slight modifications. For a discussion of this poem and its place in modern Hebrew culture, see Ariel Hirschfeld, "Locus and Language: Hebrew Culture in Israel, 1890–1990," in David Biale, ed., *Cultures of the Jews: A New History* (New York, 2002), 1013–14.

Chapter 2. Torah: The Secular Jewish Bible

1. Max Nordau, *Die conventionellen Lügen der Kulturmenschheit* (Leipzig, 1909), 59–60. For an English translation, see Nordau, *The Conventional Lies of Our Civilization* (Chicago, 1886), 60–61 (the translation in the text is mine).

2. Jonathan Sheehan, *The Enlightenment Bible: Translation, Scholarship, Culture* (Princeton, NJ, 2005). For a broad analysis of the various modern Jewish understandings of the Bible, see Jacob Shavit and Mordechai Eran, *The Hebrew Bible Reborn: From Holy Scripture to the Book of Books: A History of Biblical Culture and the Battles over the Bible in Modern Judaism*, trans. Chaya Naor (Berlin, 2007).

3. Richard Cohen, "Urban Visibility and Biblical Visions: Jewish Cultural in Central and Western Europe in the Modern Age," in David Biale, ed., *Cultures of the Jews: A New History* (New York, 2002), 762–83.

4. See Raymond Scheindlin, *Wine, Women and Death: Medieval Hebrew Poems on the Good Life* (New York, 1999).

5. Robert Alter, "The Double Canonicity of the Hebrew Bible," in David Biale, Michael Galchinsky, and Susannah Heschel, eds., *Insider/Outsider: American Jews and Multiculturalism* (Berkeley, CA, 1997), 131–49; and idem, *Canon and Creativity: Modern Writing and the Authority of Scripture* (New Haven, CT, 2000).

6. T. Carmi, ed., *The Penguin Book of Hebrew Verse* (New York, 1981), 314 (the translation is mine, with some borrowings from Carmi's).

7. Ibn Ezra on Exodus 14:27, 16:13, 34:29. See Nahum M. Sarna, "Ibn Ezra as an Exegete," in Isadore Twersky and Jay M. Harris, eds., *Rabbi Abraham ibn Ezra: Studies in the Writings of a Twelfth-Century Jewish Polymath* (Cambridge, MA, 1993), 1–27; and Irene Lancaster, *Deconstructing the Bible: Abraham ibn Ezra's Introduction to the Torah* (London and New York, 2003).

8. See Jay M. Harris, "Ibn Ezra in Modern Jewish Perspective," in Twersky and Harris, *Rabbi Abraham ibn Ezra*, 136–39.

9. He did not, however, separate them entirely. He points out a few verses in the Bible that do hint at the supralunar world. The Bible, it turns out, must be read from a dual perspective: human and divine. See my "Philosophy and Exegesis in the Writings of Abraham Ibn Ezra," *Comitatus* (UCLA Medieval and Renaissance Center), 5 (Fall 1974): 43–62.

10. See David B. Ruderman, *Jewish Thought and Scientific Discovery in Early Modern Europe* (New Haven, CT, 1995), 14–53 (on Sephardi intellectuals) and 54–99 (on Ashkenazi Jews).

11. On Ibn Ezra's scientific views, see Shlomo Sela, *Abraham Ibn Ezra and the Rise of Medieval Hebrew Science* (Leiden, 2003). On the role of astrology in medieval Jewish ideas about nature, see Ruderman, *Jewish Thought*, 21–35; and Ron Barkai, "Theoretical and Practical Aspects of Jewish Astrology in the Middle Ages" [in Hebrew], in *Maddah, Magia u-Mitologia be-Yemai ha-Beinayim* (Jerusalem, 1987), 7–35.

12. On Ibn Ezra and Krochmal, see Harris, "Ibn Ezra in Modern Jewish Perspective," 150–58.

13. For Maimonides' exegetical method, see his introduction to part 1 of *The Guide of the Perplexed*.

14. See in particular *Guide*, 2:25.

15. On the "principle of accommodation," see Amos Funkenstein, *Theology and the Scientific Imagination from the Middle Ages to the Seventeenth Century* (Princeton, NJ, 1986), 213–71; idem, *Perceptions of Jewish History* (Berkeley and Los Angeles, 1993), 88–98; and Steven D. Benin, *The Footprints of God: Divine Accommodation in Jewish and Christian Thought* (Albany, NY, 1993).

16. Maimonides' treatment of the reasons for the commandments is in *Guide*, 3:25–49. See Funkenstein, *Perceptions of Jewish History*, 137–44; and Abraham P. Socher, "Of Divine Cunning and Prolonged Madness: Amos Funkenstein on Maimonides' Historical Reasoning," *Jewish Social Studies* 6:1 (1999): 6–29.

17. Isaac Heinemann, *Ta'amei ha-Mitzvot be-Sifrut Yisrael* (Jerusalem, 1954).

18. Yosef Hayim Yerushalmi, *Zakhor* (Seattle, 1982).

19. On ibn Verga, see Yosef Hayim Yerushalmi, *The Lisbon Massacre of 1506 and the Royal Image in the Shebet Yehudah* (Cincinnati, 1976). For early modern Jewish historiography generally, see idem, *Zakhor*.

20. Lester Segal, *Historical Consciousness and Religious Tradition in Azariah de'Rossi's Me'or 'Einayim* (Philadelphia, 1989).

21. For a discussion of this question, see, for example, Nancy Levene, *Spinoza's Revelation* (Cambridge, 2004), chap. 2.

22. See Leo Strauss, *Spinoza's Critique of Religion*, trans. E. M. Sinclair (New York, 1965).

23. See the preface to Spinoza's *Theological-Political Treatise*, 2nd ed., trans. Samuel Shirley (Indianapolis, 2001).

24. I owe this insight to conversations with Yuval Jobani.

25. Spinoza, *Theological-Political Treatise*, 87.

26. Ibid., 89.

27. See Richard Popkin, "Spinoza and Bible Scholarship," in Don Garrett, ed., *The Cambridge Companion to Spinoza* (Cambridge, 1996), 383–407, and Eric Nelson, *The Hebrew Republic* (Cambridge, MA, 2010).

28. Spinoza, *Theological-Political Treatise*, chap. 3.

29. Ibid., 38.

30. Ibid., chap. 17.

31. See Levene, *Spinoza's Revelation*, chap. 2.

32. Heinrich Heine, *The Poetry and Prose of Heinrich Heine*, ed. Frederic Ewen (New York, 1948), 657. For the expression "portable fatherland," see p. 663 in Heine's essay "Moses."

33. Ibid., 678.

34. Ibid., 666.

35. Ibid., 664.

36. Ibid., 665.

37. Ibid.

38. On Heine's interpretations of Moses, see Bluma Goldstein, *Reinscribing Moses: Heine, Kafka, Freud and Schoenberg in a European Wilderness* (Cambridge, MA, 1992), 20–39.

39. Heinrich Heine, *Prinzessin Sabbat: Über Juden und Judentum* (Bodenheim, Germany, 1997), 533.

40. Heine, *Poetry and Prose*, 666.

41. Ibid., 667.

42. The literature on *Moses and Monotheism* is voluminous. Among the most important readings of the book, see Marthe Robert, *From Oedipus to Moses: Freud's Jewish Identity*, trans. Ralph Mannheim (Garden City, NY, 1976); Yosef Hayim Yerushalmi, *Freud's Moses: Judaism Terminable and Interminable* (New Haven, CT, 1991); Jay Geller, *Freud's Jewish Body: Mitigating Circumcisions* (New York, 2007); and Eliza Slavet, *Racial Fever: Freud and the Jewish Question* (New York, 2009).

43. Sigmund Freud, *Moses and Monotheism*, trans. Katherine Jones (New York, 1939), 52.

44. Ibid.

45. Ibid., 55.

46. Ibid., 67.

47. Ibid., 152.

48. Ibid., 142.

49. Ibid., 109

50. Ibid., 147.

51. Ibid., 118.

52. Ibid., 125. On the context for Freud's adoption of this theory of inherited psychological characteristics, see Slavet, *Racial Fever*, and Yerushalmi, *Freud's Moses*.

53. Freud, *Moses and Monotheism*, 128–29.

54. An English translation appears as "Preface to the Hebrew Translation," in *The Standard Edition of the Complete Psychological Works of Sigmund Freud* (London, 1955), 13:xv. The translation was not published until 1939.

55. Freud, *Moses and Monotheism*, 158.

56. Ibid.

57. Yerushalmi, *Freud's Moses*, 10.

58. Freud, *Moses and Monotheism*, 152.

59. See Ahad Ha'am, "Moses," in *Nationalism and the Jewish Ethic*, ed. Hans Kohn (New York, 1962), 206–27. The essay was written in 1904. See further Steven M. Zipperstein, *Elusive Prophet: Ahad Ha'am and the Origins of Zionism* (Berkeley, CA, 1993), 214–16. On the biblical prophets generally, see Ahad Ha'am, "Priest and Prophet," in *Selected Essays*, trans. Leon Simon (Philadelphia, 1912), 125–38. The essay is from 1894.

60. For a survey of four modern interpretations of Moses, see Goldstein, *Reinscribing Moses*.

61. Ahad Ha'am, "The Torah of the Heart" [in Hebrew], in *Al Parashat Derakhim: Kovetz Ma'amarim* (Berlin, 1921), 1:93–94.

62. Ahad Ha'am, "Transvaluation of Values," [in Hebrew], in *Al Parashat Derakhim*, 1:66–77. Translated in Ahad Ha'am, *Selected Essays*, 217–41.

63. Ahad Ha'am, "Torah of the Heart," 1:82–86.

64. See his 1891 essay, "Slavery in Freedom" in *Nationalism and the Jewish Ethic*, 44–65.

65. For Berdichevsky's explicit use of the Hebrew for "transvaluation of values" (*shinui arakhim*), see the essays under that title in Micha Yosef Bin Gorion, *Kol Kitve Micha Yosef Bin Gorion: Ma'amarim* (Tel Aviv, 1960), 27–31. Bin Gorion was Berdichevsky's pen name.

66. See, for example, "On Values" [in Hebrew], ibid., 19. And see further his denunciation of the Ten Commandments in "On Negation" [in Hebrew], ibid., 20.

67. "Contradiction and Building" [in Hebrew], ibid., 30. See also p. 38.

68. Ibid., 19.

69. "On History" [in Hebrew], ibid.

70. "The Book and Life" [in Hebrew], ibid., 30–31. For his systematic critique of Ahad Ha'am, see ibid., 32–38.

71. M. Y. Bin-Gorion, *Sinai ve-Gerizim* (Tel Aviv, 1962), 7.

72. Ibid., 132.

73. B. Shabbat 119B. The meaning of the phrase in context is that Israel will be punished by the sword of the nations if it doesn't follow the book. Berdichevsky interprets the sword to be part of Israel's own identity. See "Two Faces" [in Hebrew], *Kol Kitve Micha Yosef Bin Gorion*, 45.

74. "Old Age and Youth" [in Hebrew], ibid., 32. The word for temple and house (*bayit*) is the same in Hebrew.

75. "Contradiction and Building" [in Hebrew], ibid., 29.

76. See Eric Hobsbawm and Terence Ranger, eds., *The Invention of Tradition* (Cambridge, 1983); and Benedict Anderson, *Imagined Communities* (London, 1983).

77. For an examination of the role of the Bible in Zionist culture and the state of Israel, see Anita Shapira, "The Bible and Israeli Identity," *AJS Review* 28, no. 1 (2004): 11–41; and idem, *Ha-Tanakh ve-ha-Zehut ha-Yisraelit* (Jerusalem, 2005). See also Shavit and Eran, *Hebrew Bible Reborn*, part 4.

78. David Ben-Gurion, *Ben-Gurion Looks at the Bible*, trans. Jonathan Kolatch (Middle Village, NY, 1972), 55–109. See also the discussion on pp. 113–25, which is from 1960. See further Anita Shapira, "Ben-Gurion and the Bible: The Forging of an Historical Narrative?" *Middle Eastern Studies* 33, no. 4 (1997): 645–74.

79. On the Canaanites, see James Diamond, *Homeland or Holy Land: The Canaanite Critique of Israel* (Bloomington, IN, 1986); and Jacob Shavit, *Me-Ivri ad-Kena'ani* (Jerusalem, 1984).

80. On the debates around Ben-Gurion's biblical readings, see Michael Keren, *Ben-Gurion and the Intellectuals: Power, Knowledge, and Charisma* (DeKalb, IL, 1983), 100–117.

81. Ben-Gurion, *Ben-Gurion Looks at the Bible*, 51. The essay, "The Bible is Illuminated by its Own Light" is from 1953.

82. Ibid., 54.

83. Ibid., 67.

84. "Uniqueness and Destiny" in ibid., 25. This was from an address to the General Staff of the Israeli army in 1950.

85. Ibid., 78.

86. Ibid., 41.

87. Ibid., 43.

88. For an example of Jabotinsky's effort to ground his social policies in the Bible, see his essay "Chapters on the Social Philosophy of the Bible" [in Hebrew], *Umah ve-Hevrah* (Jerusalem, 1959), 181–91.

89. For the English version, see Jabotinsky, *Samson the Nazarite*, trans. Cyrus Brooks (London, 1930). For a close reading of the novel, see Michael Stanislawski, *Zionism and the Fin de Siècle* (Berkeley, 2001), 221–27.

90. See Nurit Govrin, *Me'orah Brenner: Ha-Ma'avak al Hofesh ha-Bitui* (Jerusalem, 1985), which includes Brenner's original essay from *Ha-Po'el Ha-Tza'ir* (22 Heshvan 1911). I will return to this essay in chapter 4.

91. Ibid., 137.

92. Ibid., 136–37.

Chapter 3. Israel: Race, Nation, or State

1. See Salo Baron, *The Jewish Community* (Philadelphia, 1942); my *Power and Powerlessness in Jewish History* (New York, 1986), chap. 3; and most recently, Ruth R. Wisse, *Jews and Power* (New York, 2007).

2. See my *Power and Powerlessness*, chap. 2; and further Michael Walzer, Menachem Lorberbaum, and Noam J. Zohar, eds., *The Jewish Political Tradition* (New Haven, CT, 2000), chap. 8.

3. M. Baba Batra 1.5. See also the more extensive discussion in the Tosefta Baba Metziah 11; and Walzer, *Jewish Political Tradition*, chap. 8.

4. Menachem Lorberbaum, *Politics and the Limits of Law: Secularizing the Political in Medieval Jewish Thought* (Stanford, CA, 2001). See also Gerald Blidstein, *Political Concepts in Maimonidean Halakhah* [in Hebrew] (Ramat Gan, 1983); and Howard Kriesel, *Maimonides' Political Thought* (Albany, NY, 1999).

5. Maimonides, *Mishneh Torah, Book of Judges*, "Law of Kings and Wars," 3.8.

6. Ibid., 3.7.

7. See Amos Funkenstein, *Perceptions of Jewish History* (Berkeley and Los Angeles, 1993), 131–54.

8. B. Sanhedrin 91b.

9. Maimonides, *Mishneh Torah, Book of Judges*, "Laws of Kings and Wars," 11.1 and 12.1.

10. Ibid., "Laws concerning Rebels," 2.4.

11. B. Yevamot 90b.

12. Carl Schmitt, *Die Diktatur, von den Anfängen des modernen Souveränitätsgedanken bis zum proletarischen Klassenkampf* (Berlin, 1921); and, more generally, idem, *Political Theology*, trans. George Schwab (Cambridge, MA, 1985).

13. Lorberbaum, *Politics and the Limits of Law*, 93–149.

14. Spinoza, *Theological-Political Treatise*, 205.

15. My analysis here is similar to that of Steven M. Smith, *Spinoza, Liberalism and the Question of Jewish Identity* (New Haven, CT, 1997), chap. 6.

16. Spinoza, *Theological-Political Treatise*, 213.

17. See George E. Mendenhall, *The Tenth Generation: The Origins of the Biblical Tradition* (Baltimore, 1973).

18. Spinoza, *Theological-Political Treatise*, 190 and 214.

19. Ibid., 213.

20. Ibid., 199.

21. Ibid.

22. Ibid., 198.

23. Ibid., 217.

24. Ibid., 45–46.

25. For this suggestion, see Josef Kastein, *Shabbtai Zewi: Der Messias von Ismir* (Berlin, 1930), 230.

26. Spinoza, *The Letters*, trans. Samuel Shirley (Indianapolis, 1995), letter 33. See also Steven Nadler, *Spinoza: A Life* (Cambridge, 1999), 254. There is no record of Spinoza's response, so the extent of his knowledge of Sabbatianism must remain speculative.

27. Mendelssohn may have taken the German word *Judenthum* from Johann Andreas Eisenmenger's *Entdecktes Judenthum* (Königsberg, 1711), an anti-Semitic compendium of real and purported texts from rabbinic literature.

28. Moses Mendelssohn, *Jerusalem, or On Religious Power and Judaism*, trans. Allan Arkush (Hanover, NH, 1983), 61 and 70.

29. Ibid., 57–59.

30. Ibid., 73.

31. Ibid., 45.

32. Ibid., 128.

33. Alexander Altmann, "Introduction" to ibid., 12. See further Alexander Altmann, *Moses Mendelssohn: A Biographical Study* (Tuscaloosa, AL, 1973).

34. Mendelssohn, *Jerusalem*, 90.

35. Moses Hess, *The Holy History of Mankind and Other Writings* (Cambridge, 2004), 93. For a commentary on this important early work, see Shlomo Avineri's introduction. See further Shlomo Avineri, *Moses Hess: Prophet of Communism and Zionism* (New York, 1985). For another reading of Hess's essay and his early work in general, see Shulamit Volkov, "Moses Hess: Problems of Religion and Faith," *Zionism* (1981): 1–15.

36. Moses Hess, *Rom und Jerusalem: Die letzte Nationalitätsfrage* (Leipzig, 1899), 16. English translation: *Rome and Jerusalem*, trans. Meyer Waxman (Lincoln, NE, 1995), 65. The translations here and elsewhere are largely my own.

37. Ibid., 2 (English, 44).

38. Ibid. and n. 1.

39. Ibid., 32.

40. Ibid., 12. As was common, Hess uses "tribe" (*Stamm*) interchangeably with "race" (*Race* or *Rasse*).

41. Ibid., 2.

42. Ibid., 57.

43. Ibid., 107.

44. Ibid., 12.

45. Kenneth Koltun-Fromm, *Moses Hess and Modern Jewish Identity* (Bloomington, IN, 2001), 76–84.

46. See my *Blood and Belief: The Circulation of a Symbol between Jews and Christians* (Berkeley, CA, 2007), 197–98. The idea that Adam was only the father of the Jews was also the position of Isaac La Peyrère, the seventeenth-century writer who may well have come from a Marrano background. La Peyrère developed a theory of "pre-Adamites" who fathered the rest of the human race. See p. 72 above, as well as Richard H. Popkin, *Isaac La Peyrère (1596–1676): His Life, Work and Influence* (Leiden, 1987).

47. Hess, *Rom und Jerusalem*, 109.

48. Ibid., 12; see also ibid., 171–73.

49. For Hess's views of intermarriage, see Avineri, *Moses Hess*, 73.

50. For an analysis of Hess's use of blood language, see my *Blood and Belief*, 175–82.

51. *Rom und Jerusalem*, 19–20.

52. Ibid., 13.

53. Ibid., 39.

54. Ibid., 41.

55. Ibid.

56. Ibid., 135.

57. Ibid., 136.

58. See John Efron, *Defenders of the Race: Jewish Doctors and Race Science in Fin-de-Siècle Europe* (New Haven, CT, 1994). On Zionist ideas on a Jewish race, see Raphael Falk, "Zionism and the Biology of the Jews," *Science in Context* 11, nos. 3–4 (Autumn–Winter 1998): 587–608. The most influential assimilationist response was by the Jewish anthropologist Maurice Fishberg, *The Jews: A Study of Race and Environment* (London and New York, 1911). A classic Marxist statement against a Jewish race based on Fishberg is Karl Kautsky, *Are the Jews a Race?* (New York, 1926). For the connection between blood language and various Jewish thinkers, see my *Blood and Belief*, 175–213.

59. Israel Zangwill, *The Melting Pot*, rev. ed. (New York, 1926), 127. For a more extensive interpretation of the play, with bibliography, see my "The Melting Pot and Beyond: Jews and the Politics of American Identity," in David Biale, Susannah Heschel, and Michael Galchinsky, eds., *Insider/Outsider: American Jews and Multiculturalism* (Berkeley, CA, 1998), 17–33. For the most recent study of Zangwill and his plays, see Edna Nahshon, ed., *From the Ghetto to the Melting Pot: Israel Zangwill's Jewish Plays* (Detroit, 2006).

60. Zangwill, *Melting Pot*, 204.

61. Ibid., 207.

62. See Michael Stanislawski, *Zionism and the Fin de Siècle: Cosmopolitanism and Nationalism from Nordau to Jabotinsky* (Berkeley, CA, 2001).

63. Zeev Jabotinsky, "Race" [in Hebrew], in *Umah ve-Hevrah* (Jerusalem, 1959), 130. For three excellent treatments of Jabotinsky's ideology, see Mitchell Cohen, *Zion and State: Nation, Class and the Shaping of Modern Israel* (Oxford, 1987), 184–97; Shlomo Avineri, "Jabotinsky: Integralist Nationalism and the Illusion of Power," in *The Making of Modern Zionism* (New York, 1981), 159–86; and Eran Kaplan, *The Jewish Radical Right: Revisionist Zionism and Its Ideological Legacy* (Madison, WI, 2005).

64. Jabotinsky, "Self-Government of National Minorities" [in Hebrew], in *Umah ve-Hevrah*, 13–72. On the "iron wall," see "On the Iron Wall (The Arabs and Us)" and "The Ethics of the Iron Wall" [both in Hebrew], in *Ba-derekh la-Medinah* (Tel Aviv, 1959), 251–66. See further Kaplan, *Jewish Radical Right*, 47–50.

65. Emma Lazarus, *An Epistle to the Hebrews*, centennial ed. (New York, 1987), 80. For a recent biography of Lazarus, see Esther Schor, *Emma Lazarus* (New York, 2006).

66. Lazarus, *Epistle to the Hebrews*, 11, quoting Claude Montefiore, "Is Judaism a Tribal Religion?" *Contemporary Review* (September 1882).

67. Ibid., 14.

68. Ibid., 25–26.

69. Ibid.

70. Ibid., 15 (italics in original).

71. On physical strength, see ibid., 31; on manual labor and productive occupations, see ibid., 16–21.

72. Emma Lazarus, "The Jewish Problem," in Morris U. Schappes, ed., *Emma Lazarus: Selections from Her Poetry and Prose*, 3rd ed. (New York, 1967), 77.

73. See Schor, *Emma Lazarus*, 129–30, 132, 172.

74. Lazarus, *Epistle to the Hebrews*, 27.

75. Ibid., 55.

76. See "The Poet Heine" in Schappes, *Emma Lazarus*, 93–94; and Schor, *Emma Lazarus*, passim.

77. The quotation is from a sonnet written in 1867 as a reply to Longfellow's poem on visiting the synagogue at Newport. See Schor, *Emma Lazarus*, 15–20.

78. Theodor Herzl, *The Jews' State*, trans. Henk Overberg (Northvale, NJ, 1997), 145. For the original German, see Theodor Herzl, *Der Judenstaat: Versuch einer modernen Lösung der Judenfrage*, ed. Ernst Piper (Berlin, 2004).

79. Herzl, *The Jews' State*, 143.

80. Ibid., 141.

81. Ibid.,

82. Ibid., 145.

83. Ibid., 133.

84. See Justinian, *Institutes*, bk. 3, title 27. Overberg brings this text and a translation on pp. 220–22. See further *L'état des juifs*, trans. Claude Klein (Paris, 1990).

85. Herzl, *The Jews' State*, 189.

86. Ibid., 187.

87. Ibid., 191.

88. Ibid., 194.

89. Ibid., 196.

90. See Jonathan Frankel, *Prophecy and Politics: Socialism, Nationalism and the Russian Jews, 1862–1917* (Cambridge, 1981); Ezra Mendelsohn, *On Modern Jewish Politics* (New York, 1993); and Eli Lederhendler, *The Road to Modern Jewish Politics: Political Tradition and Political Reconstruction in the Jewish Community of Tsarist Russia* (New York, 1989).

91. See the thorough biography of Phillipe Oriol, *Bernard Lazare* (Paris, 2003).

92. Ibid., 329–30.

93. Bernard Lazare, "The Revolutionary Spirit of Judaism," in *Antisemitism, Its History and Causes* (London, 1967), 141–48.

94. Ibid., 145.

95. Bernard Lazare, "Jewish Nationalism," in *Job's Dungheap*, ed. Hannah Arendt (New York, 1948), 55.

96. Bernard Lazare, *Le Fumier de Job* (Paris, 1928), 28. The English translation is incomplete and I have relied on the French original instead.

97. See the essays titled "The Race" and "Nationalism and Antisemitism" in Lazare, *Antisemitism*, 119–40.

98. Lazare, "Jewish Nationalism," in *Job's Dungheap*, 57.

99. Ibid., 73.

100. Ibid., 79.

101. Quoted in Oriol, *Bernard Lazare*, 366.

102. Ibid., 358.

103. Lazare, "Nationalism and Jewish Emancipation," in *Job's Dungheap*, 86.

104. Oriol, *Bernard Lazare*, 341.

105. Lazare, "Revolutionary Spirit," 148.

106. See Lazare's open letter to M. Tarieux, quoted in Oriol, *Bernard Lazare*, 355.

107. Lazare, *Fumier de Job*, 54–55.

108. Ibid., 37.

109. Ibid., 59–60.

110. Ibid., 31. For Mahler's (1899–1977) philosophy of Jewish history, see his *A History of Modern Jewry, 1780–1815* (London, 1971).

111. Lazare, *Fumier de Job*, 78.

112. Ibid.

113. Ibid., 75.

114. Ibid., 76–77.

115. Ibid., 85.

116. Ibid., 66.

117. Ibid., 49.

118. Bernard Lazare, *Juifs et antisémites* (Paris, 1992), 177

119. See Oriol, *Bernard Lazare*, 367–73, 387–91.

120. Quoted in ibid., 350.

121. Hannah Arendt interview with Günter Gaus on German television (1964). See Elisabeth Young-Bruehl, *Hannah Arendt: For Love of the World*, 2nd ed. (New Haven, CT, 2004), 11. On Arendt's Jewish identity, see further Pierre Birnbaum, *Geography of Hope: Exile, the Enlightenment, Disassimilation*, trans. Charlotte Mantell (Stanford, CA, 2008), chap. 5.

122. Young-Bruehl, *Hannah Arendt*, 10.

123. See Steven E. Aschheim, *Scholem, Arendt, Klemperer: Intimate Chronicles in Turbulent Times* (Bloomington, IN, 2001).

124. See the summary of the dissertation in Young-Bruehl, *Hannah Arendt*, 490–500.

125. See Richard J. Bernstein, *Hannah Arendt and the Jewish Question* (Cambridge, MA, 1996).

126. See Seyla Benhabib, *The Reluctant Modernism of Hannah Arendt* (Thousand Oaks, CA, 1996), esp. chap. 2; Peg Birmingham, *Hannah Arendt and Human Rights* (Bloomington, IN, 2006); Dana R. Villa, *Arendt and Heidegger: The Fate of the Political* (Princeton, NJ, 1995); and Margaret Canovan; *Hannah Arendt: A Reinterpretation of Her Political Thought* (Cambridge, 1992).

127. Although much of this argument was already present in *The Origins of Totalitarianism* (New York, 1951), she developed it more fully in *The Human Condition* (Chicago, 1958).

128. See Ronald Beiner, "Arendt and Nationalism," in Dana Villa, ed., *The Cambridge Companion to Hannah Arendt* (Cambridge, 2000), 44–64.

129. Arendt, *Origins of Totalitarianism*, 301.

130. Beiner argues in "Arendt and Nationalism" that Arendt's political philosophy was not communitarian, but he offers no argument to show how it was

essentially different, even if arising from her own idiosyncratic theories of the state and the nation.

131. Arendt, *Origins of Totalitarianism*, 296–97.

132. Hannah Arendt, *Eichmann in Jerusalem* (New York, 1964), 268–69.

133. Arendt, *Origins of Totalitarianism*, 240.

134. Ibid., 22.

135. See her 1940 essay "The Minority Question," in Hannah Arendt, *The Jewish Writings*, ed. Jerome Kohn and Ron Feldman (New York, 2007), 130.

136. Arendt, *Origins of Totalitarianism*, 68–79.

137. On the question of Arendt's ambivalent relation to modernity, see Benhabib, *Reluctant Modernism*.

138. Arendt, *Origins of Totalitarianism*, 8.

139. Hannah Arendt, "Jewish History, Revised" in *Jewish Writings*, 377–78.

140. Arendt, *Origins of Totalitarianism*, 120.

141. Arendt, "To Save the Jewish Homeland," in *Jewish Writings*, 400–401.

142. See Arendt, *On Revolution* (New York, 1965).

143. Arendt, "To Save the Jewish Homeland," 401.

144. Arendt, *Eichmann in Jerusalem*, 262–63

145. On the historical background of monism and Jabotinsky's use of it, see Stanislawski, *Zionism and the Fin de Siècle*, 217 and Kaplan, *The Jewish Radical Right*, 31–50.

146. David Ben-Gurion, *Mi-ma'amad le-Am* (Tel Aviv, 1974), 247. Translated in Cohen, *Zion and State*, 175.

147. Ben-Gurion, *Mi-ma'amad*, 252.

148. Ben-Gurion, *Medinat Yisrael Hamehudeshet* (Tel Aviv, 1969), 5.

149. See Benny Morris, *Israel's Border Wars, 1949–1956: Arab Infiltration, Israeli Retaliation, and the Countdown to the Suez War* (Oxford, 1993).

150. For an excellent discussion of the evolution of this doctrine, see Cohen, *Zion and State*, 201–59. On Ben-Gurion's abandonment of socialism, see ibid. and also, more polemically, Zeev Sternhell, *The Founding Myths of Israel: Nationalism, Socialism, and the Making of the Jewish State* (Princeton, NJ, 1998).

151. David Ben-Gurion, *The New Tasks of World Zionism* (London, 1949), 3. See further Cohen, *Zion and State*, 205.

152. See Cohen, *Zion and State*, 205, on Ben-Gurion's speech to the Knesset in June 1953 on the question of which flags would fly over state institutions.

153. Ben-Gurion, *Medinat Yisrael*, 2.

154. For the text of the Declaration of Independence, see Paul Mendes-Flohr and Jehuda Reinharz, eds., *The Jew in the Modern World: A Documentary History*, 2nd ed. (New York, 1995), 629–30.

Chapter 4. Israel: History, Language, and Culture

1. For the biographical context, see Jeffrey L. Sammons, *Heinrich Heine: A Modern Biography* (Princeton, NJ, 1979), 94–96 and 243–44.

2. Heinrich Heine, *The Rabbi of Bacherach*, trans. E. B. Ashton (New York, 1947), 61–62.

3. See Mark H. Gelber, "Herzl and Nordau: Aspects of the Early Zionist Reception," in Mark H. Gelber, ed., *The Jewish Reception of Heinrich Heine* (Tübingen, 1992), 139–52.

4. On Zamenhof, see René Centassi, *L'homme qui a defié Babel: Ludwik Lejzer Zamenhof* (Paris, 2001); and Marjorie Boulton, *Zamenhof: Creator of Esperanto* (London, 1960).

5. Max Weinreich, "The Language of the Way of the SHaS," in *History of the Yiddish Language*, trans. Shlomo Noble (Chicago, 1980), 175–246.

6. See Wilfred Cantwell Smith, *The Origin and Meaning of Religion* (San Francisco, 1978); and Talal Asad, *Genealogies of Religion: Discipline and Reasons of Power in Christianity and Islam* (Baltimore, 1993), chap. 1.

7. See David Biale, ed., *Cultures of the Jews: A New History* (New York, 2002), especially my preface. For some qualifications to this argument, see Moshe Rosman, *How Jewish Is Jewish History?* (Oxford, 2007).

8. See Ivan Marcus, "The Culture of Ashkenaz," in Biale, *Cultures of the Jews*, 449–516.

9. See David Ruderman, *The World of a Renaissance Jew: The Life and Thought of Abraham Ben Mordecai Farissol* (Cincinnati, 1981), appendix; and Shalom Sabar, "Bride, Heroine and Courtesan: Images of the Jewish Woman in Hebrew Manuscripts of the Renaissance in Italy," *Proceedings of the Tenth World Congress of Jewish Studies*, division D, vol. 2 (1990): 68. I thank Shalom Sabar for drawing the text from the Jewish Theological Seminary Library to my attention.

10. For an ambitious attempt to do this, see Yermiyahu Yovel, David Shaham, and Yair Tzaban, eds., *Zeman Yehudi Hadash: Tarbut Yehudit be-Edan Hiloni* (Jerusalem, 2007).

11. For some crucial background, see Steven J. Zipperstein, *The Jews of Odessa: A Cultural History, 1794–1881* (Stanford, CA, 1985).

12. See Steven J. Zipperstein, *Elusive Prophet: Ahad Ha'am and the Origins of Zionism* (Berkeley, CA, 1993); and David H. Weinberg, *Between Tradition and Modernity: Chaim Zhitlowski, Simon Dubnow, Ahad Ha-Am, and the Shaping of Modern Jewish Identity* (New York, 1996), chap. 4.

13. Ahad Ha'am wrote many essays arguing this position. See, for example, his 1903 essay "Spiritual Renewal" [in Hebrew], in *Al Parashat Derakhim* (Berlin, 1921), 2:111–43.

14. Ahad Ha'am, "Slavery within Freedom" [in Hebrew], *Al Parashat Derakhim* (Berlin, 1921), 1:132.

15. Ahad Ha'Am, "Zionism and Jewish Culture," in *Essays, Letters, Memoirs*, trans. Leon Simon (Oxford, 1946), 96.

16. Ahad Ha'am, "Slavery within Freedom."

17. Weinberg, *Between Tradition and Modernity*, 262.

18. Ahad Ha'Am, *Essays, Letters, Memoirs*, 270 (letter of 30 March 1913).

19. Ibid., 269 (18 September 1910).

20. Ibid.

21. See his letter to B. Benas and I. Raffalowich in ibid., 272 (26 October 1915).

22. Ahad Ha'am, "Zionism and Jewish Culture," 91.

23. Ahad Ha'am, "Diaspora Nationalism," in *Essays, Letters, Memoirs*, 226.

24. Ibid.

25. Ahad Ha'am, *Al Parashat Derakhim*, 1:169–77.

26. Ahad Ha'am, "Zionism and Jewish Culture," 98–99.

27. Ahad Ha'am, "The Supremacy of Reason," in *Nationalism and the Jewish Ethic: Basic Writings of Ahad Ha'am*, ed. Hans Kohn (New York, 1962), 275–76.

28. Ibid., 288.

29. Quotes in Zipperstein, *Elusive Prophet*, 49.

30. For this essay, see Hayim Nahman Bialik, *Kol Kitve H. N. Bialik* (Tel Aviv 1938), 197–201. On the essay, see Chana Kronfeld, *On the Margins of Modernism* (Berkeley, CA, 1993), 83–85. Kronfeld shows that even though the essay became first widely known from its appearance in *Hashiloah* in 1907, it was, in fact, first published in *Ivriya* in 1905.

31. See Yitzhak Bacon, *Bialik: Ben Ivrit le-Yiddish* (Beersheba, Israel, 1987).

32. Bialik, *Kol Kitve Bialik*, 197–98. Translated in Kronfeld, *On the Margins*, 83.

33. Bialik, *Kol Kitve Bialik*, 198.

34. Ibid., 199.

35. Bialik, "On the Collection of the Aggadah" [in Hebrew], *Kol Kitve*, 213–16.

36. Louis Ginzberg, *Legends of the Jews* (Philadelphia, 1909–38).

37. Bialik, "Halakhah and Aggadah" [in Hebrew], *Kol Kitve*, 216–22.

38. Ibid., 217.

39. B. Eruvin 13b, Gittin 6b.

40. Bialik, "Halakhah and Aggadah," 221.

41. Ibid., 222.

42. See Jeffrey Veidlinger, "Simon Dubnow Recontextualized: The Sociological Conception of Jewish History and the Russian Intellectual Legacy," *Jahrbuch des Simon-Dubnow-Instituts* 3 (2004): 411–27.

43. See Anke Hilbrenner, "Simon Dubnov's Master Narrative and the Construction of a Jewish Collective Memory in the Russian Empire," *Ab Imperio* 4 (2003): 143–64.

44. Simon Dubnow, "The Sociological View of Jewish History," in Michael A. Meyer, *Ideas of Jewish History* (New York, 1974), 263.

45. Ibid., 262–63.

46. Ibid.

47. See my *Gershom Scholem: Kabbalah and Counter-History* (Cambridge, MA, 1979), esp. chap. 9. See also Amos Funkenstein, "Anti-Jewish Propaganda: Pagan, Medieval and Modern," *Jerusalem Quarterly* 19 (Spring 1981): 56–72; and later, idem, *Perceptions of Jewish History* (Berkeley and Los Angeles, 1993), 36–40, 169–201.

48. M. Y. Bin-Gorion [Berdichevsky], *Zefunot ve-Aggadot* (Tel Aviv, 1956), 11.

49. M. Y. Bin-Gorion [Berdichevsky], *Kol Kitve M. Y. Bin-Gorion*, 43.

50. Ibid., 34.

51. Ibid., 181–84.

52. Ibid., 87–88.

53. See Emanuel bin Gorion, "Micha Joseph bin Gorion (Berdyczewski)" in *Mimekor Yisrael*, trans. I. M. Lask (Bloomington, IN, 1990), xvi.

54. Bin-Gorion [Berdichevsky], *Kol Kitve*, 49.

55. See my "Historical Heresies and Modern Jewish Identity," *Jewish Social Studies* 8, no. 2/3 (2002): 112–32; and "Shabbtai Zvi and the Seductions of Jewish Orientalism," *Jerusalem Studies in Jewish Thought* 17 (2000) 2:85–110 (English section).

56. Gershom Scholem, "The Science of Judaism—Then and Now," in *The Messianic Idea in Judaism and Other Essays in Jewish Spirituality* (New York, 1971), 310. Translation revised on the basis of the original, "Wissenschaft des Judentums, Einst und Jetzt," in idem, *Judaica* (Frankfurt, 1968), 1:158. See further my *Gershom Scholem*, chap. 9.

57. Gershom Scholem, "The Messianic Idea in Judaism," in *Messianic Idea*, 21.

58. Gershom Scholem, *Sabbatai Sevi: The Mystical Messiah*, trans. R.J.Z Werblowsky (Princeton, NJ, 1971).

59. Gershom Scholem, "Über die Theologie des Sabbatianismus im Lichte Abraham Cardozos," in *Judaica* (Frankfurt, 1963), 146. By "reality of the Hebrews," Scholem is referring to a book of magical neo-Kabbalism by Oskar Goldberg, *Die Wirklichkeit der Hebräer* (1925; republished Wiesbaden, 2005). See my *Gershom Scholem*, 265, n. 46.

60. Gershom Scholem, "Redemption through Sin," in *Messianic Idea*, 78–141.

61. Ibid., 137–41.

62. Ibid., 84.

63. See in particular his 1945 essay, "Reflections on the Science of Judaism" [in Hebrew], in *Devarim be-Go*, 2nd ed. (Tel Aviv, 1976), 385–403. A much abbreviated and restrained English version, "The Science of Judaism—Then and Now" appeared in *Messianic Idea*, 304–13.

64. See my *Gershom Scholem*, chap. 8.

65. See Joseph Hayim Brenner, "The Faithful One (On the Image of Bialik)" [in Hebrew], in *Ketavim* (Tel Aviv, 1985), 4:1391–1421. For an analysis of Brenner's literary method, see Menahem Brinker, *Ad ha-Simta ha-Teverianit: Ma'amar al Sippur ve-Mahshava be-Yitzirat Brenner* (Tel Aviv, 1990).

66. Brenner, "On Halakhah and Aggadah" [in Hebrew], in *Ketavim*, 4:1507.

67. Ibid., 4:1510. The reference is to Bialik's poem, "Shirati" which immortalizes his mother, condemned to raise her children in poverty after she was widowed.

68. Ibid., 4:1503.

69. Ibid., 4:1502.

70. Brinker, *Ad ha-Simta*, 168–72.

71. Brenner, "Evaluation of Ourselves in Three Volumes" [in Hebrew], in *Ketavim*, 4:1225.

72. Ibid., 4:1242.

73. Ibid., 4:1254.

74. Ibid., 4:1253.

75. Ibid., 4:1284.

76. Ibid., 4:1246–47.

77. Ibid., 4:1282.

78. Ibid., 4:1284.

79. Ibid., 4:1295–96.

80. Ibid., 4:1296.

81. On Gordon, see Eliezer Schweid, *Ha-Yahid: Olamo shel A. D. Gordon* (Tel Aviv, 1970).

82. Brenner, "Evaluation of Ourselves," 4:1244.

83. Ibid., 4:1240.

84. Ibid., 4:1405.

85. See Nurit Govrin, *Me'orah Brenner: Ha-Ma'avak al Hofesh ha-Bitui* (Jerusalem, 1985), for a history of the controversy and relevant documents, including Brenner's original essay in *Ha-Po'el Ha-Tza'ir* (22 Heshvan 1911).

86. Quoted in Brinker, *Ad ha-Simtah*, 164.

87. Govrin, *Me'orah Brenner*, 135.

88. Ibid., 136.

89. See Matthew Hoffman, *From Rebel to Rabbi: Reclaiming Jesus and the Making of Modern Jewish Culture* (Stanford, CA, 2007), chap. 2.

90. The best treatment of Zhitlowsky's life and thought is in Weinberg, *Between Tradition and Modernity*, chap. 2. On Zhitlowsky's relationship to the movement of Yiddishism, see Emanuel S. Goldsmith, *Architects of Yiddishism at the Beginning of the Twentieth Century* (Rutherford, NJ, 1976).

91. Discussed in Weinberg, *Between Tradition and Modernity*, 92–93

92. Chaim Zhitlowsky, *Yid un velt* (New York, 1945), 191.

93. Ibid., 97. For Zhitlowsky's initial view of Zionism (1898), see "Zionism or Socialism?" [in Yiddish], in *Gezamelte Shriften* (Warsaw, 1931), 5:47–76.

94. See Tony Michels, *A Fire in Their Hearts: Yiddish Socialists in New York* (Cambridge, MA, 2005), chap. 3.

95. See Chaim Zhitlowsky, "Why Especially Yiddish?" [in Yiddish], in *Gezamelte Shriften*, 5:31–43.

96. Zhitlowsky, "Zionism or Socialism," 72–73, translated in Michels, *Fire in Their Hearts*, 133.

97. See Weinberg, *Between Tradition and Modernity*, 105–6.

98. Zhitlowsky, "Job, Poem of Jewish Free Thought," [in Hebrew], in *Ketavim*, trans. Yaakov Rabi (Merchavia, Israel, 1961), 313–42.

99. Ibid., 328–30.

100. Zhitlowsky, "The Poetic-Nationalist Renewal of the Jewish Religion" [in Hebrew], in *Ketavim*, 223–57.

101. Zhitlowsky, "What Is a Nation?" [in Yiddish], in *Der Sozializm un die natzionale Frage, Gezamelte Shriften* (Warsaw, 1935), 13:68–98.

102. Ibid., 71.

103. See the discussion of this essay by Matthew Hoffman, "From *Pintele Yid* to *Racenjude*: Chaim Zhitlowsky and Racial Conceptions of Jewishness," *Jewish History* 19 (2005): 65–78.

104. See Michael Silber, "The Emergence of Ultra-Orthodoxy: The Invention of a Tradition," in Jack Wertheimer, ed., *The Uses of Tradition: Jewish Continuity in the Modern Era* (New York and Jerusalem, 1992), 49.

105. See Zhitlowsky, "What Is a Nation?" 88.

106. See Michels, *Fire in Their Hearts*.

107. See my "The Melting Pot and Beyond: Jews and the Politics of American Identity," in David Biale, Susannah Heschel, and Michael Galchinsky, eds., *Insider/Outsider: American Jews and Multiculturalism* (Berkeley, CA, 1998), 17–33.

108. Judah L. Magnes, "A Republic of Nationalities," *Emmanuel Pulpit* (February 13, 1909), 5, reprinted in Paul Mendes-Flohr and Jehudah Reinharz, *The Jew in the Modern World* (New York and Oxford, 1980), 392.

109. Reprinted in Horace Kallen, *Culture and Democracy in the United States* (New York, 1924), 67–125. See further Mitchell Cohen, "In Defense of Shaatnez: A Politics for Jews in a Multicultural America," in Biale, *Insider/Outsider*, 34–54.

110. Kallen, *Culture and Democracy*, 112–13.

111. *Ibid.*, 114–15.

112. *Ibid.*, 122.

113. Isaac B. Berkson, *Theories of Americanization: A Critical Study, with Special Reference to the Jewish Group* (New York, 1920). See further Milton Gordon, *Assimilation in American Life* (New York, 1964), 149–52.

114. See his "Can Judaism Survive in the United States?" (1925), reprinted in *Judaism at Bay* (New York, 1932), 177–220. On Kallen's change in position, see Gordon, *Assimilation*, 151.

115. Mordecai Kaplan, *Judaism as a Civilization* (New York, 1967), 312. On Kaplan, see Arnold Eisen, *The Chosen People in America: A Study in Jewish Religious Ideology* (Bloomington, IN, 1983); and my "Louis Finkelstein, Mordecai Kaplan and American 'Jewish Contributions to Civilization,'" in Jeremy Cohen and Richard I. Cohen, eds., *The Jewish Contribution to Civilization: Reassessing an Idea* (Oxford, 2008), 185–98. Much of this section is drawn from the latter essay.

116. On Ahad Ha'am's influence on American Zionists, see Evyatar Friesel, "Ahad Ha-Amism in American Zionist Thought," in Jacques Kornberg, ed., *At the Crossroads: Essays on Ahad Ha-am* (Albany, NY, 1983), 133–41.

117. Kaplan, *Judaism as a Civilization*, 178.

118. Ibid., 79.

119. Ibid., 418–19.

Epilogue: Legacy

1. For this concept of legacy, see Hermann Levin Goldschmidt, *The Legacy of German Jewry*, trans. David Suchoff (New York, 2007), esp. 236–44.

2. See, for example, Peter Berger, ed., *The Desecularization of the World: Resurgent Religion and World Politics* (New York, 1999).

3. Amos Oz, *In the Land of Israel* (New York, 1983), 9.

4. Ibid., 6.

5. Ibid., 16.

6. See Amos Oz, "Full Wagon, Empty Wagon?" *Contemplate: The Journal of Cultural Jewish Thought* 3 (2005–6): 60–72.

7. See Chana Bloch and Chana Kronfeld, "Amichai's Counter-Theology: Opening *Open Closed Open* (Yehuda Amichai)," *Judaism* 49, no. 2 (Spring, 2000), 153–67.

8. Yehuda Amichai, *Shirim, 1948–1962* (Jerusalem and Tel Aviv, 1969), 71.

9. Yehuda Amichai, "Gods Change, Prayers Are Here to Stay," in *Open Closed Open*, trans. Chana Bloch and Chana Kronfeld (New York, 2006), 40.

10. Yehuda Amichai, "Tourists," in *Selected Poems*, trans. Chana Bloch and Stephen Mitchell (New York and San Francisco, 1986), 137–38.

11. See Adi Ophir, "Jew-Goy" [in Hebrew], in *Avodat ha-Hoveh: Masot al Tarbut Yisraelit ba'Zeman ha-Zeh* (n.p., 2001), 52–84.

12. Adi Ophir, "The Passover Haggadah: A Deconstructed Reading" [in Hebrew], in *Avodat ha-Hoveh*, 85–116.

13. See Jonathan Sarna, *American Judaism: A History* (New Haven, CT, 2004).

14. Will Herberg, *Protestant, Catholic, Jew: An Essay in American Religious Sociology* (Garden City, NY, 1955).

15. Philip Roth, *The Plot against America* (New York, 2004), 220.

16. Hana Wirth-Nesher, "Jewish Culture USA" [in Hebrew], in Yermiyahu Yovel, David Shaham, and Yair Tzaban, eds., *Zeman Yehudi Hadash: Tarbut Yehudit be-Edan Hiloni* (Jerusalem, 2007), 3:293.

17. Leon Wieseltier, *Kaddish* (New York, 1999).

18. Andrea Most, "Postmodernism and Jewish Identity" [in Hebrew], in *Zeman Yehudi Hadash*, 4:126–29.

19. Rebecca Goldstein, *Betraying Spinoza* (New York, 2006).

20. See Shalom Auslander, *Foreskin's Lament: A Memoir* (New York, 2007); and Nathan Englander, *For the Relief of Unbearable Urges* (New York, 1999).

Index

Abraham bar Hiyya, 65
Abrahams, Israel, 141
Abramowitsch, S. Y. (Mendele Mokher Sforim), 140
accommodation, principle of, 66
"acosmic" view, 32
acquired intellect, 28
active intellect, 28
Adam, as father of the Jews, 107, 209n46
aggadah, 148–50, 157–58
Ahad Ha'am (Asher Ginzberg), 60, 82–84, 123, 139–45, 153, 161–62, 172, 185, 189, 214n13; "Imitation and Assimilation," 143; influence of, 145–47; "Transvaluation of Values," 82
ahavat ha-shem, 28
Akhenaten (Egyptian pharaoh), 77–78
al-Andalus, 61–62
Aleichem, Sholem. *See* Sholem Aleichem
alienation, xii, 101–2
Alter, Robert, 61
Altmann, Alexander, 103
Americanization, 169–75
American Jewish community, 169–75, 187–93
Amichai, Yehuda, 184–85; *El Maleh Rahamim*, 184
Amsterdam, Portuguese "nation" of, 22–24, 27–28, 93, 119
anarchism, 123, 155, 158; cultural, 118–19
Ansky, S., 150, 164
anti-Catholicism, 173. *See also* Catholicism
antijuif, 118
anti-Nietzscheans, 51
antinomianism, 147
anti-Semitism, 104, 107, 110, 114–15, 118, 160
anti-Zionism, 182–83. *See also* Zionism
apikoros, 5, 166
Apollo (pagan deity), 38–39, 57–58
apostasy, 30, 108, 155–56
Arendt, Hannah, 92, 122–29, 133–34, 176, 179, 212n130; *Eichmann in Jerusalem*, 125; "The Jew as Pariah," 124; *The Origins of Totalitarianism*, 125–29
army, Israeli, 131, 186
Asad, Talal, 10
Asch, Sholem, 163
Ashkenazim, 9, 29–30, 138, 180
assimilation, 109–10, 115, 118, 124, 127, 141, 143–45, 159
astrology, 65
atheism, 15, 20, 22, 28–29, 32, 37, 40, 45, 177
Auerbach, Berthold, 35
Augustine, 124; *City of God*, 2
Auslander, Shalom, 191
autonomism, 118, 123, 129, 134, 151
autonomy, human, 8
axial age, 3
ayin, 47

baal teshuva, 166–67
Barcelona, 96
Barth, Karl, 53
bat kol, 7–8, 18
Bayle, Pierre, 29
Beiner, Ronald, "Arendt and Nationalism," 212n130
belief, principles of, 12
Ben-Gurion, David, 43, 60, 86–90, 93, 130–34, 179, 182, 190
Benjamin, Walter, 55
Berdichevsky, Micha Yosef, 57, 60, 83–86, 139–40, 152–54, 185; "On the Book," 84; *Sinai und Gerizim*, 85
Berger, Peter L., 3, 5–6
Berlin, Jewish community of, 29–30
Bernstein, Leonard, *Kaddish* Symphony, 189
berurim, 95
Betteljuden, 29
Bialik, Hayim Nahman, 15, 47–51, 83, 137, 139–40, 145–50, 176–77; "The Birth Pangs of Language," 146; "Halakhah and Aggadah," 148–50; influence of, 157, 161; Mishnah commentary, 148; "Rev

Bialik, Hayim Nahman (*cont'd*)
elation and Concealment in Language,"
47–51, 146; *Sefer ha-Aggadah* (with
Ravnitsky), 148
Bible, 6, 178; as cultural text, 59–60, 136;
and definition of "Israel," 93; Freud on,
76–81; Heine on, 74–75; as historical
text, 73, 97–99; interpolations in, 62–63;
of Jewish Enlightenment, 59–60; Maimonides on, 72; as nationalist text, 86,
89; as political document, 74–75; as portable fatherland of Jews, 74–75; speaks
the language of human beings, 64–66,
72, 88; Spinoza on, 69–74; Zionism and,
81–91. *See also* biblical books; Torah
biblical allegories, 63–65
biblical books: Deuteronomy, 7, 16, 63,
85, 89; Ecclesiastes, 17; Esther, 16–17;
Exodus, 7, 16, 87; Genesis, 62–63, 87;
Job, 17–18, 166; Leviticus, 196n14; Song
of Songs, 61–62, 88
biblical exegesis, 19, 63–65, 121, 178
biblical metaphors, 71–72
Bildung, 36, 40
Birnbaum, Pierre, *Geography of Hope*, 195n7
Bloch, Ernst, 42
blood community, 107
blood libel, 136, 160
Blumenberg, Hans, 12, 196n8
Born, Max, 43
Brenner, Joseph Hayim, 60, 90–91, 139,
157–63, 175–76, 178, 183–85, 187, 192;
Breakdown and Bereavement, 160; "Evalu-
ation of Ourselves in Three Volumes,"
158–59
Brenner Affair, 162–63
Brinker, Menahem, 158
Brod, Max, 55
Buber, Martin, 53, 128; *I and Thou*, 54
Buddhism, 3
Bundism, 11, 118, 134, 164

Cahan, Abraham, 169
Calvin, John, 98
"Canaanite" writers, 87
capitalism, 106, 120
Cardozo, Abraham, 155
Catholicism, 3, 22, 173. *See also* Christianity
Chalier, Catherine, 22
chosen people, concept of, 73, 77, 97,
126–27, 160, 164

Christianity, 1–4, 97–99, 103, 105, 119,
121, 149, 162–64; conversion to, 22, 30,
35–36, 135, 139, 141, 162–64
circumcision, 100
civic religion, 70–71
class struggle, Jewish history as, 121–22,
133
Cohen, Hermann, 33–34
Cohen, Richard, 60
collective memory, 11, 197n33
collector, as historian, 150–52
commandments: distinguished from laws,
103; historical interpretation of, 19,
67–68, 178; Mendelssohn's theory of,
102–3
communism, 11
"conscious pariah," 123–24, 127
conversion to Christianity, 22, 30, 35–36,
135, 139, 141, 162–64
conversos, 22
cosmopolitanism, 74–75, 112–14, 165
counterhistory, 139, 152–57
covenant, divine, 94–95, 98
Crescas, Hasdai, 65
crimes against humanity, 126
crucifix debate, 163–64
culture: as basis for Jewish identity, 136–37,
140–45; Israeli, 175; Jewish, 136–38;
Ahad Ha'am and, 140–45; and secularism, 11–13
curse of Eve, 50

Da Costa, Uriel (Gabriel), 23, 27, 154
Damascus Blood Libel, 136
Darwin, Charles, 168
dat, 138
democracy, 98–100, 117, 171
Democratic Party, 169
determinism, 21, 26
deus absconditus, 55–56, 177
deus sive natura, 25, 43
Deutscher, Isaac, xii, 9–10, 176; "The
Non-Jewish Jew," 1
Diaspora, 87, 104, 118, 127–28, 144,
159
Disraeli, Benjamin, 109–10, 126
diversity, 122, 125–27
Dos naye Leben (periodical), 163
dos pintele Yid, 168
Dreyfus, Alfred, 118
Dreyfus Affair, 118, 127, 180

Dubnow, Simon, 123, 129, 134, 139–40, 150–52, 164; *World History of the Jewish People*, 151
Duran, Profiat, *Efodi*, 198n15
Durkheim, Émile, xii

Eastern European Jews, 47, 112–14, 134, 179
Egypt, ancient, 77–78, 89
Eichmann, Adolf, 126, 128
ein sof, 47
Einstein, Albert, 15, 41–44, 46, 177; "On Spinoza's Ethics," 42
Eisenmenger, Johann Andreas, *Entdecktes Judenthum*, 209n27
Eliezer, Rabbi, story of, 7–8, 18
Elisha ben Abuya (Aher), 1, 138, 154, 176
emergency powers, rabbinic courts and, 96, 117
Englander, Nathan, 191
Enlightenment, European, 1–2, 6, 29–30, 156, 166, 200n38
Enlightenment, Jewish, 9, 31, 166
Epicurus, 5
excommunication, 102–3; of Spinoza, 27–28, 70, 93, 108, 132
Exile, negation of, 160
exiles, ingathering of, 131, 133, 144
existentialism, 145
Ezra the Scribe, 69

family, Jewish, 106–7
Feiner, Shmuel, xi, 30
fellow-unbeliever (*Unglaubensgenossen*), 40
Fichte, Johann Gottlieb, 34
First Temple period, 16
Fishberg, Maurice, 210n58
folk culture, 150, 168, 173
France, 180
Frankists, 155–56
Freud, Sigmund, xii, 15, 40–41, 46, 60, 176–77; on the Bible, 76–81; "Civilization and Its Discontents," 40; *The Future of an Illusion*, 40–41; *Moses and Monotheism*, 76–81; and racial theory, 79–80, 109–10; *Totem and Taboo*, 41, 78–79, 81
Funkenstein, Amos, 3, 9

Gans, David, 68
Gauchet, Marcel, 6; *The Disenchantment of the World*, 3

Gay, Ruth, 30
Geiger, Abraham, 65
German Jews, 29–34, 36
Germany: Nazi era, 77–78, 124–25; Weimar era, 45, 53
Gerondi, Nissim, 96–97, 178
Ginsberg, Allen, "Kaddish," 188–89
Ginzberg, Louis, 148
Gnosticism, 15, 32, 55–56, 177
God: and Apollo, 58; biblical, 16–18; dehumanizing of, 26; does not have a body, 66; of Einstein, 42–43; existentialist, 33; of Heine, 37–39; hidden, 55–56, 177; of history, 16; as idea of perfection, 33; identified with nothingness/death, 47; infinite, 24, 47; of Kabbalah, 47; of Kabbalists, 20; of Maimon, 32–34; of Maimonides, 19–22; name of, 52; as necessity, 21, 37; of the philosophers, 16; as psychological projection, 177; Spinozan, 25–26; as spirit of nature, 174; transcendent, 16–22; as the void, 49
God, Torah, and Israel, as Jewish "trinity," 12, 92
Goetschel, Willi, 24
Goldstein, Herbert S., 42
Goldstein, Rebecca, 24, 190–91, 199n25
Gordon, Aaron David, 161
Gordon, J. L., 157
goy/Jew binary, 185
Graetz, Heinrich, xii, 17, 198n3
Great Revolt against Rome, 153
Great Separation, 2
Greece, ancient, 16–17, 79

Ha'am, Ahad. *See* Ahad Ha'am
Haganah, 131–32
Haggadah (Passover), 186
hakham, 95
ha-Kohen, Joseph, 68
halakhah, 148–50, 157–58
Halbwachs, Maurice, 11
Halevi, Judah, *Kuzari*, 35
Haman, 60
Hashomer Hatzair, ix–x, 193
Hasidism, 141
Haskalah, Maimon and, 31–34
Hebrew language. *See* language, Hebrew
Hebrew literature. *See* literature, Hebrew
hefker bet-din, 94
Hegel, G.W.F., 34, 105

Heine, Heinrich, 15, 35–40, 46, 60, 114, 137, 177; on Bible, 74–75; "Germany: A Winter's Tale," 36–37; *The Rabbi of Bacherach*, 135–36; "Religion and Philosophy in Germany," 36–37
Heisenberg, Werner, 43
Herberg, Will, 188
Herder, Johann Gottfried, 83
herem, 103
heresy, 1, 5, 176. *See also* Sabbatianism
heretics: and counterhistory, 153–57; as secularists, 5–6
hermeneutics, 54–55, 68–69, 71–72
Herod the Great, 198n3
Herzl, Theodor, 60, 92, 114–17, 120, 133–34, 137, 164, 176, 179, 187, 189–90; *Altneuland*, 117, 186; *Der Judenstaat*, 114, 116–17; and Zionism, 115–17, 123
Hess, Moses, 92, 104–9, 119, 133–34, 179; *The Holy History of Mankind*, 35, 105; *Rome and Jerusalem*, 105–8
Hibbat Zion, 150
hiloni, 5, 196n16
Hirschfeld, Ariel, 48
historical consciousness, 53–54
historical fiction, Jewish, 135
historicism, 45
historiography, Jewish, 68–69
history, and secularism, 11–13. *See also* counterhistory
Hiwi al-Balkhi, 63
Hobbes, Thomas, 72
Hoffman, Matthew, 168
hofshi, 196n16
hol, 4–5
Holocaust, 126, 169, 183, 189
Hovevei Zion, 137
human freedom, 54–55
humanism, 10, 183–84
hyphenated identities, in contemporary America, 173

Ibn Adret, Solomon, 96–97, 178
Ibn Ezra, Abraham, 62–66, 72, 178
Ibn Gabirol, Solomon, 62, 113
Ibn Verga, Solomon, *Shevet Yehudah*, 68
Ichud group, 128
idealism, 33–34
identity, Israeli, 131, 133
identity, Jewish: based on culture, 136–37, 140–45; based on race, 104–11, 119–20,

167–68, 171–72; based on religion, 119; Einstein and, 41–44; as individual decision, 162–63
imitation, and assimilation, 143
immigrants, Jewish, to United States, 169, 179–80, 188
immigration, Kallen's theory of, 171
immortality, and Jewish belief, 104–11
immortality of the soul, Spinoza on, 27–28
individualism, 24, 158, 162–63
Inquisition, Catholic, 22
intermarriage, 107, 110, 170, 173, 192
internationalism, 122
Irgun Zvai Leumi, 131–32
Islam, 4, 9, 79
Israel, ancient, 73, 93; Ben-Gurion on, 86–87; Berdichevsky on, 85–86; Spinoza on, 97–99
Israel, Jonathan, *Radical Enlightenment*, 200n38
Israel, state of, 89, 91–93, 128–29, 139, 144, 178, 181–88; Ben-Gurion and, 131–34; and Bible interpretation, 86–90; Declaration of Independence, 132–33
Israelites, distinguished from Jews, 118
Italy, Fascist, 77–78

Jabotinsky, Vladimir, 90, 111, 130–31, 134, 179; influence of, 131–32; *Samson*, 90
Jacobi, Friedrich Heinrich, 29
Jaspers, Karl, 3
Jesus, 75, 154
"Jew by choice," 191
Jewish studies, as academic discipline, 190–91
Jews: Ashkenazim, 9, 29–30, 138, 180; Eastern European, 47, 112–14, 134, 179; German, 29–34, 36; Mizrahi, 143, 182; Portuguese, 22–24, 27–28, 93, 119; Sephardim, 9, 29, 35, 112, 114, 118
Job (biblical figure), 121
Jobani, Yuval, 205n24
Joseph (biblical figure), 87
Josephus Flavius, 68
Joshua (biblical figure), 85
Joshua, Rabbi, 7–8
Judaism: as civilization, 172–74; emergence of, 3; as ground for Jewish secularism, 4–6; as most modern religion, 103; as most religious religion, 174; as noncoercive religion, 102; search for "essence"

of, 12; and social justice, 121. *See also* Orthodoxy; Reform Judaism
"Judaizers," 22–24
Judenthum, 209n27
Judeomania, 167
Jung, Carl, 80

Kabbalah, 4, 46–47, 52, 177, 199n25, 203n105; doctrine of contraction, 32; and Sabbatianism, 100–101
Kabbalists, 20, 61; secular, 15, 46–56
kaddish, 188–89
Kafka, Franz, 15, 55–56; "Before the Law," 56
Kallen, Horace, 139, 175; "Democracy *versus* the Melting Pot," 171
Kant, Immanuel, 10
Kaplan, Mordecai, 139, 175; *Judaism as a Civilization*, 12, 172–74
Karaites, 18
Karelitz, Rabbi Abraham (Hazon Ish), 182
Kaufman, Yehezkel, 89
kibbutz movement, 128
Kierkegaard, Søren, 49
Klausner, Joseph, 5
Koltun-Fromm, Kenneth, 107
Krochmal, Nahman, 65
Kronfeld, Chana, *On the Margins of Modernism*, 215n30
Kushner, Tony, *Angels in America*, 189

Labor Zionist movement, 89–90
Ladino dialect, 12
laïcité, 180
Lamarckism, 79–80, 167–68
language: Bialik on, 47–51; of Bible, 64–65; and culture, 139–40; spoken, 146–47
language, English, 139, 174–75, 188
language, Esperanto, 137
language, German, 174
language, Greek, 174
language, Hebrew, 12, 54, 91, 140, 146, 161, 175, 182; as biblical language, 64–65, 72; as national language, 142–43; revival of, 51–52, 137
language, Israeli, 175
language, Russian, 90
languages, European, 12
language wars, 137, 140, 142–43, 146–47, 149–50, 160–61, 179

La Peyrère, Isaac, 72, 209n46
laws of nature, 20–21, 26–27, 34, 43
laws of sacrifice, 67
Lazare, Bernard, 92, 118–23, 129, 133–34, 164, 179; influence of, 124, 127; *Job's Dungheap*, 119, 121; "The Revolutionary Spirit in Judaism," 119
Lazarus, Emma, 35, 92, 112–14, 119, 133
Lazarus, Moritz, *Ethics of Judaism*, 44
Lazier, Benjamin, 45
legacy, concept of, 181
Lehi group, 132
Leibniz, Gottfried Wilhelm, 29, 33
Lenin, V. I., 115, 151
Lessing, Gotthold, 29–30
Levi ben Gershon (Gersonides), 28, 65; influence of, 25–26
Levites, 99
liberalism, 11
Lilien, Ephraim Moses, 60
Lilienblum, Moses Leib, 35, 140
Lilla, Mark, 2
linguistic creation, 146–47
literature: Hebrew, 60–61, 185; Yiddish, 165–66
Locke, John, 101
Lorberbaum, Menachem, 95–97
Löwith, Karl, 3
Luria, Isaac, 47, 49
Luzzato, Samuel David, 108–9

Magnes, Judah L., 128, 141–42, 170–71
Mahler, Raphael, 121
Maimon, Salomon (Shlomo ben Joshua), 15, 29–34, 46, 144, 176–77; *Lebensgeschichte*, 31
Maimonides, Moses, 15, 18–22, 52, 65, 72, 88, 117, 176–78; and allegorical exegesis, 66–68; *Guide of the Perplexed*, 18–19, 35; historical interpretation of the commandments, 19, 67–68, 178; influence of, 18–19, 25–26, 29–34, 66, 144; on Jewish political theory, 95–97; *Mishneh Torah*, 67–68, 148; negative theology, 9, 19–20, 22, 26
majority rule, principle of, 7–8
majority status, and Jewish politics, 133
mamlakhtiyut, 131
Mapu, Avraham, 81; *Ahavat Zion*, 60
marginality, 152
Marranos, 22–24, 27–28, 155

Marx, Karl, "On the Jewish Question, xii, 120
Marxism, 115
materialism, 10
mathematics, 33, 48
Meir, Rabbi, 1
Meiri, Menachem, 97
"melting pot" theory, 170–72
memory traces, 79–80
Menasseh ben Israel, 102
Mendelssohn, Moses, 10, 29–30, 93, 101–4, 116, 134, 192, 198n7; *Bi'ur*, 60; *Jerusalem*, 101–4
Mercier, Pierre, *Essai sur la littérature juive*, 106
Messiah, 62, 163
messianism, 95–96. *See also* Sabbatianism
metaphysics, 10–11, 21
Michels, Tony, 169
Middle East, 180
midrash, 61, 64–65
minhag, 138
miracles, biblical, 21, 26–27, 34
miscegenation, 111
Mizrahi Jews, 143, 182
modernity: Arendt on, 124–29; Herzl on, 114–15; Lazare on, 122–23; Lazarus on, 113–14; and religion, 1–4; and secularism, ix–xiii
modernization, 6
monism, 130–31
monotheism, 3–4, 6, 28; Egyptian, 77–78
Montefiore, Claude, 112
More, Henry, 2
Moser, Moses, 38
Moses, 69, 75, 82, 87, 99, 116–17; murder of, 76–79
Most, Andrea, 190
multiculturalism, 122, 125–27, 189

Nabatean Agriculture, 67
Nadler, Steven, 27
Nagel, Thomas, 24
Nahmanides, Moses, 96–97, 178
Nahman of Bratslav, 49–50
Narboni, Moses, 21, 25–26, 198n15
Narodniki, 165
nationalism, German, 36
nationalism, Italian, 111
nationalism, Jewish, 36, 86, 89–90, 92, 106, 121–23, 137, 168; and Jewish identity,

112–17; Lazare on, 118, 120; Lazarus on, 112–14; and race, 104, 107, 179; and Zionism, 82, 128, 130. *See also* Zionism
nationalism, linguistic, 142–43
nature, 19–22, 45–46, 65, 71
necessity, 21, 37, 73
negation of a privation, 20
"negation of the exile," 86
negative theology, 9, 19–20, 22, 26
negotiorum gestio, in Roman law, 116
Neoplatonism, 2, 62, 65, 113
Newton, Isaac, 33
Nietzsche, Friedrich, 82–84, 147; *Beyond Good and Evil*, 166; "On Truth and Lie in a Non-Moral Sense," 51
Nissim of Gerona, 117
non-Zionism, 182
Nordau, Max, 90, 137, 177–78; *The Conventional Lies of Our Civilization*, 59
North Africa, 180
nothingness, 47, 49–51
Novalis, 28

Odessa, 47, 90, 139–40, 145, 150
olam, 2
Oldenburg, Henry, 100
Olympia Academy, Bern, 42
Onkelos, 5
Ophir, Adi, 185–87
organicism, 151
Oriol, Philippe, 123
Orthodoxy, 134, 179, 182, 191–92
Ottoman empire, 101
Oz, Amos, 183–84, 192

paganism, 15, 38–39, 56–58, 178
palace (*hekhalot*) literature, 56
Palestine, xi, 51, 82, 114, 123, 128, 139, 142, 144–45, 157, 164. *See also* Israel, state of
Palmach, 132
panentheism, 65
pantheism, 15, 29, 32, 36–37, 113, 177–78
Passover, 167, 186
peasantry, as source of revolution, 164–65
"people of the book," 82–83
Pfister, Oskar, 40
philosophy: Greek, 16–17; Islamic, 18, 21, 63, 65; Jewish medieval, 18–19; separated from religion, 70
physics, 21, 41–44
pluralism, 12, 152; cultural, 171–72

poetic-nationalist, 167
poets and poetry, 47–51, 146–47; Muslim, 61–62. *See also* Bialik, Hayim Nahman; literature, Hebrew
Poland, 155–56
political sovereignty, 133
political theory, Jewish, 93; Arendt on, 127, 129; Lazare on, 122–23, 129; Maimonides on, 19, 95–97; rabbinic, 94–95; Spinoza on, 70, 97–101, 179
polygeneticism, 107
Portuguese Jews, 22–24, 27–28, 93, 119
Posen, Felix, xiii
Posen Foundation, xiii
positivism, 111
postmodernism, 191–92
postsecularism, 181, 193
post-Zionism, 185–87
Prado, Juan (Daniel) de, 23–24
pre-Adamites, 209n46
prophecy, biblical, 7–8, 18
Protestantism, 3, 75; American, 173. *See also* Christianity
proto-Zionism, 104–9
psychoanalysis, 40–41, 76–81

quantum mechanics, 43

rabbinical authorities, 94, 153–54
rabbinic courts, 94–95
race, as basis for Jewish identity, 104–11, 119–20, 167–68, 171–72
racial theory, Freud and, 79–80
Rakovsky, Puah, xi
Rashi, 88
Ravnitsky, Y. H., *Sefer ha-Aggadah* (with Bialik), 148
Reform Judaism, 30, 68, 83, 92
religion: as basis for Jewish identity, 119; and modernity, 1–4; and subordination of state, 99–101
religious culturalism, 172–74
Renaissance, 68–69
renunciation, instinctual, 78–80
revelation, divine, Scholem's rejection of, 53–54
Revisionist Betar, ix–x
Revisionist Zionism, 90, 111, 129–31
Reznikoff, Charles, 189
Rieff, Philip, 80
Roman law, Herzl's use of, 116

Romanticism, 35–40
Roosevelt, Franklin D., 169
Rosenzweig, Franz, x, 51, 74
Rossi, Azariah dei, *Me'or Einayim*, 68–69
Roth, Philip, *The Plot Against America*, 188
Rousseau, Jean-Jacques, 116
Rubenstein, Jeffrey, 8
Rubenstein, Richard, 57
Russia, 162
Russian empire, 115, 134, 140–45, 151, 169
Russian Social Democratic Party, 115

Saadia Gaon, 64, 67; *Book of Beliefs and Opinions*, 18
Sabar, Shalom, 214n9
Sabbatianism, 23, 100–101, 127, 155–56, 209n26
Sabeans, 67
saeculum, 2
Sammons, Jeffrey, 201n70
Schlesinger, Rabbi Akiva, 168
Schmitt, Carl, 3, 96
Schocken, Salman, 55
Schoeps, Hans Joachim, 53; *Wir deutschen Juden*, 203n104
Scholem, Gershom, 9, 15, 51–56, 100, 124, 137, 139, 147, 154–57, 176–77, 203n105; biography of Zvi, 155; "Mitzvah ha-Ba'ah be-Averah," 155–56
School of Hillel, 153
School of Shammai, 153
Schor, Esther, 114
science, and Jewish state, 132
Science of Judaism, 156
Scott, Sir Walter, 135
Second Temple period, 16–17, 94
secular, use of term, 2–3, 10
secularism, 3, 10; and modernity, ix–xiii
secularization, 6, 166–67; use of term, 3, 113
secularization theory, 1–2
seculatio, 2
Sefer Yitzirah, 52
sefirot, 47
separation of church and state, 70, 101, 134, 187–88
Sephardim, 9, 29, 35, 112, 114, 118
Seven Years War, 30
Sforim, Mendele Mokher, 159
shaatnez, 130
Shammas, Anton, *Arabesques*, 185
Shapiro, Lamed, 163

Shavuot, 187
Sheehan, Jonathan, 59
shelilat ha-gola, 160
Shimoni, Yalkut, 148
Shochat, Azriel, 30
Sholem Aleichem, 169
Slavophilism, 151, 165, 167
Socher, Abraham, 31
social contract, 94–95, 98, 101, 116
social Darwinism, 111
socialism, 75, 90, 104, 118, 164–65, 169–70
social justice, 120–23
Social Revolutionary Party, 165
Society for the Culture and Science of Judaism, 36
Soloviev, Vladimir, 151
Sorkin, David, *Moses Mendelssohn and the Religious Enlightenment*, 197n26
Soviet Union, 77–78
Spain, 46, 96; Muslim, 61–62
Spencer, Herbert, 114
Spinoza, Baruch (Bento/Benedict), xii, 9–10, 15, 22–28, 65, 116, 177; on ancient Israel, 97–99; and atheism, 28–29, 32, 37; on the Bible, 60, 69–74, 178; *Ethics*, 24–28, 154; excommunication of, 27–28, 70, 93, 108, 132; influence of, 34–46, 58, 104–6, 108–9, 113, 132, 154, 185, 190–91, 200n38; on Jewish political theory, 70, 93, 97–101, 179; and Kabbalah, 199n25; on laws of nature, 26–27; and Maimonidean tradition, 25–26, 66; and pantheism, 29, 113; and Sabbatianism, 209n26; *Theological-Political Treatise*, 16, 27, 69–74, 76, 81, 93–94, 99–101
Stanislawski, Michael, 110
state, Jewish, concept of, 182. *See also* Israel, state of; Palestine
statelessness, 124–26, 128
state of exception, 96
Strauss, Leo, 45–46, 177; *Natural Right and History*, 45; *Persecution and the Art of Writing*, 45; *Spinoza's Critique of Religion*, 45
subordination of religion to state, 99–101, 132
substance, Spinozan concept of, 25, 29
Sukkot, 167
superstition, Spinoza on, 99

tarbut, 138
taxation, rabbinic courts and, 94–95

Tchernikhovsky, Saul, 57–58; "Facing the Statue of Apollo," 57–58
territorialism, 11
Teutomania, 167
theocracy, 97–98
theology, Jewish, 39–40, 53; emergence of, 16–18
theology, secular, 3, 9
tohu, 49–51
Torah, 60–61; authorship of, 69; as name of God, 52; "of the heart," 82
tradition, invented, 86
transvaluation of values, 84
Trepp, Leo, 12

ultra-Orthodox, 182–83
uncertainty principle, 43
United States: and Jewish immigrants, 169, 179–80, 188, and secular Jewish culture, 169–75, 187–93
universal identity, Spinozan, 24–25
universalism, 1, 24–25, 107, 111, 137, 163–64
"unsynagogued, the," 11
Usque, Solomon, 68

Varnhagen, Rahel, 124, 127
"view from nowhere," 24
Virgin Mary, 106
Volksgeist, 83
Volozhin, Lithuania, 47

Weber, Max, 3
Weinrich, Max, 138
Wieseltier, Leon, *Kaddish*, 189
Wirth-Nesher, Hana, 188
Włocławek, Poland, ix
Wolfson, Harry, 28
women, Jewish, 106, 109, 138, 158
working class, Jewish, 118
world, as God's "attributes of action," 20, 41–44
world history, Dubnow and, 151–52
World War I, 125
World War II, 129

xenophobia, 112

Yadin, Azzan, 51
Yermiya, Rabbi, 7
Yerushalmi, Yosef Hayim, 68, 80; *Zakhor:*

Jewish History and Jewish Memory, 197n33
yeshiva training, 47, 83, 158, 187
Yiddish dialect, 12, 137, 142–43, 146, 161, 163–69. *See also* language wars
Yiddishkayt, 168
Yom Kippur, x
Young Hegelians, 104
Yovel, Yirmiyahu, 24, 28

Zaddik, 49
Zamenhof, Ludwig L., 137
Zangwill, Israel, *The Melting Pot*, 110, 170
zar, 5

Zhitlowsky, Chaim, 139, 142, 163–69, 192; "Jews and Jewishness," 168; "Thoughts on the Historical Destiny of Judaism," 164; "What Is a Nation?" 167
Zionism, 11, 179, 182; Arendt and, 123–29; Ben-Gurion and, 130–34; and the Bible, 81–91; cultural, 82–83, 123; Freud and, 81; Herzl and, 115–17; Jabotinsky and, 111; messianic, 182; Scholem and, 51–53, 156–57; Zhitlowsky and, 164. *See also* post-Zionism; Revisionist Zionism
Zohar, 12
Zoroastrianism, 3
Zvi, Shabbtai, 9, 23, 100–101, 154–55, 176. *See also* Sabbatianism